The Casablanca Companion

The Movie Classic And Its Place In History

The Casablanca Companion

The Movie Classic And Its Place In History

by

Richard E. Osborne

Riebel-Roque Publishing Company
Indianapolis, Indiana

Library of Congress Number 97-92578

ISBN: 0-9628324-3-X

Date of Publication 1997
Published and Printed in USA

Cover Design by Alan Brown

Other Books by Richard E. Osborne
TOUR BOOK FOR ANTIQUE CAR BUFFS
WORLD WAR II SITES IN THE UNITED STATES

Acknowledgments

Josephine N. Osborne, the author's wife, for her patient editing and review of the manuscript and for her endless reserve, patience, tolerance and support.

Warner Bros.: The author is deeply grateful to the makers and scriptwriters of this marvelous and historically factual movie for their many ideas and clever words. Without their consent for the use of materials from the movie, this book could not have been written.

Aljean Harmetz, author of the book *Round Up the Usual Suspects* for her advice and help in the beginning stages of this endeavor.

Stan Cohen, President of Pictorial Histories Publishing Co., Missoula, MT for his technical assistance.

Wayne Sanford, publisher of *The World War II Chronicle,* for his advice on historical matters and for his encouragement and help in advancing my writing career.

Steve Miller, founder and CEO of SM Design, for his help and suggestions in designing this book and its cover.

Billie Felix Jeyes, for help shaping this book.

Stills from *Casablanca* used in this book and on the cover © 1943 Turner Entertainment Co. All Rights Reserved.

Research Associates:

Roger A. Godin, Curator of the Ordnance Museum, Aberdeen Proving Ground, Maryland.

Dr. Russell Parke, Internet Specialist.

Raymond Featherstone, Research Associate

Liliane Krasean, Teacher of Languages

CONTENTS

Introduction

The 1943 movie *Casablanca* was entirely a product of World War II. But, like World War II, it had its roots in the time before and during World War I. *Casablanca* was conceived, written and produced by individuals who, in one way or another, had experienced those early years—and those events were within their living memory. Some of those pre-World War II events were incorporated into the movie's script, along with many references to World War II.

The movie was produced for the wartime audiences of North America and a secondary market in Latin America. At the time, there was virtually no market for it in Europe.

Because *Casablanca* was a wartime movie, it was heavily endowed with the rhetoric of World War II. In the case of *Casablanca*, that endowment was extremely generous and accurate. But now that the movie is being viewed by a new generation, the references to World War II and the time before may have become somewhat foggy and unclear. The purpose of this work, then, is to explain in some detail the meanings of the many World War II-related words, phrases and sentences so that the present-day viewer can better comprehend what is being said and shown and appreciate the richness and historical depth embodied within the movie's content. With this added insight, today's viewers can enjoy the movie to its fullest—as did the viewers of 1943. After reading this book, readers will discover that the next time they view *Casablanca*, they will see and hear things they have never seen and heard before.

The events in *Casablanca* will be followed in this book in the order they appear on the screen. They begin on Tuesday December 1, 1941, the day of the couriers' murder, and end on December 4—three days before the Japanese sneak attack on Pearl Harbor, Hawaii. Those were some of the darkest days of the war for the Allied Nations.

During the first two days of the *Casablanca* story, this is what was happening world-wide:

December 1, 1941

•**MOSCOW**: German and other Axis forces are assaulting Moscow in an attempt to surround the city. The Red Army has taken terrible losses in six months of heavy fighting and many believe it is all but beaten. The Germans have pushed to a point nine miles from the Kremlin—German troops can see its spires—and the Soviet Government is on verge of fleeing the city. Bitter winter weather makes fighting all along the eastern front horrible and costly for both sides.

•**LENINGRAD**: The Soviet Union's second largest city (now called St. Petersburg) is besieged by German and Finnish forces. Food and fuel are running out fast and thousands of civilians are dying of starvation and frostbite.

•**LIBYA**: There is heavy fighting in eastern Libya between German and Italian forces on the one hand and British forces on the other as Axis forces advance toward Cairo, Egypt and the Suez Canal.

•**WASHINGTON, DC**: High-level talks are underway between the U.S. and Japanese governments. The Japanese can see that a new world order is about to emerge and they have expansion plans to take control of the lightly protected Far East colonial interests of France, Britain, the Netherlands and Portugal. With that plan in mind, they are proposing that Japan and the United States work jointly to free the colonial lands of Southeast Asia from their masters and turn the area into a joint American-Japanese economic zone in which the two nations would dominate economically, politically and militarily. The U.S. rejects the idea because it would betray the trust of America's friends, Britain, France, The Netherlands and Portugal. The U.S. counters with demands that Japan pull her troops out of northern China which she had invaded in 1937. By now both sides realize that their positions are too far apart and that the talks, which have been going on for several weeks, are about to break down.

•**WESTERN PACIFIC**: The Japanese naval task force destined to attack Pearl Harbor is four days out of its Japanese ports, sailing slowly, awaiting the results of the Washington talks and final word to proceed with the attack, should those talks fail. The attack is planned to knock out the American Pacific Fleet, the only military force capable of challenging Japan's ultimate plan of conquering the lands of Southeast Asia by force. The leaders in Tokyo fully realize that such an attack would mean war with America.

•**TOKYO, JAPAN**: Later in the day, the decision is made that the Washington talks have failed. So, an Imperial Council, headed by Premier Hideki Tojo and held in the presence of Emperor Hirohito, decides unanimously to attack the U.S. fleet at Pearl Harbor.

•**MALAYA** and **SINGAPORE**: British authorities, fully alert to the situation, fear a Japanese attack, and declare a State of Emergency.

December 2, 1941

•**SOVIET UNION**: The German onslaught continues to inch its way around Moscow to the north and the south in an effort to encircle the city. The soldiers of the Red Army fight heroically. The hard fighting and worsening weather continues to take a heavy toll of lives on both sides.

•**WASHINGTON, DC**: The Japanese/American talks continue. President Roosevelt personally intervenes and asks the Japanese envoys to explain the meaning of the recent buildup of Japanese military forces in Indo-China. This is seen as a threat to the American-controlled Philippines and all of Southeast Asia. The envoys are unable to explain the buildup and defer the question to Tokyo—stalling for time.

•**WESTERN PACIFIC**: The commander of the Japanese naval strike force heading towards Hawaii receives a coded message, "Climb Mount Niitaka." This is the order that

Secretary of State Cordell Hull (front center) with the Japanese negotiators, Special Envoy Saburu Kurusu (front left) and Admiral Kichisaburo Nomura, the Japanese Ambassador. The Japanese's code name for Hull was "Miss Umeko" and for President Roosevelt, "Miss Kimiko."

he has been waiting for. It tells him that the Washington talks have failed and he is to proceed as planned and carry out the attack on Pearl Harbor on the morning of December 7, 1941—the day war would begin between the Empire of Japan and the United States of America.

•**TOKYO**: the Japanese Cabinet is reshuffled to bring in more military men in preparation for the war that is about to begin. Orders are sent to the Japanese Embassy in Washington for the embassy staff to begin burning all but its most secret papers.

•**LIBYA/EGYPT**: On the Libyan/Egyptian border, in the Tobruk area, heavy fighting continues between the Axis forces under General Erwin Rommel and the British 8th Army. Losses are mounting on both sides and the outcome is still undecided.

Events of the final two days in the movie's time frame will be presented later in the book.

Chapter One

The Refugee Trails

The movie *Casablanca* opens with a view of a spinning globe and the ominous voice of a narrator telling of the coming of World War II. As the camera zooms in, the globe comes to a halt, showing a map of Axis-occupied Europe during the latter part of 1941. Upon closer examination, the map reveals three tones of gray for the land mass. The lightest tone identifies Great Britain which, with her Empire and a few Governments-in-Exile, stands alone in the west against the combined might of the Axis nations. In the east, and out of the map, is the Soviet Union, Britain's only ally. The middle tone shows the neutral nations: Sweden, Switzerland, Eire (Ireland), Spain and Portugal. The darker tone shows the Axis nations of Germany, Italy and their allies: Hungary, Rumania, Slovakia and Croatia. The same color tone also shows the areas conquered by the Axis Powers: Belgium, The Netherlands, Norway, Denmark and the remnants of the nations that no longer existed in 1941: Poland, Luxembourg, Czechoslovakia and Yugoslavia.

France is shown in both tones of gray. The northern and western portions in darker gray indicate German-occupied France, and a southern portion in the middle tone of gray indicates Unoccupied France, a neutral zone.

French North Africa—consisting of Tunisia, Algeria and French Morocco—are also shown in the middle tone of gray, indicating that those areas are unoccupied and neutral, too. It is here, in French Morocco, that the action in the movie *Casablanca* takes place.

To the viewers of 1943, the map was enough to tell them that the events in the movie took place during one of the darkest hours of World War II. They knew that, by this time in the war, France had been beaten, was under the thumb of the Axis Powers, and it was undesirable to be anywhere in the French Empire, including Casablanca. Furthermore, the viewers of 1943 knew the movie took place immediately before the United States became involved in the war as a result of the Japanese attack on Pearl Harbor, Hawaii, on December 7, 1941. After that date, the whole nature of the war changed dramatically.

A map of Paris appears on the screen and the narrator describes the torturous and roundabout trail that European refugees are taking to get out of Europe. The trail begins in Paris and a line is traced on the maps showing the refugee route to Casablanca:

"Paris to Marseilles, across the Mediterranean to Oran, then by train, or auto, or foot, across the rim of Africa into Casablanca in French Morocco."

From July, 1940, to late 1941, this (see italics) was the primary escape route for refugees from western Europe trying to get to freedom in the west.

After the Axis Powers conquered vast areas of western Europe between April and June, 1940, virtually all other escape routes to the west were closed because the Axis leaders wanted non-Jews to remain in Europe to serve as workers for the Axis war effort. As for the Jews, the Nazis welcomed their departure at first, but later changed their minds, realizing that many would support the Allied cause, especially young men of military age. Despite the controls imposed by the Axis Powers, though, refugees of all types continued to find ways to escape.

Those who could escape to neutral Sweden or Switzerland were often trapped there for the duration of the war. Neither country had easy access to the west. Sweden was virtually surrounded by the Axis, had halted all sea traffic to the west, and had only very limited westward air connections. Land-locked Switzerland, of course, had no sea connections and very limited commercial air connections to the west. Switzerland did have a short common border with Unoccupied France, so it was possible to cross into Unoccupied France provided one met the necessary conditions laid down by both governments. These conditions were very stringent, however. Neither the Swiss Government nor the defeated Government of Unoccupied France, known as the Vichy Government, wanted to see large numbers of refugees fleeing to the west for fear of incurring the wrath of the Axis Powers. Unoccupied France was awash with refugees and discouraged any more from leaving Switzerland. The best way out of Switzerland was via commercial air lines direct to Lisbon, Portugal. This air route was maintained throughout most of the war but getting a seat on a plane going to Lisbon was a very difficult thing to do.

Refugees who slipped out of Sweden and Switzerland, without proper travel documents, risked arrest or incarceration in jails or refugee camps in the countries to which they escaped. Conditions such as these were common for every nation in Europe.

This was the best way out of Switzerland to Lisbon, via Swiss-Aire. This plane, a tri-motor German-built Junker Ju 52/3m, shown with Swiss military markings, was one of the most popular transports in Europe during the war. Many nations used them. Swiss-Aire's planes were boldly marked by white crosses with a bright red background similar to this aircraft.

In order for refugees to get out of Europe in any direction, they had to have an open route across which they could travel, the proper travel documents for each country they entered and left, and some idea of a final destination. Consequently, the longer the escape route and the more borders that had to be crossed, the more difficult it became. The route from France to French Morocco, although rather long, was the easiest route of all because one never left French territory. This eliminated the need to cross international borders and the cumbersome problem of getting entrance and exit visas. Therefore, getting into French territory legally was one of the primary goals of most refugees. Getting beyond French territory, though, was another problem.

Shopping For Freedom

While traveling the Casablanca route, refugees went through several large cities with sizable charitable and relief organizations that helped all refugees in need. Furthermore, in most of these cities, the local Jewish communities had established organizations to help Jewish refugees in transit. Algeria, for example, had about 130,000 Jewish residents and French Morocco had 175,000, the largest of any country in Africa and the 13th largest Jewish population in the world at the time. The larger cities had foreign consulates where the refugees could "shop," as it were, for a country in which to settle. The standard international procedure for would-be immigrants was to obtain entrance visas from the foreign consulate of the country of their choice before departing for that country. Upon arrival in that country, they would then be recognized by their visas and allowed to enter.

Upon receiving an entry visa, the visa holders could leave at once for their new destinations. Traveling on to Casablanca was not necessary, but leaving for the west from any of the larger cities bordering the western Mediterranean Sea was very difficult. Because that area was an active war zone, virtually all commercial airline and shipping operations had ceased. The best that the refugees could hope for would be to find passage on a French ship, or a ship of another neutral nation, that had ventured into the war zone and was heading west to Tangier (an international sea port on the north coast of Morocco opposite Gibraltar), or to Lisbon, or beyond. For the first ten months after France's defeat, up until May 1941, there were four French ocean liners that sailed beyond: the "Winnipeg," the "Alsina," the "Wyoming" and the "Monte Viso." These ships sailed from the various French Mediterranean ports, sometimes stopped at Casablanca or Lisbon, and then traveled on to the West. The usual destination was the island of Martinique in the West Indies. From Martinique, refugees could travel to their final destination providing they had the necessary documents to do so. Arriving at Martinique without such documents was very risky for refugees because there were very few foreign consulates on the island.

On May 10, 1941, the British, who were engaged in an undeclared sea war with their former French ally, captured the liner "Winnipeg." With this, the French ceased transatlantic service on the remaining ships. At the time the "Winnipeg" was captured, the "Monte Viso" was at Casablanca and was scheduled to go on to Martinique. But,

Casablanca, French Morocco, in 1942 was a large and modern city.

the Vichy Government canceled the schedule and the passengers had to disembark, becoming stranded in Casablanca with all the other refugees.

Three other French ships, "Lyautey," "Ville Jouran" and "General Gambon," continued to sail for a while between Marseilles and Casablanca, but not beyond.

During 1941, the sea war in the eastern North Atlantic Ocean intensified, and more and more merchant ships, from both belligerent and neutral nations, were being sunk. Maritime insurance rates sky-rocketed for this part of the world and merchant ships sailing to and from Portuguese, Spanish and French ports became fewer and fewer. By the end of 1941, the few American ships that had sailed to ports in this part of the world stopped altogether. By January, 1942, only a few Portuguese ships ventured to cross the Atlantic with any regularity, and only occasionally could ships of other neutral nations be seen coming and going in Portuguese, Spanish and Moroccan ports along the Atlantic. Of all the seaports in the area, Lisbon was, by far, the most active. Therefore, for refugees hoping to get to America or other places in the Western Hemisphere, Lisbon offered the best opportunities.

Upon arrival in Casablanca, those refugees who had not yet obtained immigration documents to a final destination had to begin making the rounds of the foreign consulates there. The more fortunate refugees, who had acquired entrance visas to their future country of residence beforehand, were ready to leave, usually for Lisbon, on the first transportation they could find. All they needed at this point was an exit visa from French territory. But then, as will be seen in the movie, they may run into an unforeseen obstacle—Captain Louis Renault, *Casablanca*'s corrupt Prefect of Police, played in the movie by Claude Raines.

Casablanca had wide avenues, typical of those in France, and multi-storied buildings.

Casablanca: The City

In its pre-colonial days, Casablanca was a totally Moroccan city, with a sizable and well-guarded International Settlement in which foreigners, traders and businessmen of many nationalities lived. When the French took over this part of Morocco and created the Protectorate of French Morocco in the early 1900s, Casablanca became France's base of operations for pacifying the areas of central and southern Morocco. These areas, mostly in the interior of the country, were in a state of anarchy resulting from years of tribal warfare. They were unsafe for Europeans.

After the French became entrenched in the city, Casablanca took on a more European appearance, yet maintained its Moroccan and international flavors.

Strategically, Casablanca and the other Moroccan ports along the Atlantic coast were important to the well-being and security of all of French North Africa because these ports provided access to the Atlantic Ocean for French-controlled Algeria and Tunisia avoiding the narrow Strait of Gibraltar where likely enemies could make maritime travel difficult, or even impossible.

In December 1941, the time frame of the movie, this was the case. France had been knocked out of the war by the Germans and Italians, and had become a neutral country very much under the influence of Berlin and Rome. Political relations between defeated France and her former ally, Great Britain, were strained. Great Britain controlled access to the Strait of Gibraltar from its bastion on the Rock of Gibraltar, and the British could close the Strait to French shipping any time they chose to do so. Casablanca would then become one of French North Africa's life-lines to the west.

During World War I, the French had made substantial improvements in the city, its harbor and the highways and rail lines connecting Casablanca with other parts of Morocco.

By the time World War II began, in September, 1939, Casablanca was Morocco's largest city and had all the amenities of any city of comparable size in Europe. There were wide avenues typical of cities in France, modern multi-storied buildings, European and native market places, amusement centers and a wide variety of economic and industrial operations, manufacturing and warehousing.

Within the city was a large native quarter, a sizable Jewish quarter and an area where Europeans and Westerners lived.

The French Navy had taken a part of the harbor and built a modern naval base. In late 1941, the French battleship "Jean Bart" and an assortment of other French warships were anchored, more-or-less permanently, in the harbor, with their guns at the ready, serving as the city's first line of defense against air raids and attacks from the sea. So far in the war, though, Casablanca had not been attacked. The "Jean Bart" was a new battleship, not yet completed, but her guns were fully operational.

All along the Atlantic coast of the Casablanca area were numerous modern coastal defenses. South of the city was a modern airport which was used by both the civil air authorities and the French military.

Casablanca had operated under wartime conditions from the beginning of the war and those restrictions were still in place at the time of the movie. The city had blackouts, curfews, air raid drills, rationing and various other wartime controls. There were numerous French soldiers, sailors and airmen in the city. The movie makes use of this historical fact and shows a considerable number of French servicemen frequenting Rick's Cafe Americain.

The Refugee Trail Through Spain

There was another refugee route out of southern France to the west which ran through Spain and into Portugal. But, this route was difficult. The three-year-long Spanish Civil War had ended in April, 1939, and, by late 1941, the time-frame of *Casablanca*, Spain was still suffering badly from the results of that war. The Spanish economy was weak and the country's infrastructure was in shambles. There was an acute shortage of food and fuel. And bridges, power plants, railroads and the other essential structures for a functioning society were out of commission. There were thousands of displaced Spaniards moving about within Spain. Available transportation facilities and accommodations were usually overwhelmed. Furthermore, some areas of the country were dangerous because die-hard Loyalist soldiers were still carrying on guerrilla warfare. Jewish refugees could expect virtually no help from Spain's very small Jew-

Refugee Escape Routes to the West from Vichy France

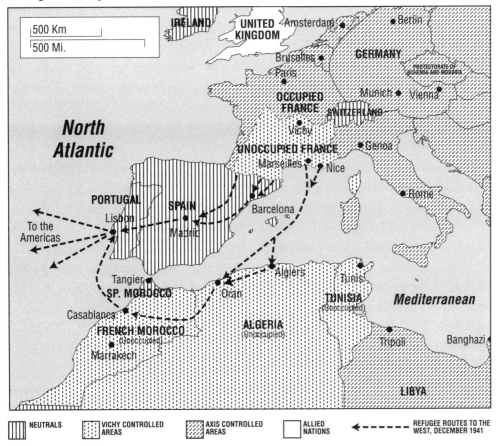

The two most viable escape routes for European refugees to the west from July, 1940, to the latter part of 1941, the time frame of the movie, were the Marseilles/Nice/Oran/Algiers/Casablanca route and the route through Spain. Of the two, the all-French Marseilles to Casablanca route was the easiest to traverse.

ish community which totaled only about 4,000. International charitable and relief organizations were operating in Spain, but they too were overwhelmed by the immensity of Spain's post-civil war problems.

In late 1940, as a concession to Germany and Italy, who had helped the Spanish Nationalists win their Civil War, the Nationalist Government closed its border with France to all male refugees of military age. This deterred, or at least delayed, their joining the armed forces of the Allies. In 1941, though, Spain began granting transit visas to those possessing valid immigration visas to countries of final destination. This granting of transit visas made it possible for thousands of refugees to cross Spain to reach Lisbon, Portugal.

Refugees who did choose the Spanish route were urged by the authorities to keep moving no matter what awaited them in the next town or at the next river-crossing. Inspections were frequent and those without proper papers could find themselves thrown into makeshift refugee camps, usually former prisoner-of-war camps, where they languished under deplorable conditions with little or no contact with the outside world.

There were some Spanish freighters with passenger accommodations leaving at various times from Spanish ports. Until the end of 1940, the United States Line had freighters occasionally servicing Vigo, Santander, Gijon and Bilbao. Departing refugees had to have entrance visas into whatever country these ships were traveling to and such visas were difficult to obtain inside Spain. Not all nations had re-established their consulates in Spain following the end of the civil war.

There was yet another reason for refugees to avoid the Spanish route—the conditions in southwestern France. All along the French/Spanish border on the French side were refugee camps holding some quarter of a million Spanish Loyalists who had fled from Spain into France during the Spanish Civil War. This number was down from a peak of about half a million refugees during early 1939, but this number was still the largest concentration of refugees in the world at that time. In February 1939, with the Spanish Loyalist forces collapsing rapidly, the French opened the border at Perthus and some 200,000 Loyalist soldiers streamed into France for safety. Most came without passports, visas or other documents and were herded by the French authorities directly into refugee camps. The victorious Nationalist Government in Madrid wasn't anxious to take these people back, especially all at once, so the Loyalist refugees languished in the French camps living off charity from the French Government, the local people and the international relief agencies there. The presence of so many people in a relatively small area put a severe strain on the resources of this region of France. Thus, new refugees coming into this area from France on their way to Lisbon were not really welcomed.

"Here the fortunate ones through money or influence or luck, might obtain exit visas."

Actually, it could be said that those who made it to Casablanca were among the lucky ones simply because they made it that far. The trip from southern France was long and arduous and those who did not make it were more numerous than those who did arrive in Casablanca.

There, refugees from Nazi-controlled areas were the most destitute of all. The Nazi Government had passed stringent laws forbidding Jews and others who emigrated from Germany from taking virtually anything of value with them. Those who were forced to leave, as well as those who chose to leave, literally walked across the German border with the clothes on their backs and a suitcase or two of personal belongings which had been thoroughly searched by the German border guards. A few of those leaving Germany had the opportunity and foresight to stash money abroad in Switzerland or other countries, but the majority were not that fortunate. From the minute most of the refugees walked across the German border, they lived on charity, help from friends and relatives or from whatever temporary employment they could find. Fortunately, there were various international relief organizations, Jewish organizations and some government agencies that kept these unfortunate individuals alive and sheltered, albeit meagerly.

When the German Army invaded The Netherlands, Belgium, Luxembourg and northern France in May, 1940, a new surge of refugees from these nations emerged and virtually all of them streamed into southern France. Some of those who fled had been

This is the way many refugees traveled to southern France: on foot pushing or pulling various wheeled vehicles filled with their belongings. It is doubtful that most of these people ever tried to reach Casablanca, being content instead to accept whatever refuge they found along the way in southern France or Algeria. Some of these people returned to Occupied France after the Armistice. Scenes such as this are blended into the first part of the movie in double exposures as the maps are being explained.

refugees before. They were Germans, Austrians, Czechs and Poles who had sought asylum in those areas from previous Nazi aggressions. There were estimates at that time that one fifth of the population of northern France fled the advancing Germans. By the end of May 1940, the Red Cross estimated that there were two million Frenchmen, two million Belgians, 70,000 Luxembourgers and 50,000 Dutch streaming southward through France. On this exodus, though, the refugees were somewhat more fortunate than those who had earlier fled Nazi-controlled areas because they could take with them whatever they could carry on foot, in a car, wagon, or on a bicycle.

In June, 1940, as the Germans overran Paris, central France and the Atlantic coast of France, the refugee wave surged again. This was the surge the movie's Rick and Sam participated in—without Ilsa (Madeleine Le Beau, who played Yvonne, and her husband, Marcel Dalio, who played the croupier, actually fled in this wave).

By the end of 1940, the flow of refugees to Casablanca slowed considerably. Most of those who wanted to go there had arrived and the others had found refuge elsewhere or along the way.

On October 4, 1940, the French Government at Vichy decreed, as a sop to the Nazis, that all non-French Jews still in southern France be interned in camps or relocated in small towns and villages under Vichy's supervision. This decree all but ended the flow of Jews to Casablanca. Non-Jews, though, could travel on to Casablanca or elsewhere as they wished. The decree of October 4 also required that all French citizens over 16, including Jewish French citizens, carry identification cards to differentiate them from the refugees. This was, most certainly, one of the documents the Casablanca Police checked for when they rounded up the usual suspects.

At this point in time, the French Government at Vichy didn't want to keep the non-French Jews in southern France indefinitely yet didn't want them to move on into the French colonies. So, the Vichy Government allowed Jewish relief agencies and other organizations into Unoccupied France to work with the non-French Jews to relocate them outside French territory. Certain French officials, with much the same scruples as *Casablanca*'s Captain Renault, saw in this scheme the opportunity to make money. They used delaying tactics, or made unreasonable demands on those wishing to leave which could only be overcome with bribes. Unfortunately, the Vichy Government did little to stop this practice and bribing an official to get out of France became common-place.

Despite these and other problems encountered by the non-French Jews in Southern France, the relief agencies were able to help some 10,000 reach Lisbon by the end of 1940. Others were sent eastward to Palestine. Relief agencies helped thousands of others get out of France during 1941 and the first ten months of 1942. Many other non-French Jews, unable to find a country of refuge, were forced to abide by the decrees of the Vichy Government or to live a tenuous existence trying to find a way out of France on their own.

When the refugees reached Casablanca, conditions for some of them improved. There were a number of relief agencies in the city working with refugees, including one headed by a Jewish woman named Helene Cazes-Benathar working specifically with Jews. Her organization provided temporary shelter, food and information on how Jews might find sanctuary overseas. Cazes-Benathar's group set up a receiving center at Ain Sebra, a few miles from Casablanca, in a building that had formerly been a children's summer camp and dance hall. The center could temporarily house up to 600 people. Residents were charged 50 francs a day (about one dollar) and could stay up to ten days. Then they would have to move on into the city. Some Jewish refugees who had, by now, exhausted their funds or for other reasons had little hope of moving on, were dispersed by Cazes-Benathar's people to various parts of French Morocco and absorbed by the Jewish communities in Casablanca, Fès and Marrakesh.

The French administration in Morocco welcomed such agencies because they kept many of the refugees from becoming burdens to the community and helped the refugees move elsewhere in an orderly fashion.

Unfortunately, the agencies could handle only a small percentage of the refugees that arrived at Casablanca. For the others, the French were obliged to build refugee camps. Camp Sidi al-Ayyashi, near Assemour, 65 miles southwest of Casablanca, was the largest refugee camp in Morocco. Camp Oued-Zem, another large camp, was 80 miles southeast of Casablanca. Three more camps—at Kasrah Tadla, Oued Akreuqi and Berguent—were situated in eastern Morocco along the new Algiers-to-Dakar Road which was under construction. These camps held ordinary convicts. Both the refugees and the convicts were put to work on roads. Another camp at Missour housed refugees unable to work.

Jewish refugees arriving in Morocco were surprised to learn they had a most unlikely friend: the Sultan himself. The Sultan of Morocco, the figurehead leader of the nation under the protectorate agreements with both the French and the Spanish, was required to cooperate with them in most matters pertaining to governing the nation.

In the mechanics of these foreign relationships, the Sultan was obliged to convert for Southern Morocco the French decrees into Moroccan laws and to do likewise with Spanish decrees in the north. In most cases he cooperated. But, he still retained some authority over social, cultural and religious matters. When the Vichy Government began issuing anti-Semitic decrees (clearly a religious matter) the Sultan exercised his authority and refused to convert many of them into Moroccan law. This meant that the few authorities still under his rule did not have to enforce such decrees. Officially, the Vichy authorities objected and continued to put pressure on the Sultan to accept the decrees. But, since most of the Vichy officials were less than sympathetic towards such decrees themselves, the matter was allowed to slip into a political limbo. As a result, foreign Jews lived a freer existence in French Morocco than in southern France.

For one thing, Jews were not rounded up in French Morocco and shipped off to German concentration camps, but neither were they permitted to hold important jobs or practice any profession. Only the lowest level of jobs were open to them. In the movie, Rick could hire Jewish refugees as waiters, cooks, bartenders, doormen and bellboys without coming into conflict with the law. He could not hire Jewish musicians or bookkeepers since those were considered professional positions. He might have had a problem in his gambling room, too, because gambling was one of the professions denied to Jews.

One decree from Vichy, though, which the Sultan readily accepted restricted where Jews could live in French Morocco. That decree, issued as a Moroccan dahir (law) on August 22, 1941, ordered all foreign Jews who had arrived in French Morocco after September 1, 1939, with a few exceptions, to terminate their residency in the European sections of French Morocco's larger cities. They were given a month to move out. This was done for two reasons: 1) Neither Vichy nor the Sultan wanted foreign Jews to settle permanently in French Morocco; and 2) all of Morocco's major cities had been segregated for centuries with clearly defined sections for natives, Jews and Europeans. With newly-arrived Jews moving into the European sections rather than into the traditional Jewish sections, the lines of segregation were blurred and the status quo upset.

Destination: Lisbon

Many countries, including the United States, had consulates in Casablanca. America's Consul General in Casablanca during the time frame of the movie was H. Earle Russell. His consulate was fully staffed with diplomatic personnel and a small secret unit of the OSS (Office of Strategic Services, forerunner to the Central Intelligence Agency). While the consulate officials conducted legitimate business with the Vichy officials, the OSS agents carried out spy missions and kept in touch with Free French operatives in Morocco and other pro-Allied individuals. It may well be that Victor Laszlo, the Czechoslovakian resistance leader played by Paul Henreid in the movie, was in contact with an OSS agent in Casablanca.

In addition to the American consulate officials, there were twelve special American vice-consuls, all United States Army and Navy officers, serving officially in various areas of French North Africa as inspectors under the American-Vichy food agreement known as the Weygand/Murphy Plan of March, 1941. This plan was a humanitarian program that allowed the Americans to supply food and other necessary consumer goods to the people of French North Africa. The official duties of the twelve inspectors were to see that the food and consumer goods were actually consumed in French North Africa and did not reach any Axis nations. Unofficially, and it was an open secret, the inspectors also acted as U.S. spies. The Vichy Government welcomed these people because they served as an unofficial communication link with the Allies and acted as a small, but very visible, counterbalance to the intense political pressures from Germany and Italy.

There was also a fully-staffed American consulate at Rabat, Morocco's capital, and a consulate at Tangier with a reduced staff headed by a First Secretary.

The U.S. consulate at Casablanca was, without doubt, the busiest consulate in Morocco because, as the movie makes very clear, nearly every refugee wanted to go to America. At the U.S. consulate, refugees could inquire as to their chances of emigrating to America. If they qualified and the immigration quota for them was open, they could obtain one of the most cherished documents of all in Casablanca, an American immigration visa. If they qualified but the quota was full, they could put their name on a waiting list for the next year, or the next, or the next—and wait. In the meantime, the refugees could apply for admission to Mexico or some other Latin American country from which they could more readily enter the United States. Refugees could not get into Canada or any of the other British possessions from Casablanca because there was no British consulate there, or anywhere else in French North Africa. This came about because of the rupture of diplomatic relations between Vichy France and the British Empire in July 1940. To apply for entrance into Canada, or any other part of the British Empire, including Great Britain itself, refugees had to wait until they reached Lisbon.

At the time of the movie, Casablanca had no direct air connections to overseas destinations, but some merchant ships from neutral countries called at Casablanca and carried some refugees to the west. The number of such ships, though, was small and their schedules erratic. A few American merchant ships, too, called at Casablanca but, like the others, their schedules were erratic and many of them were not equipped to carry passengers. When an American ship arrived in Casablanca's harbor, it could easily be identified because every American ship sailing in West African waters before December 7, 1941, had huge American flags painted on either side of the hull with the flags brightly illuminated at night. This was to prevent the ship from being attacked by the Axis submarines prowling the same waters.

For most of the refugees all of these problems added up to one thing: the best hope in getting to the west was still through Lisbon.

Why Lisbon?

After June 1940, the capital of Portugal was the only large neutral city in western Europe that had reliable sea and air communications to the Western Hemisphere. Lisbon had embassies from all the major nations of the world. For refugees who made

Even after reaching Lisbon, refugees had to wait. But waiting in Lisbon was more comfortable and pleasant than in most other places.

it to Lisbon, the hardest part of their journey was over. Once there, they could work with the various embassies to get visas and transportation to their new homelands. They could even shop around to see what country would suit them best. Meanwhile, if they had the money, they could live in relative comfort and safety in this clean and beautiful old city of 600,000 people.

People could reach Lisbon from Casablanca in three different ways: by regularly scheduled air service, by sea or by land. The land route was the least desirable because it required obtaining an entrance visa into Spain, then traveling north through Spanish Morocco, across the Strait of Gibraltar, through southern Spain and into Portugal.

Wartime Lisbon was many things to many people. It was a major center for currency exchange which meant that refugees from Germany could take the *Reichmarks* they had smuggled in the lining of their clothing and convert them into Portuguese *escudos* or American dollars. Those with diamonds and other gems to sell who felt they couldn't get fair value in Casablanca could try again in Lisbon. Those with money in foreign banks could usually retrieve that money once they reached Lisbon. In Lisbon, refugees could get money from relatives abroad or secure help from a variety of relief organizations. Prospects of getting a job in Lisbon were slim because Portuguese law forbade refugees from taking permanent jobs.

For those without money, the Portuguese Government had established refugee camps. They were far from elegant, but they were clean and safe.

Before the United States went to war, Lisbon was the gateway to Europe for Americans going to Spain, Unoccupied France or Axis-controlled areas. Ernie Pyle, the famous American war correspondent, took note of the city's refugees and wrote that Lisbon was "a city that harbors 10,000 distresses of spirit." His estimate was low. By mid-1940, the city had an estimated 20,000 refugees and was becoming the "refugee capital of Europe." Housing was hard to find, in part due to the influx of refugees and also due to the fact that 1940 was the 800th anniversary of Portugal's founding and the 300th anniversary of Portugal's independence from Spain. Many people had traveled to Lisbon to take part in the festivities. Of course, if refugees had enough money, they could buy or lease a home in Estoril, Lisbon's posh western suburb, and sit out the war in relative comfort. King Carol of Romania and his mistress, Madam Lupescu, lived in Estoril for a while as did Ignace Pederewski, Poland's first President, and Don Juan, Pretender to the Throne of Spain. Lisbon was also home to about 565 Americans in 1940.

Various charitable and relief organizations operated in Lisbon and were a great help to refugees. As in Casablanca, the local Jewish community of Lisbon formed an organization to help fellow Jews. This group, headed by Moses Amzalak, a friend of Portugal's Premier Salazar, cared for up to 4,000 people a year.

Quite naturally, Lisbon became a city full of intrigues. Spies, saboteurs, assassins, diplomats, diplomatic couriers, secret agents, black-marketeers, arms merchants and many other characters, honest and dishonest, passed through Lisbon. The city was also an exchange point for prisoners of war between the Allied and Axis nations.

For those in the know, Hotel Aviz was where citizens from the Allied nations gathered while Axis citizens congregated at the plush Palacio Hotel in Estoril. There were so many Germans in Lisbon that rumors persisted that they were part of a secret advance military force preparing for a German invasion of Portugal. Newspapers, books and the like were readily available in Lisbon from both Allied and Axis nations.

The fascinating goings-on in Lisbon were noticed by Hollywood which produced several movies set in this exotic location. Edwin Small's *International Lady* (1941) starred George Brent as an FBI agent operating in Lisbon who falls in love with an Axis spy, played by Ilona Massey. Also that year, Paramount made *One Night in Lisbon* starring Fred McMurray as an American flyer who falls for a British socialite (Madeleine Carroll) being used by the British as a decoy to catch German spies. In 1942, Paramount produced *The Lady Has Plans* starring Ray Milland and Paulette Goddard. Milland played a reporter in Lisbon mistaken for a Nazi spy. In 1944, Warner Bros. did a sequel to *Casablanca* based in Lisbon entitled *The Conspirators*. It had a generous supply of *Casablanca* personnel. The film starred Paul Henreid, with Sydney Greenstreet and Peter Lorre in supporting roles, and was filmed by Arthur Edeson and scored by Max Steiner. The leading lady was Hedy Lamarr, who helped her lover, an escaped Dutch resistance leader, played by Henreid, clear up a nasty Nazi conspiracy in Lisbon. That same year, Republic Studios, attempted to cash in on *Casablanca*'s success and Lisbon's exotic image by producing *Storm Over Lisbon* with Erich von Stroheim and Vera Hruba Ralston. This was the story about an international spy master who runs a night club in Lisbon and sells secret documents to the highest bidder.

Ironically, there really was a restaurant owner in Lisbon spying for the Allies. He was Frederick Danielski, a native of Vienna, Austria. Danielski had moved to Lisbon in 1932 and, five years later, opened "Freddy's Viennese Restaurant." During the war, the restaurant became a favorite hangout for Germans and Austrians in Lisbon because it served German food. The British approached Danielski, who spoke seven languages, and asked him to spy on his German and Austrian customers. Danielski, who hated

The Vienna Connection

The city of Vienna is not mentioned in *Casablanca* but many of the individuals associated with the film had strong connections to that city. Some of them lived in the city, others worked there and two indiviuals, Max Steiner (musical score) and Helmut Dantine (Jan, the Bulgarian man) were born there. Another man who had strong connections to Vienna was the man who was responsible for starting World War II — Adolph Hitler.

When Hitler turned 17, he went to Vienna, Austria's capital, with the intent of enrolling in the Royal Academy of Fine Arts and becoming an artist. He had a small inheritance from his father who had died several years earlier but he did not have the full support of his mother who called him "pig-headed" for wanting to become an artist. Hitler presented his dossier to the Academy's admissions committee, and, much to his surprise, his application was rejected because his paintings simply weren't good enough. It was a devastating blow to Hitler—one he would never forget or forgive. He did well painting buildings and scenery, but very

These are typical of the paintings made by A. Hitler in his youth in Vienna. He loved painting buildings. When Hitler became Chancellor of Germany in 1933, his paintings soared in value. He didn't paint in later life although he spoke of doing so again in retirement.

poorly with the human figure. The official report from the academy read "Adolph Hitler, born Braunau/Inn, Upper Austria on 20 April 1889 …Catholic, Father: Civil Servant, Sample drawings inadequate, few heads."

He tried to get into an architectural school but was rejected because he didn't have a high school diploma. He tried a year later to once again get into the Royal Academy of Fine Arts and was rejected a second time. To add to his woes, his mother, to whom he was devoted, died of breast cancer when he was 18. She was 47.

With an inheritance from his mother's estate and a small orphan's pension from the Government, Hitler was able to live on in Vienna, albeit frugally, hoping, somehow, to make a life for himself in the arts. He tried writing plays and failed. He tried writing an opera and failed again. Hitler, then living in a boarding house with a roommate who had a piano, would pick out chords and melodies late into the night as he composed. He even designed some of the stage settings. Once, when his roommate teased him about his opera, Hitler took offense and angrily reminded him that the famous German composer, Wagner, like himself, had been a high school drop-out and was mainly self-taught. Thereupon, Hitler went into a long and angry dissertation on the uselessness of formal education.

When Hitler's money ran out, he tried living on his orphan's pension. It didn't work. When he couldn't pay his boarding house rent, he skipped out and lived on the streets. At this time he became known to the Vienna Police who recorded his name in their log with the notation "Address unknown."

Eventually, more out of desperation than anything, he teamed up with a friend and formed a partnership in which he made paintings that his partner would sell and they split the profits 50-50. Together, these two entrepreneurs found a small market for hand-painted postcards for tourists, paintings for frame makers, and paintings on cloth that were sold to furniture makers for the backs of divans. Hitler and his partner also acquired some work in advertising. On his own, Hitler found some contract work in the construction field doing gilding and decorative painting.

In this manner, Hitler was able to support himself and moved into a YMCA-type facility called the Mannerheim where a man could rent a small private room for a modest fee and share lavatory, laundry, kitchen and lounge facilities. Hitler staked out a spot for himself in the lounge, set up his easel, and spent many hours painting for his clients. But, despite this newfound measure of prosperity, he was still an angry and frustrated man. Nothing could ease the pain he felt at being rejected by the Royal Academy and the architectural school. Hitler found other things to be angry about too. He learned to hate Vienna. In his opinion, it was old and ugly and he told friends that it should be torn down and rebuilt. It was also full of Jews. Twenty-five percent of the population was Jewish and they were prominent in the political and economic structure of the city and the nation. As a proud Austrian, Hitler felt that these positions should be reserved for Germanic people like himself.

He also became disgusted with his nation's Government. He spent time in the visitors' gallery of the Reichsrat, the nation's parliament, listening to representatives of the various parts of the Empire speak. Their heavy accents, foreign mannerisms and, in his opinion, lesser culture, made him angry. It drove home the fact that his country was a nation of foreigners and they all had the right to speak and vote in the Reichsrat. If this was what the democratic way was all about, Hitler concluded, he wanted nothing to do with it. Hitler wasn't alone in his dislike for foreigners. The Germans had long had a word for the Nazis, agreed to do so. Danielski later said that he would ply the Germans and Austrians with champagne and after the third bottle or so they would usually open up. After seeing the movie *Casablanca*, Danielski said that the activity in Rick's cafe was "like a piece of my life." After the war, Danielski emigrated to America and settled in Palm Beach, Florida, where he became a food and beverage manager. For the rest of his life he was known as "Mr. Casablanca." Danielski died in Florida in 1993.

War Scare In Portugal

During 1940 and the first half of 1941, there was great concern that Spain would join the Axis and take the British-held bastion at Gibraltar, thus opening the door to a British invasion through Portugal to outflank such an attack. The American Government felt that the situation was so uncertain that a U.S. warship was anchored permanently in the Lisbon harbor ready to evacuate Americans on short notice.

The Portuguese people heavily favored the Allied nations in the war although their Government acted otherwise. During the dark days of late 1940, when Britain

peoples of lesser culture: *untermenchen* (undermen).

Hitler also grew to dislike the Royal family. The Habsburgs had, at one time, been of pure Germanic stock but they had tainted their own blood by intermarrying with *untermenchen*.

In his disgust for his country, Hitler refused to register for the compulsory military draft. This was to be his undoing in Vienna. If caught, he could face immediate induction into the Army, or fines and imprisonment. Furthermore, his draft obligation would last until he was 36. Realizing that his position in Austria was untenable, he began saving his money for a move to Germany which, in his opinion, was the motherland of all German peoples. He would go to Munich where there weren't so many Jews and where there was another art school that might accept him as a student.

When Hitler left Vienna, he was an angry young man; angry that he had not been accepted as a serious painter, angry at his country's royal family and political system, and angry that there were so many Jews in the world.

While Hitler was in Vienna, several individuals who would become associated with the movie

Casablanca were there too. Some of them were Jews.

Peter Lorre (Ugarte), born Laszlo Loewenstein June 26, 1904, of Jewish parents in Rozsahegy, Hungary was there. Loewenstein's mother died when he was still a baby, and, in 1906, he and his father moved to Vienna, where his father had secured a good job as general manager of an automobile factory. Loewenstein grew up in Vienna and considered it his home town. He didn't know it of course, but a lot of people with whom he would become associated later in life, would become his neighbors in Vienna.

When the Loewensteins arrived in Vienna, Max Steiner, another Jew, who would compose the musical score for *Casablanca*, was already there, having been born in the city.

Paul von Henreid (Laszlo), four years younger than Loewenstein, would also come to live in Vienna soon after World War I, and Helmut Dantine (the Bulgarian man) was born in Vienna. Michael Curtiz (director) took refuge in Vienna after fleeing a Communist revolution in his native Hungary and S. K. Sakall (Carl) also spent time there.

stood alone against the Axis powers and was undergoing the terrible air blitz, a group of Portuguese citizens started a fund to pay for a British Spitfire fighter plane. Those who contributed were given a lapel pin bearing either Churchill's likeness or the Union Jack. The Germans protested and the Portuguese Government responded by outlawing the lapel pins. Soon afterwards, a new lapel pin appeared showing a hat and a cigar.

The war scare surfaced again in Portugal in July, August and September, 1941, after Germany and her Axis Allies had invaded the Soviet Union (June 22, 1941). The Axis military successes were so spectacular that many thought the Soviet Union would collapse in a matter of months. If that came to pass, the Axis nations would be in control of the European continent and could then use their mighty war machines to resolve some, or all, of the remaining unsettled issues in Europe—including Gibraltar. This created, once again, the same unpleasant military situation for Portugal that had been seen in 1940. This time, though, the Salazar Government approached the United States, still a neutral nation, asking for military aid if such a scenario came about. Washington did not say no and secret talks began between the Americans and Portuguese. The talks were not encouraging for the Portuguese, though, because the American military leaders concluded that with the combination of Axis forces released from the eastern front and a probable collaboration of Spanish forces, the Portuguese homeland could not be held. Discussions even covered the possibility of the Portuguese Government withdrawing to the Portuguese-owned Azores Islands in the central Atlantic Ocean and continuing their struggle from there.

If such a scenario came about and Lisbon, the last neutral large city in western Europe, fell to the Axis it would be a disaster of the first order for those refugees in Casablanca and elsewhere hoping to get to the west.

Salazar: Portugal's Dictator

Upon arriving in Lisbon, refugees found themselves in yet another dictatorship. But it was unlike the dictatorships from which they had fled.

For the first three decades of the 20th century, Portugal had been a democratic nation, but her economy and governments were never strong. In the late 1920s, a series of dictators came to power. In 1928, Portugal's economy was on the verge of collapse so General Carmona, the country's President and then-current dictator, appointed Dr. Antonio de Oliveira Salazar, a relatively unknown professor of economics from Coimbra University, as the country's Finance Minister. Carmona gave Salazar extraordinary powers to correct Portugal's faltering economy. Salazar did an excellent job, and, by 1932, in spite of the effects of the Great Depression, Portugal's economy was stronger that it had been in living memory.

Carmona then appointed Salazar to the post of Premier. Together, the two men formed the "União Nacional" (National Union), the only political party permitted in the country, and used it as a vehicle to carry forward their programs and reforms. Carmona and Salazar, both religious men, claimed that their new party would guide

Dr. Antonio de Oliveira Salazar, ruler of Portugal for 30 years.

Portuguese boys of the "Mocidade" in the green-shirted uniforms giving the Fascist salute.

the nation according to the "clerico-corporativist" philosophy set forth in several Papal encyclicals from the 19th and 20th centuries, and on the more modern theory of integral nationalism espoused in Charles Maurras' *Action Française*.

For all practical purposes, Salazar became Portugal's dictator with the full approval of Carmona. Salazar took unto himself the ministries of foreign affairs and war, and ruled by decree. He made no attempt to glorify his regime with gaudy trappings or paramilitary organizations such as Mussolini and Hitler had done. Salazar was a political technocrat and not a glory-seeker. He was a quiet man seldom seen in public and he issued his decrees without fanfare through the government-controlled news media. He was a lifelong bachelor, having taken a vow of chastity after a failed love affair in his youth. When asked why he didn't marry, he gave the same reason Hitler gave: that he was devoting his life to his country. He openly courted the Catholic Church and attended Mass regularly. Salazar was not overtly anti-Semitic but espoused the principle that one of the duties of government was to protect the state "from the clutches of audacious minorities." Neither was he a believer in democracy, describing it as a "life subordinated to politics." His regime had an official motto, "Deus, Patria e Familia" (God, Country and Family), but it was said that the real motto he stressed was "Futebol, Fado e Fatima" (football, the traditional music of Portugal called fado, and religion). These activities were designed to keep the minds of the people off politics.

Salazar hated Communism, ran the country through "corporative organizations" and syndicates, controlled the unions, outlawed strikes and lockouts, and established labor courts to settle labor disputes. In 1933, Salazar created a new constitution requiring that the President, the nation's Head of State and the man who would re-appoint him, stand for election every seven years by voters who had attained a prescribed degree of education. The new constitution called for freedom of religion, separation of church and state, imprisonment without formal charges for cases of f*lagrante delicto* for the safety of the State, military conscription, a 120-member National Assembly, and a

Corporative Chamber of an unspecified number of members to serve as an advisory body to the Head of State. Salazar called the political regime created by the new constitution the "Estado Novo" (New State). He took a very modest salary of $208 a month and made a serious effort to keep himself politically below President Carmona.

In foreign affairs, Salazar steered a neutral course while maintaining strong economic and political ties with both Great Britain and Spain. When the Spanish Civil War started in July 1936, Salazar was openly supportive of Franco and the Nationalist rebels. He allowed Portuguese men to volunteer for service with the rebels and let war supplies from Germany flow through Portugal into Spain. Republicans who escaped to Portugal during the Civil War were forcibly returned to Spain. A few were executed by the Portuguese. Naturally, he and Generalissimo Franco of Spain became close friends. In some quarters, Salazar was labeled a Fascist, a label he made no effort to renounce.

With final victory for the Nationalists in Spain nearing and the creation of a neo-Fascist government in Madrid a near certainty, Salazar saw that he was going to have a Fascist neighbor heavily indebted to Germany and Italy. So, as a gesture of friendship towards the Franco regime, he decided to take on some of the trappings of the Fascists. This was also seen as a gesture of friendship towards Spain's supporters, Germany and Italy, whose political and military powers were undeniably on the rise in Europe.

One of the first things Salazar copied from Fascism was to issue a decree requiring all Portuguese civil servants and teachers—he had been a teacher—to swear loyalty oaths to him personally. He then created a state-run youth movement for boys, the "Mocidade Portuguê," and a parallel organization for girls patterned after those in Germany and Italy. Membership was compulsory from ages 10 through 14. All members wore green shirts in keeping with the Fascist tradition of using various colored shirts to identify various organizations. In Italy the Fascists had used black shirts, the Nazis used brown shirts, the Spaniards used blue shirts and the American Fascist fringe used silver shirts.

The British and pre-armistice French Governments took little comfort in Salazar's Fascist-like maneuverings, but in London and Paris appeasement was the policy of the day and they let Salazar have his way without interference.

When the Spanish Nationalists gained final victory in Spain during the Spring of 1939, Salazar was delighted and made several political moves to strengthen his friendship with Generalissimo Franco, who was now calling himself the Caudillo (Protector) of Spain. This included giving Portugal's support for Spain's territorial claims against the French in North Africa. Franco responded by appointing his brother Ambassador to Lisbon.

At the same time, Salazar made pronouncements stressing that Portugal's strong traditional ties with Great Britain were still a mainstay of Portugal's foreign policy. Salazar played it both ways.

When World War II broke out in September 1939, Salazar announced a policy of strict neutrality for Portugal. He did not want to see the war come to the Iberian Peninsula and strongly urged Franco to keep Spain out of the war. After the fall of France in June 1940, he confided to a German envoy that he believed Britain could no longer win the war. He also predicted that the United States would not enter the war on its own, but would support Britain to the end.

This was the political atmosphere the refugees in the movie experienced when they reached Lisbon. They found a dictatorial but neutral government with some very visible fascist trappings, but yet not oppressive or racist. On the personal level, this meant that the Portuguese authorities with whom the refugees had to deal were firm but fair and relatively honest. And, fortunately for all concerned, Lisbon did not have a Captain Renault. Salazar wouldn't have tolerated it.

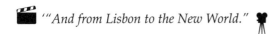 *'"And from Lisbon to the New World."*

The movie's narrator made it sound all so easy. But it wasn't. To get to Lisbon in the first place, refugees had to convince the officials at Portugal's foreign consulates that they would not stay long. This was done by producing an entrance or immigration visa from some other foreign country. Furthermore, the refugees had to prove that they had transportation out of Portugal. This latter was very hard to prove because transportation out of Lisbon was erratic and ever-changing. The Portuguese consular officials recognized this and tended to accept whatever plausible explanations the refugees offered.

Upon arriving in Lisbon, refugees had to register with the Portuguese immigration officials, find a place to live—which was difficult—change money, contact the embassy of the country to which they were to travel and look for transportation.

There were ways to get out of Lisbon by air, but air facilities were extremely limited and refugees were near the bottom of the priority list. The most likely way to get out of Lisbon was by ship. During the early part of World War II, from September 1939, to July 1940, there were enough ships calling at Lisbon to handle the needs of most refugees. After July 1940, when France surrendered and Italy entered the war, the situation changed for the worse. About this time, submarine warfare intensified and sea travel became less safe for neutrals and belligerents alike. Since maritime insurance rates went sky-high for merchant ships operating in European waters, many shipowners simply stopped sending their ships to Europe. Passenger liners were the first to go. By the end of 1940, virtually all of them had been requisitioned by their governments or leased by their respective governments and converted into troop or hospital ships. This meant that passenger-carrying freighters were virtually the only means of transportation still available to refugees. More and more freighters, though, began traveling in protected convoys which were slow, and those ships usually gave top priority to passengers other than refugees. Passengers with high priorities were servicemen,

Merchant ships sunk by Axis submarines in the Atlantic, during the nine month period from March, 1941, to December 6, 1941. During the first week of December, 1941, the time frame of Casa-blanca, *the Germans had 25 submarines working the waters off Mo-rocco, Gibraltar and Portugal. Italy had several submarines in the area too.*

Merchant ships sunk by U-boats in the Atlantic
18 March 1941–6 December 1941

3000 Km
3000 Mi.

Scale at the Equator.

their families, war wounded, government officials and citizens of the same nationality as the ship's owners. Because of this priority system, those with lower priorities, such as refugees, could be bumped at any time right up to the moment of sailing.

On February 14, 1940, the Germans made sailing on merchant ships even more risky. On that day, Berlin announced that German submarines would begin sinking any ship, neutral or not, steaming into or out of a port of an Allied nation. The next day, the British countered this announcement by declaring that they would begin allowing ships of neutral nations to join their convoys. This was not good news for refugees in Lisbon. It meant that more ships would now be sailing in convoys and convoys seldom came to Lisbon or went where the refugees wanted to go, with one great exception—America.

By the end of 1940, American Export Lines was the only American steamship line calling at Lisbon, and this was with freighters, some of which didn't carry passengers. United States Lines had a few freighters still calling in Spanish ports.

In July 1940, German submarines began operating out of French Atlantic ports meaning that more submarines were, from then on, operating in waters close to Portugal.

Ships of neutral nations often chose not to join convoys and continued to sail alone. Being neutral they were relatively safe and not intentionally attacked by Axis submarines, but mistakes were made and Portuguese ships became victims. On June 1, 1941, the Italian submarine "Marconi" accidentally sank the Portuguese trawler "Exportador I" 137 miles southwest of Cape St. Vincent, Portugal. Then, on June 20, 1941, the German submarine U-123 accidentally sank the Portuguese freighter "Ganda" 260 miles west-north-west of Casablanca. On October 12, 1941, U-83 sank the Portuguese steam ship "Corte Real" only 80 miles off Lisbon, and on December 14, 1941, the German submarine U-108 sank the Portuguese freighter "Cassequel" 250 miles northwest of Casablanca. Incidents such as these continued to occur throughout the war and every neutral nation had one or more of its ships accidentally sunk or damaged.

Chapter Two

Round Up All Suspicious Characters

🎬 *"To all officers. Two German couriers carrying important official documents murdered on the train from Oran."* 🎥

The roundup of the suspects is one of the historically accurate differences between Unoccupied and Occupied France. Even though two Germans had been murdered, the Germans had no authority investigating a crime in Unoccupied France, a neutral country. That was clearly the responsibility of the French Police. If the Germans had been murdered in Occupied France, the Gestapo would have taken the lead in the investigation and the French Police would have taken their orders from them. And, the Gestapo could be ruthless. They could, and often did, take and execute hostages in such situations. But, in Unoccupied France, the best the Gestapo could do was send their own people to assist in the investigation and keep pressure on the French Police authorities to do their duties, hence the presence of the Gestapo's Major Strasser in the movie.

In the round-up scenes, only men in European clothing are taken into custody. This is obviously to highlight the precarious situation of the refugees. In all likelihood, native Moroccans would have been suspects, too.

Petain is one of only three real-life individuals whose name or likeness appears in the movie. The others are Adolph Hitler and Charles De Gaulle. Petain is never mentioned by name, Hitler is mentioned only when the Nazis exchange "Heil Hitlers," and De Gaulle is mentioned even though he shouldn't have been.

Petain was the dictator of France, and, like most dictators, ruled by decrees backed up by force and justified his actions with high-sounding slogans. The man who was

Fleeing suspect played by actor Paul Andor, whose papers are not in order, is shot and killed as he tries to escape the Casablanca Police. Behind him is a likeness of Marshal Henri Petain, the dictator of Unoccupied France. The slogan reads, "I keep my promises, just as I keep the promises of others."

Marshal Henri Petain, French Head of State.

shot and killed beneath his portrait was, as will soon be revealed, a member of the Free French, an organization headed by Petain's arch rival, General Charles De Gaulle. It was Petain who, in June, 1940, as the Premier of France, surrendered to the Germans and Italians and took France out of the war. General De Gaulle, a relatively low level member of Petain's Government, refused to accept that surrender, fled to England, and announced that he would continue to fight on against the Axis powers. To carry out that struggle, De Gaulle formed an organization called the "Free French" and set up his headquarters in London.

In 1943, when *Casablanca* was released to the American public, Petain was a well-known figure, one of about a dozen individuals whose picture appeared regularly in newspapers, magazines and newsreels.

Marshal Petain was one of France's greatest heroes from World War I (1914-1918) and became French Premier on June 16, 1940, at the age of 84. At that time, France was on the verge of military collapse. The French Army was in general retreat, the Germans had occupied Paris, Italy had declared war on France, and, together, the two Axis Powers were rapidly overrunning the whole country. The French Government that preceded Petain, headed by Paul Reynaud, had fled to Bordeaux. There, the Reynaud Government fell into disagreement and was unable to decide whether or not to fight or to surrender. Reynaud and his Cabinet resigned and Petain was appointed Premier of

U.S. Citizen Shot in *Casablanca*

When Wolfgang Zilzer decided to go to America, he applied for his immigration visa and was pleasantly surprised to learn that he was already an American citizen. His German parents, also actors, had been on tour in the U.S. when he was born and that qualified him for American citizenship. He later changed his name to Paul Andor and appeared in *Casablanca* as the man shot by the Casablanca police.

General and Madame Charles De Gaulle in London. Madame De Gaulle escaped from France separately from her husband in June, 1940, just a few steps ahead of the advancing German troops.

France by France's President, Albert Lebrun. It was hoped that this honored hero of World War I, could somehow save France. Petain had saved France once before during the prolonged and costly Battle of Verdun in 1916. At that time, the Germans had launched a major offensive against the Verdun front with the objective of breaking through the French lines and marching on to Paris. Petain commanded the French troops on the Verdun front and directed a masterful defense that held the Germans to small advances of only a few miles after almost six months of extremely heavy fighting. During the height of one battle he made the dramatic statement, "Ils ne passeront pas" (they will not pass). The French lines held and Petain and his statement became famous. Eventually, the Germans gave up the offensive and Petain became known thereafter as "The Hero of Verdun." Soon afterwards, he was promoted to Field Marshal. The Battle of Verdun was one of the worst battles of World War I, costing the Germans 540,000 casualties and the French 430,000.

Thus, in July 1940, 24 years after Verdun, Petain was called upon again to save France. But, this time there would be no heroic defense. He "saved" France by asking for an armistice. In doing so, he saved about one third of metropolitan France from being occupied and retained French control over the sprawling French Empire. By this action, though, he broke his Government's pledge to Great Britain that neither country would seek a separate peace without the approval of the other. In the eyes of the British, the Americans and most other western leaders, Petain had betrayed France's honor. They argued that he could have continued the struggle honorably and effectively from bases in the French Empire, especially from French North Africa.

The Armistice Petain was forced to sign all but made him and his government puppets of the Germans, and to a lesser degree, the Italians. When the Petain Government moved to Vichy, he prevailed upon the demoralized French Assembly, the nation's parliament, to give him extraordinary powers to rule the country by decree. He was given the authority to write a new constitution that placed most political powers in the hands of a single leader to be known as the Head of State, a euphemism for dictator. After a lengthy and heated debate, the Assembly voted Petain the powers he sought. Within the next few hours, Petain issued three decrees that officially ended democracy in France as well as in the French Third Republic. These three decrees were issued pending the creation and ratification of the new constitution which, it was expected, would make them permanent. In the first decree, Petain declared himself Head of State. In the second, he decreed that the Head of State shall be given the "totality of Governmental Power," and in the third, he dismissed the French Assembly indefinitely. Petain thus became the absolute dictator of France.

Throughout the movie, nothing more of Petain will be said, but the word "Vichy" will be mentioned often. To the moviegoers of 1943 it was well known that these words were synonymous. Now, the moviegoers of this era know it too. "Vichy" and the man on the wall mean the same thing: the dictatorial government of wartime France.

The Cross Of Lorraine

When the audiences of 1943 saw the Cross of Lorraine, they knew in an instant that one of the good guys had fallen. The Cross of Lorraine was almost as well known as the swastika of Nazi Germany and the hammer and sickle of the Soviet Union.

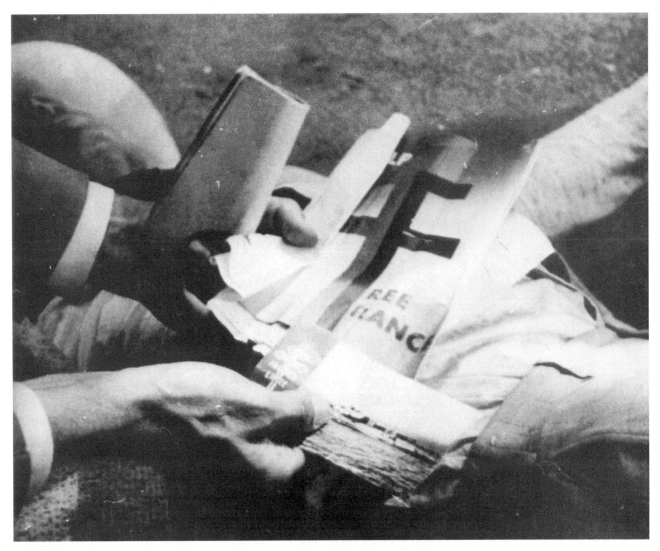

It was not always that way, though. Up to July, 1940, the Cross of Lorraine was just one of hundreds of obscure symbols used worldwide for political, religious and other purposes. In this case, the Cross of Lorraine was the age-old symbol of the French province of Lorraine in northeastern France and it was seldom seen outside its regional area. Lorraine and the adjoining province to the north, Alsace, bordered Germany and had a mixed population of French- and German-speaking citizens. Both Germany and France had claimed the two provinces as their own over the years and had fought over them for generations. Since 1870, the two provinces had changed hands three times. In 1939, at the beginning of World War II, the provinces belonged to France.

During the German conquest of Northern France, the two provinces were over-run by German troops and became part of Occupied France. Soon after their conquest, the Germans announced that they would be annexed by the German Reich. In July 1940, the German Government began the systematic expulsion of the provinces' 70,000 French families, all their Jews, Gypsies and other undesirables. In November 1940, Germany formally annexed the provinces. Alsace became a part of the neighboring German state of Baden and Lorraine was renamed "Westmark." The use of the French

Papers found on the body of the fleeing suspect bore the "Cross of Lorraine," the symbol of the Free French.

A poster published by the France Forever Movement in America displays the Cross of Lorraine. This was one of many ways Americans became familiar with the symbol of the Free French.

language was thereafter forbidden. German families with French surnames were ordered, by law, to change them to the German versions.

This was a bitter pill for the entire French nation to swallow. The Petain Government sheepishly acknowledged the loss of Alsace and Lorraine and announced that space would be found in Unoccupied France for those expelled.

From London though, De Gaulle and his Free French organization took a more determined stand. They refused to acknowledge the loss of the provinces and announced that, as a constant reminder to Frenchmen everywhere that the provinces were still French territory, the Free French movement would, henceforth, use the Cross of Lorraine as its symbol. The Free French modified the traditional tri-colored flag of

France by placing the Cross on the center white panel. This became the Free French flag. All Free French servicemen wore the symbol somewhere on their uniforms and all Free French official documents, letterheads, publications, news releases etc. bore the symbol. And, as might be expected, the Cross of Lorraine was used extensively in Free French propaganda.

In the Allied nations and in neutral America, the activities of De Gaulle were being followed with great public interest because the creation of the Free French movement was one of the few bright spots in the Allied war effort. De Gaulle and his Free French were given generous and positive press coverage and the Cross of Lorraine became a well-known symbol. By 1943, when *Casablanca* was released, everybody who could read had seen the Cross of Lorraine numerous times. Hollywood acknowledged the symbol in 1944 when MGM made a movie called *The Cross of Lorraine* starring Gene Kelly, Jean-Pierre Aumont and *Casablanca*'s Ugarte (Peter Lorre). This was a thriller in which French soldiers escape from a German prisoner-of-war camp and lead a local village in an uprising against the Germans.

Behind the scenes, in the Government halls of London and Washington, De Gaulle and his movement were not as readily accepted as the public was led to believe. These differences, though, were kept secret, and, as far as the Allied public was concerned, De Gaulle was the undisputed leader of France's resistance movement. The Cross of Lorraine was seen, not only as the symbol of De Gaulle and his Free French, but as the symbol of that movement.

The Battle of the National Slogans

The scene quickly changes from the policeman viewing the fallen man's papers to an ornate sign, etched in stone over a doorway. The signs reads "Liberté, Egalité, Fraternité" (Liberty, Equality, Fraternity), the time-honored and well-known slogan of the French Republic. Then, the next frames show more of the roundup in progress and the suspects being led into a building bearing the sign "Palais de Justice" (Palace of Justice).

By juxtaposing the slogan of the French Republic, "Liberté, Egalité, Fraternité" (Liberty, Equality, Fraternity), with the roundup of the suspects, the screenwriters are inserting a bit of sarcastic wartime propaganda at the expense of the Vichy regime because the activities of the Casablanca Police certainly belie the meanings of that hallowed French slogan and the democratic concept of justice it conveys.

In reality, though, the French Republic was dead and so was the slogan. The Vichy regime had replaced it with one of its own: "Travail, Famille, Patrie" (Work, Family, State). The old slogan of the Republic, though, was still the one seen by the great majority of the French because the Vichy Government simply hadn't had time enough to replace all of the signs throughout the Empire bearing the old slogan with new signs bearing the new slogan.

Mers el Kebir:
Britain and France Go to the Brink of War

The English couple watching the roundup of suspects, who eventually fall prey to the pickpocket, might appear to be tourists or perhaps a businessman and his wife in town on business—and well they might have been originally. But not now. In this first week of December 1941, they were simply two individuals out of thousands of British subjects stranded in Vichy-controlled areas around the world as a result of the unfortunate naval battle between the British and French Navies on July 3, 1940, at a place called Mers el Kebir.

The battle of Mers el Kebir came about as a direct result of the collapse of France and the fears the British had that the Axis Powers might gain control of the large and still very powerful French Navy.

When, in late June 1940, it became obvious to the British that the French were out of the war permanently and that the new Petain Government was strongly under the influence of the Axis Powers, the British military leaders became even more concerned about the future of the French Navy. The French Army and Air Force had been decimated and were of little value to anyone, However, the French Navy, fourth largest in the world, was still a formidable fighting force. The British feared that the Axis Powers would gain control of the French Navy. Together with the Italian Navy, the world's fifth largest, and the German Navy, the sixth largest, they would pose a serious threat to the British Navy, the world's largest. (The American Navy was the second largest and the Japanese Navy was third). Furthermore, the British could see that such a combined naval force could facilitate an Axis invasion of England which, they knew from various intelligence reports, the Germans were planning.

During the last days of the struggle in France, the British conveyed their fears to the French by warning them that London would not accept, under any circumstance, the Axis Powers gaining control of the French Navy. The French replied, more than once, that they would not welcome such a situation either and would do all in their power to prevent it from happening, even to the point of scuttling their own ships to keep them out of the enemy's hands. The German/French Armistice Agreement gave further assurances about the French Fleet in article #8 which stated that the German Government would not seize the French ships as long as they remained disarmed in their home ports.

These assurances were not good enough for the British. They demanded that all of the French warships either join the British by sailing immediately to British ports, or neutralize themselves by sailing to neutral ports to be interned for the duration of the war or be scuttled by their crews. The French refused to do any of these things and a political stalemate developed. The British then concluded that they had to put teeth into their demands and, at the insistence of Winston Churchill, England's Prime Minister, it was decided to make a determined show of force against the French. This decision was opposed by many of Churchill's advisors and remains to this day one of the most controversial decisions of the war. It was, nevertheless, carried out. The British chose to make their show of force by launching a naval attack on the French fleet at some suitable location and confiscating French warships whenever the opportunity presented itself. The place chosen for the naval attack was Mers el Kebir, the large French naval base in Algeria five miles northwest of Oran. Some of France's largest warships were anchored there.

On the morning of July 3, 1940, a powerful British naval force, commanded by Admiral Sir James Somerville, sailed into sight of the French naval base and took up positions off shore with guns at the ready. A British delegation went ashore, met with the French base commander, Admiral Marcel Gensoul, and ordered him to choose, under threat of attack, one of several options, all of which would neutralize the French ships for the duration of the war. Gensoul quickly conferred with the Petain Government which was then en route to Vichy. Petain rejected all the British demands and the British delegation returned to inform Somerville. After a brief delay, the British ships opened fire. The French responded in kind and for the better part of an hour the navies of the two former allies blasted away at each other. Losses and casualties were inflicted on both sides, but the French losses were greater.

Meanwhile, throughout the British Empire, French ships at anchor in British ports were boarded and taken over by British sailors, soldiers and marines. The most significant action was in Great Britain at Plymouth and Portsmouth where, after a brief skirmish, two French battleships, nine destroyers and several dozen other ships were secured. At Alexandria, Egypt, where French and British warships were anchored within several hundred yards of each other, the French refused to let the British board. After a tense standoff, the French finally gave in and accepted the British demand that their ships be disarmed.

At Mers el Kebir, one French battleship, the "Bretagne," was sunk, two others were badly damaged and 1,400 French seamen were killed.

During the *mêlée* at Mers el Kebir, the French battleship "Strasbourg" and five destroyers managed to slip out of the harbor, fight their way through the British fleet, and sail on to the major French naval base at Toulon, France.

The attack on Mers el Kebir was clearly an act of war and the French had every right to declare war on Britain. There were those in Petain's Government who advocated that action. Petain, though, wisely hesitated. Clearly, a French response was called for and Petain began exploring his options.

On July 4, Petain asked Hitler to suspend article #8 of their Armistice Agreement so that the French Navy could retaliate against the British. Hitler promptly agreed.

By the evening of July 4, though, cooler heads had prevailed. Clearly the Petain Government was in no position to declare war on England and see itself thrust into the arms of the Axis more than they already were. The French wanted no more naval battles like Mers el Kebir. Their Navy was the only powerful weapon they had left and they didn't want to lose any more ships, especially to the British. So, a naval attack by the French Navy on the British was ruled out.

Petain and his advisors finally agreed that a proper retaliation for the attack on Mers el Kebir would be an air attack by French planes on Gibraltar. That attack was carried

The French battleship "Bretagne" sinking by the stern as a result of the attack by the British Navy on the French naval base at Mers el Kebir, Algeria.

out the next morning, July 5. In an effort to tone down the confrontation with the British, Petain instructed the French Navy not to attack any British warship unless it ventured within 20 miles of a French military installation. This order was made public.

Churchill, though, was not satisfied. He felt that the French had not been punished enough. On July 6, the British struck again at Mers el Kebir, this time with a bombing raid. Following that, Vichy severed diplomatic relations with Britain. The British responded by announcing that the naval blockade, which they had maintained against Germany since the beginning of the war, would be expanded to include France and all Vichy-controlled colonies. This action had worldwide consequences. First of all, it meant that Vichy's supply of food and raw materials from her overseas colonies would all but cease—and the French were already very short of food. Furthermore, the extension of the British blockade meant that supplies from America and other neutral nations would now be restricted by the will of the British.

By July 12, 1940, Churchill was satisfied. He announced that the British Navy would no longer interfere with the operations of the French Navy unless French ships tried to sail to Axis-controlled ports. With this, the tensions of the Mers el Kebir crisis began to subside. The French, though, felt it prudent to keep their warships as immobile as possible lest they raise again the ire of Mr. Churchill.

As for the naval blockade, the British eventually clarified that they would allow food, consumer goods, humanitarian supplies and other non-military items to flow through the blockade so long as those goods did not reach the Axis nations. They reserved the right, though, to inspect any ship carrying goods to the French and to confiscate those ships and their cargoes if it was determined that they were carrying contraband.

During the Mers el Kebir crisis, one of the measures the Vichy Government took against Britain was to forbid all British males from leaving Vichy-controlled territory.

A Vichy anti-British poster from late 1940 or early 1941 shows Churchill as an octopus with the words "His amputations continue systematically." Note that the octopus' tentacles still reach out to the west to America, to the east to India, and hold Ireland, the Arabian Peninsula and South Africa firmly in their grasp.

The British had been making it very difficult for male French citizens to leave England. Most of the Frenchmen in England were servicemen stranded there when France fell. The British put pressure on them to join De Gaulle's Free French and if they refused they found it difficult to get back home.

This, then, accounts for the middle-aged British couple's presence in Casablanca. The man was not allowed to leave French territory so his dutiful wife chose to remain with him.

Throughout the movie, there is no mention of the strong anti-British feeling felt by the Vichy French as the result of the Mers el Kebir incident. Nevertheless, it did exist and had an adverse effect throughout the war on relations between the Allies and the Vichy French, especially those in French North Africa.

This ill will between Vichy and London was another factor in the decision by the United States to try to keep on good terms with Vichy so as to provide a political counter-balance and a communications conduit between Vichy and London. Fortunately, Vichy wanted that too, so the Vichy-American relationship remained on relatively good terms serving the interests of both sides.

Another reason why the hard feelings between the British and the Vichy French were not mentioned in the movie was due to American censorship. When *Casablanca* was made in 1942, the American movie industry had to comply with American wartime censorship regulations. At that time, the American Government wanted the American public to believe that the French people were really anti-Vichy at heart and were just waiting for their opportunity to throw off the Vichy yoke and resume the fight against the Axis. This was not necessarily true but, in 1942, it was more important to keep up the morale of the American people than to tell the truth.

S.K. Sakall (Carl) Flees The Nazis

S. K. Sakall was born Eugene Gero Szakall, February 2, 1884, in Budapest, Hungary. After writing gags for a popular Budapest comic, he became a comic himself performing under the name Szoke Szakall and moved to Germany where he became very popular in the cabarets and night club circuits with an act in which he horribly butchered the German language. Much of this was not an act. Szakall had trouble learning new languages.

When the Nazis came to power in January, 1933, and took over all aspects of the entertainment business in Germany, Szakall, who was Jewish, returned to his native Budapest. There, he found work as a comic, but virtually nothing opened up for him in the Hungarian film industry. Germany was a big market for Hungarian films and all foreign films with Jews in them were banned in Germany. Szakall stayed on in Budapest for three years, but in that time found work in only three movies. Then, in 1935, he acquired a good movie role in Vienna and moved there. After a while, he returned to Budapest and made a living for himself once again as a cabaret and night club comic.

On May 3, 1939, the pro-Axis Government of Hungary announced that all Jews in Hungary had to leave the country within five days. This applied to Szakall. Fortunately, though, a relative, Hollywood producer Joe Pasternak, contacted Szakall and urged him to come to Hollywood where he felt he could find work. Szakall agreed and traveled to the United States that spring. Pasternak was right. The Hollywood crowd fell in love with this jolly, overweight Hungarian who spoke terrible English and had flabby jowls that he could shake on command. In Hollywood he began using the name S. K. Sakall (sometimes S. Z. Sakall) but, Jack Warner gave him another name, "Cuddles." In 1940, Sakall was in his first American movie, Universal's *It's a Date*. Then he had two more movies in 1941 and more in 1942, including *Casablanca*, in which he played Rick's head waiter, Carl. That year, he signed a long-term contract with Warner Bros. and became one of their most identifiable and often used character actors in Hollywood.

For the English couple in the movie, things would get worse for them before they got better. In March 1942, in response to reports reaching Vichy that the Allies were about to invade the Atlantic coast of French Morocco, all British citizens, including the British couple, were ordered to move inland 200 miles or more. The reports in March, 1942, of a pending Allied invasion were false, but the Americans did, indeed, invade the Atlantic coast of French Morocco eight months later.

Major Strasser's Arrival

In the movie, when Jan and Annina, the Bulgarian couple, see the plane arriving at Casablanca airport, Annina wonders aloud if they'll be on it tomorrow. She believes it to be the plane from Lisbon, but it isn't. It's a German plane bringing Major Heinrich Strasser, of the Gestapo, to Casablanca to assist in the investigation of the murdered German couriers and the recovery of the stolen documents.

Strasser's plane may not have been the only plane over Casablanca that day. Since the fall of 1940, British reconnaissance planes had been flying all along the Atlantic coast of French Morocco taking photos of military installations, roads, bridges, possible landing beaches and the like. One of the several military options the British were studying was the creation of a land route through French North Africa from the Atlantic Ocean to the Mediterranean in the event Gibraltar was lost and/or the Strait of Gibraltar was closed by enemy action. To establish such a route the British would have to invade French Morocco, advance eastward into Algeria and then northward to the Mediterranean coast.

The British reconnaissance planes flew so high over French Morocco that they were seldom heard and almost never seen. The need to open an alternative land route between the Atlantic and the Mediterranean never materialized, but the information gathered by the reconnaissance planes was used by the Americans in planning their invasion of French Morocco which took place in November 1942.

After Strasser's airplane flies over Rick's Cafe Americain, it lands at the city's airport which appears to be in the middle of Casablanca. In reality, the airport was about five miles southeast of downtown on the road to Marrakech.

Strasser's plane—a single-engined high-wing aircraft with a black swastika on the vertical stabilizer and bold black letters on the sides of the fuselage and on the top and bottom of the wings—is, in fact, an American-made plane. It is a Travel-Air light transport plane manufactured in the late 1920s. Could this be historically correct? Could a Gestapo man be flying about in a ten- to twelve-year-old American-made airplane? The answer is, yes. During wartime, aircraft in general are in short supply in all the belligerent nations and serviceability, not age, is the criteria for their usefulness.

The Germans could have acquired this aircraft in several ways. They could have bought it directly from the American manufacturer before the war, because many of the Travel-Airs were exported, or they might have acquired it as war booty from one of their many conquests. Ten to twelve years was not an unusual age for a commercial aircraft of this type, although it was nearing the end of its useful life. This plane was slow and had no arms or armament. So, it was best that it not be flown in western Europe where the British Royal Air Force (RAF) was carrying out bombing missions. Nor could it be used on the eastern front where the Soviet Air Force was very active up to several hundred miles behind the front. If this plane was ever attacked by a modern-day fighter plane of the times it wouldn't have a chance. So, one of the places a plane of this type could be used was in a remote outpost, such as French Morocco.

The Armistice Commissions

When Strasser's plane comes to a halt, it is greeted by a number of waiting dignitaries. In the gathering are several French policemen, an honor guard of native Moroccan soldiers (commanded by French Army officers), an Italian honor guard, an Italian officer and several German Army officers. All of their uniforms appear to be authentic — a compliment to the Warner Bros. wardrobe department.

This scene, though, brings up one of the frequently-asked questions about the movie. Why there were German and Italian soldiers in Unoccupied French Morocco?

These were members of the German and Italian Armistice Commissions established as a result of the German and Italian Armistice Agreements signed with France in June, 1940. Those agreements, one between Germany and France and the other between Italy and France, permitted the Germans and Italians to send such commissions into certain areas of the French Empire to ensure that the French lived up to the terms of the Armistice. Casablanca was one of the most likely locations for such commissions because of the many French Army installations in the area and the presence of French warships in the harbor.

The Italians established their commission in Casablanca first, soon after the Armistices were signed, and it reported to the Italian Central Armistice Commission in Turin, Italy. The Germans had originally planned to rely on the Italian commissions to monitor the Armistice in most of French North Africa, but this didn't work out. The French had little respect for the Italians and looked upon them as jackals who had entered the war when it was obvious that France was beaten, and now wanted to feast off of the French corpse. As a result, the French snubbed and abused the Italian commissions at every opportunity and the Italians proved incapable of enforcing all of the armistice conditions. This was a great disappointment to the Germans, so, in the spring of 1941, they sent their own commission to Casablanca. The German Armistice Commissions reported to the German Central Armistice Commission in Wiesbaden, Germany.

The German Armistice Commission for Casablanca set up its headquarters in the plush Miramar Hotel in Fedala, a beach resort 24 miles northeast of Casablanca. This made them the second German agency functioning in the Casablanca area. The German Consulate was the other.

When the original play was written, after France had fallen but before the German Armistice Commission came to Casablanca, Strasser, then a Captain and not a Major, was an *attaché* of the German Consulate in Casablanca. The Warner Bros. screenwriters retained the Consulate connection in the person of Herr Heinze who is identified as "the German consul" in Howard Koch's book, *The 50th Anniversary Edition, Casablanca, Script and Legend*. Heinze wears a military uniform throughout the movie but is addressed by the civilian title "Herr."

The German Consulate, itself, is not mentioned in the movie, but it was quite an important place in the world of international politics because it was one of the few places around the world where the Germans and Americans were on relatively friendly terms. This was due to the nature of the personal relationship between Theodore Auer, the German Counsel General, and Robert Murphy, the American special envoy to French North Africa. Both Auer and Murphy were professional diplomats and knew each other from their earlier days together in Paris. In his book, *Diplomat Among Warriors*, Murphy wrote that Auer was something less than an ardent Nazi and remarked on one occasion, "That prize ass in Berlin [Hitler] does not seem aware that this area exists."

The salutes exchanged by the Nazis beside the plane are accurate and according to Nazi protocol. Heinze, the junior officer, initiates the greeting with the traditional outstretched arm and wrist salute and is the first to say "Heil Hitler." Strasser, the senior officer, acknowledges Heinze's salute by giving the receiving salute in which the elbow is bent and the wrist bent backwards. Strasser returns the greeting of "Heil Hitler." Heinze holds his salute until after Strasser has said "Heil Hitler."

Heinze then introduces Major Strasser to Captain Louis Renault, Casablanca's Prefect of Police. This is Captain Renault's first appearance in the movie.

No Ordinary Police Chief

As Prefect of police, Renault is a very important individual in the ruling hierarchy of the city, and has more authority than most Chiefs of Police else where. This fact is not mentioned in the movie. It stems from the city's history and France's position as a colonial power.

In the decade of 1900-10, when the French were first attempting to establish themselves in central and southern Morocco, Casablanca was under the control of the Moroccans and was one of the least secure cities along the Moroccan coast for Europeans. Nevertheless, it was a major trading center, and, over the years, a sizable international settlement evolved within the city housing a relatively large number of Europeans. The settlement was well-guarded and warships from France and other nations were almost always anchored in the harbor, serving as an additional means of protection. The city's Moroccan administration generally cooperated with the Europeans, but was prone to sudden and dramatic changes due to the turbulent nature of Moroccan politics. One of the more drastic political changes in Casablanca occurred during this time when a local sorcerer came to power and ruled the city for a year before being deposed, however, trade between the Moroccans and Europeans went on as usual.

By the summer of 1907, native unrest in the interior of Morocco had escalated into a full-blown colonial war. Several Moroccan chieftains had united into a sizable military force and were strong enough to threaten an invasion of Casablanca. During the Spring and early Summer of 1907, tensions were at a fever pitch. In July, several Italian and French workmen quarrying stone outside the city were attacked and murdered by Moroccan warriors. This incident, along with other ominous signs, indicated that the city was about to be invaded by the Moroccan chieftains. The French warships in the harbor quickly landed armed sailors who rushed to take up defensive positions around the international settlement, the various foreign consulates and certain other important city facilities. Fortunately, the sailors got into position before the wild Moroccan bands surged into the city. Immediately, the bands began looting, burning, murdering and committing other atrocities. The full force of the attack fell on the city's Jews and those native city-dwellers whom the invaders accused of having collaborated with the Europeans. The French positions were assaulted by the invaders but the Frenchmen held their ground. During the battle, the French ships in the harbor bombarded a section of town believed to be the stronghold of those who sympathized with the Moroccan invaders.

Eventually, the French received reinforcements and the invaders were chased back into the desert. The rape of Casablanca, though, cost the lives of nine Europeans and gave all the western nations with interests in the city and in Morocco cause for concern that a similar invasion might happen again. In response to this concern, the French took over the administration of the city while the French Government in Paris gave assurances to all that, in the future, Casablanca would be well-protected by French troops and by a large and powerful police force that would be permanently maintained in the city. This action gave Casablanca's Prefect of Police a unique international commitment to protect and defend the interests of other nations in Casablanca as well as the interests of France. To ensure that the Prefect of Police could fulfill that commitment, he had under his command a police force larger than most other cities of comparable size.

This commitment was still in force in 1941 during the time-frame of the movie, giving Captain Renault the authority to deal with international matters such as the murder of the German couriers and the theft of the important documents the German couriers were carrying.

Italy's Wartime Reputation

After being introduced to Major Strasser Captain Renault introduces his aide, Lt. Casselle. Seconds later, a man in a white uniform steps in front of Strasser and Renault and introduces himself as Captain Tonelli of the Italian service. Strasser and Renault are visibly annoyed at this intrusion and rather rudely brush him aside.

It is not known from the movie whether Tonelli was from the Italian Armistice Commission or from the Italian Consulate, but his treatment by Strasser and Renault is historically accurate. By this time in the war, Italian military prowess had been proven woefully inadequate and the political position of the Italians had eroded considerably. In 1940/41, the Italians had lost their east African colonies of Eritrea, Italian Somaliland and Ethiopia to the British and Free French. They were about to lose Libya too until Hitler sent General Irwin Rommel and two and a half divisions of well-trained, well-equipped German troops, known as the Afrika Corps, to fight alongside the Italians

and save that colony from being overrun by the British. In 1941, Hitler had to bail out the Italians in the Balkans after their unsuccessful attempt to conquer Greece. Furthermore, the Italian units fighting in the Soviet Union had proven to be a disappointment to the Germans and were always relegated to "quiet" sections of the front.

In the United States, Britain, and even in Germany, jokes were made about the inadequacies of the Italian military. As the movie progresses, the Italians will receive additional less-than-complimentary comments about their fighting abilities.

Later on in a scene in the movie where Lieutenant Casselle and Captain Tonelli are seen together entering Rick's Cafe, Lieutenant Casselle is haranguing Captain Tonelli in French about Italy's inability to win a battle without the aid of the Germans. Casselle is telling Tonelli what most of the world already suspects: that Italy is now militarily dependent on Germany. Casselle is speaking specifically about the Italian debacle in Greece, thereby chiding Tonelli about one of Italy's most embarrassing campaigns. In October, 1940, Italy provoked a war with Greece and invaded that country from Italian-held Albania. The Italian advance was soon stopped by the determined

Thousands of Italian soldiers surrendered to the British in Libya before German General Rommel and his Afrika Corps were sent to stiffen the Axis front there.

German troops raising their flag in front of the Acropolis soon after the fall of Athens.

Stalin's Siberians. These were the men attempting to stop the German advance on Moscow while Strasser and Renault spoke of the warm climate in Casablanca. The Siberians were well-trained soldiers, adequately equipped for winter warfare and inured to cold. Stalin pulled them from Siberia leaving that region unprotected against a possible attack by Japan. His gamble paid off. A few days later, Japan attacked the United States military installations at Pearl Harbor, Hawaii, and stuck south into Southeast Asia and not north into Siberia.

resistance of the Greek Army with help from the British Army. The Greeks and British then counter-attacked and drove the Italians back into Albania. The British sent in reinforcements with the intention of capturing all of Albania, a situation Hitler—who was planning his invasion of the Soviet Union—could not accept since he did not want a sizable British force on his southern flank. Furthermore, the reputation of his major European ally was at stake if Albania was lost to the Allies.

So Hitler sent powerful German forces through Bulgaria and Yugoslavia to invade Greece. Those forces, together with the tag-along Italian and Bulgarian forces, succeeded in conquering Greece and forcing the British to withdraw from the Balkan Peninsula. The Axis military situation was salvaged but not Italy's reputation. From then on, Italy's image as a major military power was badly tarnished, and remained so throughout the war.

As Strasser and Renault walk together from the airport, Renault comments os Casablanca's warm weather. Strasser then replies,

 "We Germans must get used to all climates from Russia to the Sahara."

This is an accurate reflection of Germany's attitude at the time. As Strasser spoke, Germany had strong forces fighting in Russia and in parts of the Sahara Desert in Libya and Egypt. From the German point of view, once those areas were conquered, Germans would be there to stay and would have to get used to the two extremes in climate.

Strasser's boast about German troops getting used to the Russian climate was being tested at that very moment. Hitler had planned for the war in Russia to be over by December, 1941, and hadn't bothered to equip the German Army for the rigors of the long Russian winter. Men like these, still wearing summer uniforms in December, suffered considerably from the cold and simply couldn't fight effectively in the extreme Russian winter weather.

Chapter Three

Everybody Comes To Rick's

When Strasser questions Renault about the steps he has made to find the murderer of the two German Couriers, Renault replies that the culprit will be at Rick's Cafe Americain tonight, saying those famous words, "Everybody Comes To Rick's" (the title of the original play).

The scene shifts to the front door of Rick's cafe. It is evening and people are entering the fashionable, upscale night club where men are expected to wear coats and ties, and ladies wear evening wear. A doorman opens the door and the camera moves inside. Music is heard—the kind of music one would expect to hear in an American night club in the 1940s—big band swing music. The tune being played is a typical 1940s rendition of "It Had to Be You."

When Murray Burnett, a vacationing high school teacher from New York City, and his wife entered the Cafe Aurore on the Mediterranean coast of France on a summer night in 1938, they experienced a very similar feeling. The events of that evening later inspired Burnett to collaborate on writing a play with a friend, Joan Alison, about the people and activities that Burnett and his wife saw that evening at the Aurore. Burnett and Alison changed the name of the night club to Rick's Cafe Americain and titled their play "Everybody Comes to Rick's." That play eventually became the basis for *Casablanca*.

This was the heyday of swing music and the sound of big bands. And, the movie makers of that era couldn't ignore the influence. Nor could they ignore the big bands themselves. The movie-going hep-cats wanted to hear the latest jive and see their favorite bands on the screen. It was a mellowroony time. So, the movie-makers generously obliged. Almost every big band in America appeared at one time or another in the movies.

Rick's five-piece band (six if Sam, the piano player, is included) could hardly have been called a big band but it was adequate for a swanky night spot like Rick's. More big band swing music will be heard as the movie progresses.

Once inside the nightclub, the camera focuses on Sam, the cafe's black piano player and Rick's closest friend. Sam's singing the American swing number, "Shine."

Here's another authentic scene from the late 1930s and early 1940s. During this era, black entertainers were very much a part of the entertainment scene. The French were especially receptive to black entertainers as was demonstrated by their love of jazz and swing music. Beginning in the 1920s, they readily accepted African-American entertainers such as singer-dancer Josephine Baker. She was the toast of Paris for a few glorious years and her career was widely publicized. She became a French citizen, married a wealthy Frenchman and went on in later years to raise orphaned children.

On the American scene, there were lots of well-known black piano players: Duke Ellington, Earl "Fatha" Hines, Count Basie, Teddy Wilson, Pinetop Perkins, Art Tatum and Nat King Cole. The movie character, Sam, fits the image of the time perfectly.

Diamonds For Sale

The camera then scans some of the tables at Rick's and eavesdrops on several interesting conversations.

There's woman trying to sell her diamonds to a Moor. This reflects an accurate bit of history: the problems the refugees had in bringing their wealth out of Europe. Nazi Germany had passed laws that restricted Jews and other "undesirables" from taking virtually anything of value from Germany when they left the country. Laws of this nature were not invented by the Nazis, they had been around for years. Virtually every country in Europe restricted, in some way or other, the outflow of capital and wealth in order to protect the home economy. Moreover, many of these laws had been tightened during the bad economic years of the Great Depression. When the Nazis came to power in Germany, there were such laws already on the books, but the Nazis modified them and took them to the extreme. The intent was to keep Germans at home to serve Germany and to expel the "undesirables" while retaining their wealth for the general good of the Third Reich.

What actually happened, though, was that individuals found ways to smuggle items of value out of Germany. When a person realized that they would have to leave Germany, and later Nazi-controlled Austria, they sought ways to take what wealth they could with them. Some wealthy and far-sighted individuals had been able to stash money in countries such as Switzerland, England, or the United States where banking laws were quite liberal. Most, however, hadn't done this. So, smuggling became the only option. If they had time, those planning to leave had to sell their property, investments, cars, furniture and other belongings, often at depressed prices. With cash they could acquire large denomination bank notes, diamonds and other gems and try to get out of the country with those things hidden in their clothing, in suit cases with false bottoms, in hollowed out shoe heels or in body cavities. Those who were caught had the items confiscated and very likely were sent to a concentration camp.

In the movie, the lady selling the diamonds probably smuggled them out of Germany herself. The price she accepts is 2,400 Moroccan francs. At that time, the Moroccan franc was worth about 3 cents in U.S. money making the amount she netted from the sale $72. This seems much too low for diamonds, even for the depressed conditions of 1941. Some of the other monetary figures mentioned in the movie also seem unreasonable. This leads to the conclusion that the Warner Bros. screenwriters possibly ignored the true value of the Moroccan franc and used amounts of money that sounded good. Besides, hardly anyone in America knew the actual value of a Moroccan franc. If the Moor had offered a more historically accurate sum of 24,000 francs ($720), that hefty figure might have conveyed the message to the viewer that the woman got a lot of money for her diamonds—which she didn't.

At another table, the camera reveals two men talking in hushed tones about men stuck waiting. Could this be a black market deal in the making or a scheme to smuggle refugees out of French Morocco?

Escape By Boat

At another table two other men are talking secretively about the fishing smack "Santiago". Suddenly they pause and remain silent as two German officers in uniform pass nearby. The older man then continues telling the other man that the boat leaves at 1:00 AM tomorrow and to bring 15,000 francs in cash.

One of the options the refugees had was to escape in small boats. All through the war, small boats continued to sail up and down the coast of Morocco. They could easily make it to Lisbon, or perhaps Tangier, carrying contraband, fish or people. It was a risky business for the boat owners to carry people out of Casablanca who did not have a proper exit visa. If they were apprehended by the French authorities, the consequences would certainly be dire for both parties. Thus, the seemingly high fee of 15,000 francs ($450) demanded of the refugee by the owner of the fishing smack was reasonable.

It was also risky for the refugees. If the boat crew was totally unscrupulous, they could, once out to sea, rob and murder their passengers, and dump the bodies overboard. No one would ever be the wiser.

This scene contains one of the movie's few historical errors. It concerns the two German officers. It was very unlikely that two German officers would be visiting Rick's on a Tuesday evening in uniform. The Germans, Italians and French had an understanding that whenever German and Italian military personnel were off duty—and even sometimes when they weren't—they would wear civilian clothing, especially in public places. This was done to keep from provoking certain elements of the population who might seek to do harm to their former enemies. Neither side wanted such unpleasantries, so the understanding was mutual.

As shall be seen time and again in the movie, the screenwriters ignored this because it was most inconvenient to the story line.

The German Army had issued a standing order which applied to all German soldiers in North Africa. It read, "Don't mistreat natives but carry yourself in such a way that they can't fail to recognize immediately your superiority. Don't tolerate any liberties from them but command their obedience and respect." The soldiers were further warned about false coins, native women and scorpions.

The camera pans quickly across another table where two oriental men are talking and a few words of an oriental language are heard. The encounter is so brief that it is difficult to determine what language they are speaking, but it is probably Chinese.

The Deutschebank

The man refused entrance to the gambling room was, as Ugarte will soon reveal, from the Deutschebank, one of Germany's largest banks. By 1941 it had become a tool of the Nazi Party and one of the most corrupt institutions in Europe. It was to this bank that the stolen assets of the Jews, gypsies, German communists, homosexuals and other

Chinese In Casablanca?

Here's another of the delightful surprises in *Casablanca*—Chinese refugees at Rick's. This is historically accurate because China was one of the Allied nations and Chinese citizens had every reason to flee Europe as did others.

In his book, *The Casablanca Companion: The Movie and More*, author Jeff Siegel points out that there are six languages spoken in the movie: English, German, French, Italian, Spanish and Japanese. The reference to Japanese is apparently to this brief encounter with the two Asian men at the table in Rick's. It is highly unlikely, though, that these men, and the language they are speaking, are Japanese. There are for several reasons for this.

First of all, Japan was a member of the Axis Alliance and Japanese citizens living in Europe or French North Africa had little reason to flee and become refugees. They could come and go quite freely from any Axis-dominated part of the continent, including unoccupied France. Having Japanese individuals fleeing from their German and Italian allies simply doesn't fit the script.

Secondly, by the time Warner Bros. started filming *Casablanca* on May 25, 1942, virtually all of the ethnic Japanese had been removed from the west coast, including Los Angeles, and placed in relocation camps in the interior of the United States. That relocation program began in March, 1942, and was nearly complete by late May. That meant that line-speaking extras of Japanese decent were very unlikely to have been employed for *Casablanca* because they simply weren't around.

Thirdly, given the public attitude towards the ethnic Japanese at this time of the war, it would have been politically and socially inappropriate for any of the movie studios to hire ethnic Japanese individuals for any reason. And, not surprisingly, other companies wouldn't hire them either.

There are other Asian individuals who appear in the movie as extras and it is reasonably safe to say that they, too, were not ethnic Japanese. One such instance is the scene in which an Asian woman is seen sitting at the table in Rick's gambling room with the Amsterdam Banker.

On Friday June 16, 1939, Hitler assumed complete authority over all financial matters within Germany as an emergency measure in preparation for the coming war. Therefore, when the Deutschebank re-opened for business on Monday June 19, Hitler was Germany's chief banker—and controlled Germany's financial world.

Der Angriff

When the German is denied entry into Rick's gambling room, he threatens to report the club to the Angriff. *Der Angriff (The Attack)* was one of several major newspapers in Germany put out by the Nazi Party. It was started in 1927 on Hitler's orders by Joseph Goebbels, Germany's future Minister of Propaganda and movie czar. The paper preached the Nazi political line, offered the Party's interpretation of national and international news events, and denounced Jews, Communists and anyone else the Nazis didn't like. Now, it appeared that Rick's Cafe Americain in Casablanca was going to be denounced in *Der Angriff*.

Der Angriff (The Attack) *was a newspaper founded in 1927 by Joseph Goebbels, Germany's future Minister of Propaganda and movie czar, to disseminate the Nazi Party line.*

enemies of the Third Reich flowed after having been confiscated by the Nazis. Those assets were then laundered by the Deutschebank for the benefit of the Party and high-level Party personnel. This wasn't a secret and Rick almost certainly knew about it. By standing firm against the Nazi banker, another glimpse of Rick's personality becomes evident. To be sure, he didn't want that dirty money in his gambling room.

Not Rick, nor anyone else, knew at the time just how rotten the Deutschebank really was. Full revelation came at the end of the war when Allied troops invaded deep into Germany and gained access to the bank's vaults. There, they found the stolen hoards of Europe. There were tons of gold and silver items, art treasures and other valuables, including the most disgusting hoard of all—gold fillings from the mouths of concentration camp victims.

In the original play, the character Rick would not admit to the gambling room was a deadbeat Englishman named Forrester-Smith who had left bad checks in gambling establishments from Honolulu to Calcutta. The screenwriters cleverly changed him to the Deutschebank man.

Visas and Letters of Transit

Where does Ugarte get visas that he can sell for half of Renault's price? Here, an educated guess is made. To begin with, it must be accepted that the visas Ugarte sells are genuine since there is no reference to their being counterfeit. So where does he get them? From Renault? Probably not. It is very likely that there are dozens of corrupt officials in French North Africa doing the same thing as Renault. Furthermore, it can be presumed that most of these officials have little or no access to the exit visa market in Casablanca and are willing to sell visas to a man like Ugarte at a discounted price, who would then re-sell them in Casablanca. For the original seller, it's an easy way to make a few extra francs in a market that, otherwise, would be inaccessible. If there are several of these officials offering Ugarte exit visas, this would enable Ugarte to bargain for the lowest price. He could then keep his price below Renault's.

It is also quite possible that Renault has similar arrangements with Ugarte-types elsewhere—say in Rabat, Marrakech, Tangier, Oran, and Algiers. This was nothing more than the age-old free-market system at work.

What exactly were letters of transit?

In *Casablanca Script and Legend: the 50th Anniversary Edition*, Howard Koch, one of the *Casablanca*'s screenwriters, said of this type of document that it "granted the bearer the right to travel without passport or (regular) visa." In the booklet *Casablanca: As Time Goes By: 50th Anniversary Commemorative* (Turner Publishing Co.) the letter of transit is called a "powerful exit visa."

Both explanations are correct.

In the diplomatic world, this document is called a Laissez Passer (to let pass). It is a very special type of visa, usually issued by a high authority, that allows the individual named thereon to travel in a special manner which completely circumvents the restrictions and officials associated with regular visas. Governments need such documents to allow certain individuals—such as diplomats, spies, secret agents, undercover men and the like—to move about quickly and anonymously without having to deal with regular customs officials and unsavory individuals like Captain Renault.

The letters of transit Ugarte has acquired are unique, though, in that the spaces showing the bearers' names are left blank. Since these documents were in the hands of the Germans and on their way to Casablanca, it is fairly obvious that they were intended for use by two Germans in order to leave French Morocco under whatever cover names they wished to use and at a time of their own choosing.

So, why didn't the Germans simply ask the French to declare the documents void once they learned that they were stolen?

The reason for this could be that there were other letters of transit in existence being used by the Germans, and the French customs officials, who would be ordered to watch for the stolen documents, wouldn't be able to identify them since no one knew whose names would be on them. To identify the two letters of transit, the Germans would have had to reveal to the French the names of all those who currently held letters of transit. This is something the Germans would not want to do because it would reveal the names of some of their secret operatives to the French. It follows, then, that the next best thing was to try to recover the stolen documents. This is what the Germans chose to do. They sent a high-ranking Gestapo officer to Casablanca, one who outranked the local Prefect of Police, to work with the local French police to ensure that the investigation was pursued with the greatest effort.

Ugarte's explanation about the letters of transit has one serious error in it—the most obvious error in the movie. The letters of transit could not possibly have been signed by General De Gaulle. Virtually every political and military official in French North Africa was loyal to Vichy and looked upon De Gaulle as a traitor. Furthermore, De Gaulle had been convicted in absentia by the Vichy courts and sentenced to death upon apprehension. So, any official document bearing De Gaulle's signature in Vichy territory would be worthless.

But, the screenwriters had a problem. To make the script historically accurate, Ugarte would have had to say that the documents were signed by either General Maxim Weygand, General Juin, or perhaps someone else. Weygand—the supreme military commander of French North Africa—is the most likely name to have been used, and Burnett and Alison used it in the play.

Weygand, however, was relieved of his command on November 20, 1941, eleven days before the letters were stolen, and his powerful position done away with. General Alphonse Juin assumed most of Weygand's military responsibilities while his political duties were dispersed to several people. It is possible that Weygand could have signed the letters of transit before he was dismissed but it is more likely that they were signed by Juin or someone else.

Herein lies the screenwriters' problem. Who should Ugarte say signed the letters? The decision was made to ignore historical accuracy and to use a name that every American knew—De Gaulle. It should be remembered that the American public was kept in the dark, thanks to American media censorship, about the anti-De Gaulle atti-

General Alphonse Juin assumed part of Weygand's responsibilities in French North Africa after Weygand's dismissal and the elimination of his position.

General Maxim Weygand, Delegate-General of French North Africa from June, 1940, to November, 1941.

tude of the Vichy French in North Africa. To the American public, De Gaulle was an important Frenchman and any document signed by him simply had to be important.

By early 1943, when the movie was released, most of French North Africa was in Allied hands and the French officialdom there had rallied to De Gaulle's cause. Therefore, documents signed by De Gaulle would have meaning in French North Africa at the time the American public saw *Casablanca* in their local theaters. The American movie-going public accepted this and there was not even a murmur of criticism about the movie's inaccuracy on this point. The screenwriters lucked out, thanks to a favorable flow of historical events.

American Isolationism

 "My dear Rick, when will you realize that in this world, today, isolationism is no longer a practical policy."

—Ferrari to Rick

Senor Ferrari, the head of Casablanca's black market and proprietor of a cafe called the Blue Parrot, pays a visit to Rick and offers to buy his cafe. Rick isn't interested in selling. But in the course of conversation, Ferrari makes the comment above. By doing so, he espouses a prevalent political sentiment in Hollywood. Isolationism was a nasty word there—especially at Warner Bros. For almost a decade prior to the making of Casablanca, many of the most powerful people in Hollywood, including Harry and Jack Warner, had been outspoken critics of America's isolationist foreign policy, a policy that had begun soon after World War I. The isolationists struck back calling the

Hollywood crowd such names as "wild" and "foreign-born" (a euphemism for Jewish) interventionists who wanted to drag America once again into Europe's conflicts.

By the first week in December 1941 (the time period of the story), isolationist sympathy in America had declined considerably because of the obvious threat to American interests by the Axis military victories in Europe and North Africa. But, the isolationists still had several powerful advocates, especially in the U.S. Senate. As recently as September 1941, they had lashed out at Hollywood—in the form of a hearing before a Senate subcommittee headed by isolationist Senator D. Worth Clark of Missouri. Clark's announced purpose for the hearings was to conduct an "investigation of any propaganda disseminated by motion pictures and radio or any other activity of the motion picture industry to influence public opinion in the direction of participation of the United States in the present European war."

One of the Hollywood moguls subpoenaed was Jack Warner. The subcommittee had raised objections to four recent Warner Bros. movies, *Confession of a Nazi Spy* (1939), *International Squadron* (1941), *Underground* (1941) and *Sergeant York* (1941).

Warner defended his studio's position by saying that the public demanded such films, pointing to the financial successes of these movies as proof. Furthermore he pointed out that about 70 percent of the non-fiction books being published at that time dealt with the Nazi menace.

Nothing came from the hearings and on December 7, 1941, the isolationist cause was given a final *coup de grâce* with the Japanese attack on Pearl Harbor.

In early 1942, when the movie script for *Casablanca* was being written, Jack Warner saw a chance to get in a last word against his isolationist foes. Since Casablanca was set the week before Pearl Harbor—just before the isolationist cause was smashed to bits—he had Ferrari give the isolationists a parting blast.

The Clipper To America

Rick steps out onto his front patio, sees Captain Renault sitting alone at one of the outdoor tables and joins him. As they chat the camera reveals that they are looking down the main runway of Casablanca's airport watching the plane for Lisbon depart.

Here is another inaccuracy in the movie. Rick's Cafe was in downtown Casablanca and the airport was six miles away.

Nevertheless, Renault asks Rick if he would like to be on that plane. Rick replies:

 "Why? What's in Lisbon?" Renault responds, "The Clipper to America."

Ah, yes! The Clipper to America. How many people in Casablanca would love to be on the Clipper to America? It was the only way to get to America by air.

For a refugee in Casablanca, the very best scenario for getting to America would be to have an exit visa from French Morocco, an entrance visa into Portugal, an immigration permit into the United States within the current year's quota, a rich sponsor

The Clipper to America. This Boeing 314 sea plane was the fastest and most luxurious way to get from Europe to America in the late 1930s and early 1940s.

waiting for them there, and one-way tickets on the Clipper to America. But very few—so very few—people could expect this to happen.

The Clipper, nevertheless, was real, and flew from Lisbon to America three times a week. This wondrous marvel was a huge, modern seaplane, one of the largest airplanes of its day, flown by America's Pan American Airways.

Pan Am had eight of these planes operating worldwide, capable of flying great distances and landing in harbors, rivers, lagoons and lakes. Clippers could carry about 50 passengers and some 5,000 lbs. of cargo. The seaplane design was used because, at this stage in the development of commercial air travel, very few places in the world had airports with runways long enough to accommodate large intercontinental land-based aircraft. The development of airports around the world constantly lagged behind the development of aircraft. Existing airports in major cities were often overcrowded. Lisbon's airport, Sintra Airdrome, was typical. Dozens of airlines flew into Lisbon from all over Europe, causing constant scheduling problems and a shortage of storage and terminal space. In contrast, the Tagus river, where the Clipper landed, broadens out into a fine natural harbor in front of Lisbon with a virtually unlimited expanse of calm water, ideal for the operation of seaplanes.

Clipper service between the United States and Lisbon was relatively new, having started in June 1939. At that time, there were land-based commercial aircraft flying the northern route from Gander, Newfoundland, to England, but when World War II began in September 1939, that service ended, leaving Pan Am's flights to Lisbon as the only commercial air connection with North America. This lasted until 1942 when Trans-Canada Airlines resumed land-based flights to Britain for Gander, Newfoundland.

Passengers from New York debark from the Boeing 314 Clipper upon arrival at Lisbon.

Needless to say, every Clipper flight was booked solid and there was a priority and bumping system in effect. Unfortunately for those in Casablanca, refugees and emigrants going to America were near the bottom of the list. At times, people were even bumped in favor of critical air cargoes. Other times, passengers were asked to leave their luggage behind to make room for more people or for important cargo. Their luggage would be sent later.

Those fortunate enough to obtain passage on the Clipper might find that their seat mate was a well-known personality or even a member of royalty. At various times, royalty—such as Queen Wilhelmina of Holland, King George of Greece and King Carol of Romania—used the Clipper. Famous war correspondents—such as Edward R. Murrow, Ernie Pyle, John Gunther, Inez Robb and William L. Shirer—used the Clipper, as did many other famous people.

A one-way ticket from Lisbon to New York cost $425, a princely sum in 1941. And, due to wartime restrictions, the tickets were not transferable. Some refugees fell victim to dishonest scalpers who sold them Clipper tickets at inflated prices only to learn that the tickets couldn't be used.

In America, the Clipper's home base was the newly-built LaGuardia Airport in New York City.

The Clipper flew directly from LaGuardia to Lisbon. On the return trip, the plane flew south out of Lisbon, skirted the coast of northwest Africa and landed at Bolama in Portuguese Guinea. Then it flew across the Atlantic to Port of Spain, Trinidad; north to San Juan, Puerto Rico; then to Miami, Florida; and back to LaGuardia. On the return leg, the trip was shorter as the plane had favorable winds, so the plane needed to

LaGuardia Airport, completed in 1939, was one of the most modern airports of the day. The runways were long enough for the land-based planes then operating, and the lagoon at the bottom of the picture was for seaplanes. The Clipper to Lisbon began and ended its journey here.

carry less fuel. It could, therefore, carry more passengers and freight than on the New York to Lisbon trip.

After the U.S. entered the war, Clipper passengers were asked to take shifts watching for enemy submarines. The Clippers had no means with which to attack submarines, but they could report their location and the direction in which they were heading to the proper American military authorities. During the course of the war, several German submarines were spotted by Clipper passengers and crews.

As one might expect, flying on a Clipper was a glamorous event. Many articles were written about the planes and the people who flew on them. A song, "Caribbean Clipper," became a popular swing number of the day and Universal Studios in Hollywood produced a Clipper-oriented movie named *Bombay Clipper* (1941).

The Czechoslovakian Government-In-Exile

"There is a man who's arrived in Casablanca on his way to America. He will offer a fortune to anyone who will furnish him with an exit visa."

—Renault to Rick

Renault is speaking of Victor Laszlo, the famous Czechoslovakian resistance leader. Laszlo has worked in resistance movements both in Prague, Czechoslovakia, and Paris and is an escapee from a German concentration camp. Renault has information that Laszlo is on his way to Casablanca and hopes to go on from there to Lisbon.

Renault's statement contains two historical errors, though. The first and most serious concerns Laszlo's arrival in Casablanca. According to Article 19 of the German-French Armistice Agreement, the French civil authorities were obligated to arrest any fugitive wanted by the Germans and turn them over for prosecution. Since Laszlo is an escapee from a concentration camp, he is, in every way, a fugitive from German justice. Renault, therefore, was obligated to arrest Laszlo at the first opportunity. But the screenwriters chose to ignore this very inconvenient bit of history. It's a good thing they did or the movie's story would end right there.

The Armistice Agreement further authorized the Germans to send search teams into Unoccupied France to "assist" in the apprehension of such individuals—and the Germans did just that. It is very likely that Major Strasser has come to Casablanca as a one-man search team to apprehend Laszlo.

In the original play, Burnett and Alison didn't have this historical question to deal with. The Germans were only after Laszlo's money, which, they claimed, was made at the expense of the Germans.

The second historical error in Renault's statement was that Laszlo wanted to go to America. At this point in time, December 1941, it is more likely that Laszlo would have wanted to go to London where the Czechoslovakian Government-in-Exile had established itself and had been recognized by the Allies.

During the winter of 1938-39, when Burnett and Alison were putting their first ideas together for their play, this was not the case. Laszlo would have wanted to go to America then, and, specifically, to Chicago. At that time, the state of Czechoslovakia had completely disappeared from the map of Europe, having been dismantled in two steps by Nazi Germany. The Czech part of the country had been absorbed by Germany and renamed The Protectorate of Bohemia-Moravia and the Slovak part had been converted into the independent state of Slovakia, closely allied with Germany. The western Allies, who were then following their policy of appeasement towards Germany, accepted the loss of Czechoslovakia and withdrew diplomatic recognition of the Czechoslovakian Government altogether. This made the Czechoslovakian Government a political non-entity.

In October 1938, Eduard Benes, the last legitimate President of Czechoslovakia, and a small group of followers, fled to the United States, one of the few countries in the western world where they felt welcomed. They settled in the Chicago area which had a sizable Czechoslovakian community and had been the home in exile of the nation's founder and first president, Thomas Masaryk, before and during World War I. Benes took a teaching position at the University of Chicago but remained the focus of Czechoslovakian political life. When Burnett and Alison began writing their play, it was logical that Laszlo would want to go to America to join Benes and his group in Chicago.

But things changed. Five days after World War II started (September 1, 1939), Benes announced from Chicago that he would form an armed Czechoslovakian military unit that would fight on the side of the Allies. Britain and France accepted the gesture and on September 9 jointly announced that one of their war aims would be the reconstitution of Czechoslovakia to its pre-1938 status. With this, they invited Benes to come to Paris and set up a Czechoslovakian National Committee and eventually a Government-in-Exile. Benes accepted, and the center of Czech resistance moved from Chicago to Paris. When Paris fell to the Germans in June 1940, Benes and his Government-in-Exile moved to London. Therefore, after that date the place for Laszlo to go would have been London.

But wait a minute! Maybe—just maybe—those clever screenwriters have given Laszlo a ploy to get out of French Morocco more easily. Given the hatred that existed in French North Africa towards the British after the Mers el Kebir incident of July 1940, it might be that Laszlo is intentionally making it known that he wants to go to America and is purposely saying nothing about London. The French would certainly be more sympathetic about letting him get to America rather than to London. Once in Lisbon, of course, Laszlo could then go on to London.

Rick Blaine's Past

 Oh, laugh if you will, but I happen to be familiar with your record. Let me point out just two items. In 1935 you ran guns in Ethiopia. In 1936, you fought in Spain on the Loyalists' side.

—Renault to Rick

Rick's activities in Ethiopia and Spain will be mentioned once again in the movie.

In the stage play, Rick didn't have a past and wasn't involved in either Ethiopia or Spain. During 1935-36, according the stage version, Rick is an unhappily married American lawyer living in Paris with a wife and two children and carrying on an affair with an American woman of questionable virtue named Lois Meredith. On the evening of April 12, 1936, Rick and his wife are dining at La Belle Aurore Cafe when Lois walks in with a new gentleman friend. A nasty scene ensued, Rick's wife found out about the affair, and Rick and Lois blew up at each other. This signaled both the end of Rick's marriage and his relationship with Lois. In 1937, Rick ran off to Casablanca, and 1939, Rick's wife got a divorce in Reno, Nevada, and custody of their two children.

When the screenwriters reworked the material, they stripped Rick of his wife and his law degree, transformed Lois into a Norwegian beauty of impeccable virtue, and sent Rick off to Ethiopia, Spain and some other adventures that they never make quite clear.

What was going on in Ethiopia and Spain? Why did Rick go there and what did he do?

The comments with regard to Ethiopia refer to the war between that country and Italy that began in October 1935, and lasted until May 1936. It was a war of colonial conquest in which Italy attacked and conquered the African nation of Ethiopia and added it to her existing colonial empire in east Africa.

In the fall of 1935, world attention was focused on the depression, the rise of Hitler and the spread of Communism. That attention shifted rather quickly, though, to East Africa in early 1935 when Italy's fascist dictator, Benito Mussolini, began making threatening moves towards Ethiopia.

At the time, Ethiopia was one of only two independent nations in sub-Saharan Africa. The other was the Republic of Liberia on Africa's west coast that had been founded by returning American slaves in the early 1800s. Since its inception, Liberia had strong economic and political ties to the United States. During the late 1800s and early 1900s, when the European powers were scrambling for colonies in Africa, they knew to keep hands off Liberia if they wanted to maintain good relations with the United States. This was still true in 1935.

Ethiopia, on the other hand, had no great protector and was fair game for anyone. In the rush for colonies, the British, French and Italians succeeded in establishing colonies all around Ethiopia, cutting that country off from the sea. Various European powers made attempts to add Ethiopia to their colonial empires, but failed. The Italians had the most to gain by colonizing Ethiopia because it was sandwiched between two existing Italian colonies: Eritrea and Italian Somaliland. If the Italians could acquire Ethiopia, all three areas could then be molded into one very large colonial holding. This possibility greatly interested Mussolini, and, by 1935, he felt he had gained the power and wherewithal to do it.

His fascist regime, was indeed, at the height of its power. Mussolini had taken Italy from an economically depressed and politically unstable nation in the years following World War I and turned the country into a prosperous and industrialized nation with considerable clout in southern Europe and the Mediterranean.

With much of the world engulfed in a myriad of problems and the U.S—the traditional champion of colonial rights—locked into a self-imposed state of isolationism, Mussolini felt that the time was right to move against Ethiopia. To this end, he slowly, but noticeably, began building up his military forces in both Eritrea and Italian Somaliland. The rest of the world soon realized that something was up and began to question Italy's moves. Mussolini made no secret of the fact that he wanted part of, or possibly all of, Ethiopia. He also believed, as did Hitler, that if and when a showdown came, the other major powers would fall back on their policies of appeasement and not interfere militarily to save Ethiopia.

To build his case against Ethiopia, Mussolini began making unreasonable demands on that nation and meddling into Ethiopia's internal affairs, seeking out clan leaders and others who might support an Italian takeover. Mussolini sent Italian troops across the poorly defined borders to clash with Ethiopian forces and purposely increase tensions between the two nations.

Eventually, the time came when Mussolini could announce that his patience was at an end with Ethiopia and that decisive action had to be taken. That was on October 2, 1935. The next day, Italian troops invaded Ethiopia. Haile Selassie, Emperor of Ethiopia, responded by calling his people to arms and ordering his Christian nation to pray for victory. His message was transmitted across the primitive landscape by runners and drums. Ethiopians responded by the thousands. They picked up their spears, mussel-loader rifles, bows and arrows, and went out to do combat against the Italians. The world watched with amazement as the two enemies clashed. Virtually everywhere, public sympathies were with the Ethiopians.

Mussolini guessed right though. Sympathy was all the Ethiopians got. No nation came to Ethiopia's aid. The only thing coming from the major capitals of the world was a stream of angry rhetoric directed towards Italy. The League of Nations did, however, call for economic sanctions against both nations in an effort to contain the war and minimize its effects. The sanctions, though, were full of holes. Both nations could get almost anything they wanted from someone.

This is very likely where Rick entered the picture. The Ethiopians needed arms and ammunition badly and appealed to various nations to supply them. Officially the answer was "no," but, behind the scenes, there were those who asked "What do you want?" and "How much can you pay?"

One can only speculate as to what course of action Rick took, but, from bits and pieces of the movie script, an informed guess can be made. Rick lived in New York City at the time and was having trouble finding employment. This put him in the right spot at the right time to make some big money. With a little effort and bravery, a young man like Rick could find out through the Ethiopian consulate in New York City what kind of arms that country was in need of, how much they were paying, who had arms to sell, and what ship captains in the harbor were willing to transport them.

Apparently, Rick was successful in this endeavor and made a deal with the Ethiopians to supply them with guns. He acquired the arms, found a cooperative ship captain, dispatched the goods, and went on to await their arrival at the sea port of Djibuti, French Somaliland. Djibuti was the terminus of a French-owned and operated railroad that led into Ethiopia and terminated at Addis Ababa, Ethiopia's capital. It was the only railroad in Ethiopia, and, being French-owned and operated, the Italians were not attacking it for fear of political repercussions from France. Therefore, supplies could flow, unobstructed, into the heart of Ethiopia from Djibuti. Some supplies came overland from British colonies, but Ethiopia's roads were primitive and most supplies had to be carried by slow-moving truck convoys or animal caravans. It is doubtful that Rick attempted to get his guns into Ethiopia that way because there is no mention throughout the movie of his having been associated with the British. All of his associations are with France and the French Empire. Furthermore, it is very unlikely that an American living in New York would have knowledge of the backroads and caravan routes of this part of Africa.

Djibuti, on the other hand, was a beehive of activity for westerners during the Ethiopian war. It was filled with refugees escaping the war zone, relief agencies helping them and others, mercenaries heading into Ethiopia to fight for a price, diplomats and other VIPs coming and going, as well as hundreds of foreigners doing the same thing Rick was doing. It was not unusual at that time to see a young American on the Djibuti docks taking delivery of large wooded crates labeled "bicycles." The French were universally sympathetic to the Ethiopian cause, so when the French customs officials saw crates marked "bicycles" going to Addis Ababa, they didn't question their content and passed them on through. The crates would be loaded onto a truck or wagon driven by Ethiopians which would then head off in the direction of the railroad station.

Doing this, though, was against U.S. law. Months before the conflict erupted in Ethiopia, the U.S. Government, seeing that armed conflicts might soon erupt in Ethiopia or in other places in the world, made a concerted effort to keep American citizens

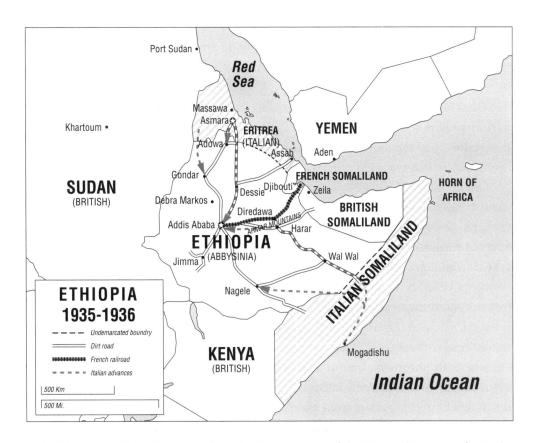

out of those conflicts. This was done by the passage of the Neutrality Law of 1935 by joint resolution of Congress on August 31, 1935. This law was entitled in part, "Providing for the Prohibition of the Export of Arms, Ammunition, and Implements of War to Belligerent Nations…" Fundamentally, it forbade American citizens from providing arms, ammunition and implements of war to whatever foreign nation the President of the United States might so designate as conditions arose. Those found guilty of violating the law were subject to fines of up to $10,000, or imprisonment for up to five years—or both. On October 5, 1935, the day after Italy invaded Ethiopia, President Roosevelt exercised his authority under the Neutrality Law and issued a proclamation forbidding the export of arms to both Italy and Ethiopia and prohibiting American citizens from participating in that activity.

The President's proclamation further ordered that "…all officers of the United States, charged with the execution of the laws thereof, the utmost diligence in preventing violations of the said joint resolution… and in bringing to trial and punishment any offenders against the same."

Here is the reason Rick was reluctant to return to America. He had violated the Neutrality Law of 1935. With his American passport now stamped and dated "French Somaliland," any alert customs agent or U.S. consular official could deduce that he had gone to Djibuti during the Italian-Ethiopian War and could detain him for questioning. This, Rick wanted to avoid.

The lopsided war in Ethiopia ran its bloody course despite the brave, and at times, suicidal defenses of the poorly-equipped and bare-footed Ethiopians.

By May 1936, Italian forces were approaching the outskirts of Addis Ababa and Emperor Haile Selassie fled. He traveled up the French-owned railroad to Djibuti and from there was whisked away to exile on a British warship. With that, the war in Ethiopia was over.

Rick, now unwilling to return to America, apparently chose to stay within French territory and possibly went to France. This way he crossed no international borders. In July 1936, just three month after the end of the Ethiopian War, civil war erupted in Spain and Rick saw another opportunity for himself.

Spain was, like most European nations, hard hit by the Depression. Actually, the country had not regained its economic health since the Spanish-American War of 1898-99. Spain became a democracy in the 1920s and soon succumbed to the plague of so many European democracies in that it simply had too many political parties. No party ever won enough votes during an election to rule on its own. So, weak coalition governments, based on compromise and negotiations, were formed by groups of political factions. With the onset of the Depression, Spanish politics became very turbulent. Between 1930 and the end of 1935, the country had 28 governments come and go. In the national elections of February 1936, the Spanish electorate did what so many other electorates in Europe had done: they abandoned the moderate centrist parties and voted heavily for the extreme left or right. This polarized the nation and brought forth the horrible specter of civil war because neither political extreme could tolerate the presence of the other.

The leftists won by a slight majority, a Popular Front Government came to power in Madrid heavily influenced by Communists and radical socialists, and immediately began implementing their revolutionary programs. The Spanish people were not prepared for this, and economic and social chaos spread across the land. During the next five months, there were 269 political murders, 113 general strikes and the fire-bombing of 170 churches, 69 political clubs and 10 newspapers. Civil war was in the air. It was only a matter of time.

On July 13, 1936, a prominent right-wing politician, Calvo Sotelo, was murdered by shock police of the central Government. This was the spark that ignited the rebellion. On July 17, elements of the Spanish Army, supporting the political right wing, rebelled in Spanish Morocco and quickly took over that area. The leader of the rebellion in Morocco was General Francisco Franco and most of his troops were Moroccans—some of them from French Morocco.

During the next two days, Army units all over Spain rebelled, but not all were successful. The Army rebellions in Madrid and Barcelona failed. Most of Spain's Army officers and about half of Spain's naval officers joined the rebellion, but virtually all of the Air Force remained loyal to the Madrid Government. It was a dreadful situation with the only option now being a long and difficult armed struggle for power. The coming civil war would last for three years, be very bloody and have worldwide consequences.

Spain's right-wing political leaders gave their support to the Army rebels, and all of the factions eventually recognized General Franco as their leader. Franco's support-

General Francisco Franco, leader of the Nationalist forces in the Spanish Civil War. Franco had some Jewish blood; a fact kept secret from Hitler.

ers became knows as the "Nationalists" and those loyal to the leftist Madrid Government were called "Loyalists." The Loyalists had a series of leaders throughout the civil war.

Both sides in the conflict appealed for help from the major powers and some responded. Clearly, Spain was more important than Ethiopia. Italy and Germany began immediately to send military aid to the Nationalists and the Soviet Union eventually came to the aid of the Loyalists. The western Allies, still counting on their policies of appeasement, stayed out of the conflict and formed the Non-Intervention Committee, a debating society based in London. The Committee was designed to discourage foreign intervention in the Spanish conflict and to provide a platform for mediation. The American isolationist ostriches kept their heads buried in the sand and stayed out of both the conflict and the Non-Intervention Committee. President Roosevelt issued another proclamation under the Neutrality Law of 1935, similar to the one he had issued at the beginning of the Ethiopian war, forbidding Americans from becoming involved on either side of the Spanish conflict.

Throughout the democratic world, the U.S. included, there arose a grass-roots support for the Loyalists, and foreign volunteers began heading for Spain by the thousands. Virtually all of them entered Spain through France whose Government was officially neutral but, in reality, very sympathetic to the Loyalists. Among the volunteers were about 3,000 Americans. Together with Canadian volunteers, they were formed into three International Brigades: the "Abraham Lincoln," the "George Washington," and the "MacKinzie-Papineau" (Canadian names) Brigades. Those brigades saw heavy fighting and suffered considerable casualties during the course of the war. At one point, the "George Washington Brigade" was so badly decimated that its survivors were merged for the rest of the war with the "Abraham Lincoln Brigade."

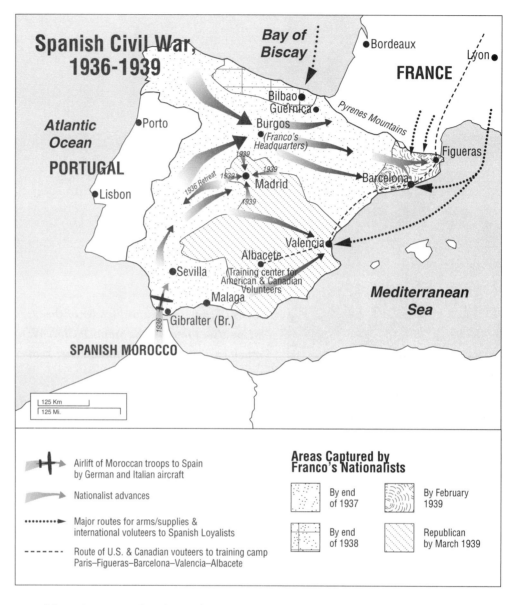

Spain during the Spanish Civil War. The war flowed generally from west to east until the Nationalists had conquered all of Spain except Madrid. Loyalists in Madrid held out until the last and its capture ended the war. American and Canadian volunteers generally reached Spain through France and were trained at Albacete.

Many foreigners fought on the Nationalist side too. Most were Italian soldiers sent there by Mussolini, but there were also Germans and Portuguese.

The movie script does not tell how Rick served in Spain but it is most likely he was not an ordinary foot soldier. For one thing, he was 32 years old which is somewhat old for an infantryman. Then too, he comments that he was "well paid" in both Ethiopia and Spain, and foot soldiers are not normally well-paid. Since Renault mentions that Rick fought "on" the Loyalists' side, it is assumed that he was one of the volunteers who went to Spain to fight rather than act as the independent entrepreneur he was in Ethiopia. Most likely, the Loyalists made use of Rick's experience in running guns and put him somewhere in their Army's supply system. Because of the Non-Intervention Committee and the facade of neutrality most nations maintained, arms and ammunition had to enter the country in a clandestine manner. Rick's experiences in Ethiopia would have been of value in this endeavor.

Loyalist troops launching an attack on the Saragossa front in 1936. It is not likely that Rick was an infantryman like these soldiers.

Rick probably left Spain in late 1938. By then, the Non-Intervention Committee had negotiated an agreement whereby both sides were to release all of their foreign volunteers. Accordingly, the American volunteers were released and transported over the Pyrenees to France. Many of them, and possibly Rick too, lost their American passports in the process. Upon arrival in Spain, the Loyalists took every foreign volunteer's passport for what they said was "safe-keeping," but it was actually to serve as a deterrent to those who might have a change of heart and want to go home.

When it came time to return the passports, most of them couldn't be found. This opened up an unforeseen opportunity for Rick, although he didn't take advantage of it. All of the Americans returning home, with or without passports, faced an uncertain future because they had all violated the Neutrality Law of 1935 by serving in the Loyalist armed forces. As it turned out, the U.S. Government chose not to prosecute the returning volunteers because public sentiment was very much against it. And those without passports were allowed to return without any problems. At this point, Rick could have returned rather safely to America by claiming that his passport had not been returned to him, whether it was true or not.

Perhaps, though, Rick did use this opportunity to obtain a new U.S. passport, most likely through a U.S. consulate in France, because later in the film he tells both Renault and Ferrari that he is going to America. Gone, apparently, is his fear of returning home.

But, alas, Rick chose not to return to America from Spain. He made his way to Paris and there met the love of his life.

Champagne and Caviar

When Strasser goes to Rick's, he orders champagne and caviar, something the Germans were consuming a lot at this time. When the Germans occupied northern France, they took over some of France's best champagne-producing regions and when they invaded the Soviet Union they captured lots of Russian caviar. These products were doled out generously to the German people as a reward for the great sacrifices their sons and husbands were making in the Soviet Union, and were visible symbols of the Nazi Government's promises of things to come. Strasser may be ordering these items to remind Renault of Germany's great military victories. Or, then again, maybe he simply likes champagne and caviar—especially when it was on the expense account.

Renault tells Strasser that the arrest is about to be made and the scene shifts to the gambling room where Ugarte is seen at the roulette tables. Policemen approach him from behind and one of them asks him to come with them. Ugarte is surprised and concerned, but agrees. He asks only to cash in his chips. The cashier gives him 2,000 francs ($60).

As the policemen escort Ugarte to the gambling room door, he bolts past the two guards and out the door slamming it closed behind him. The policemen open the door to pursue him. Ugarte pulls a gun and shoots at them but misses. Ugarte runs into Rick and begs him to help him. Rick refuses. The policemen overpower Ugarte and drag him away.

Strasser, still seated at his table, congratulates Renault.

A cafe patron comes up to Rick and says: "When they come after me, Rick, I hope you'll be more help."

Rick replies, "I stick my neck out for nobody."

Germans in London?

When Heinze asks Rick if he can imagine the Germans in London, at this point in the war such a thing was still very much a possibility. Hitler had given it very serious consideration during the winter of 1940-41, but changed his mind and began to make plans to eliminate the Soviet Union instead. Conquest of the Soviet Union held much more promise for Germany. By eliminating the Soviet Union, Germany would purge the world of Communism and gain an immense territory geographically adjacent to The Third Reich that could then be colonized for the benefit of Germany. Hitler was a colonialist of the first order and on several occasion referred to the Soviet Union as "our India," a reference to the enviable job the British had done in colonizing India. Hitler also kept alive the hopes of regaining Germany's overseas colonies taken from her after World War I.

Once the Soviet Union was eliminated, Hitler reasoned, he could deal with England and plan for the day when the world would see German troops in London. In the meantime, though, German propaganda and certain military activities had to be maintained to make it appear that the invasion of England was still very much a possibility.

New York?

When Strasser asks Rick if he thinks the Germans could take New York, this, too, was not beyond the realm of possibility in early December 1941. And, like the inva-

This bomber, the German Messerschmitt Me 264, was designed to bomb targets along the U.S. east coast from bases in Europe. Only prototypes were made and it was never put into production.

sion of England, depended upon Germany settling the unfinished business in the Soviet Union.

The Germans had in their files two long-standing plans for the invasion of the United States—one from 1899 and the other from 1900. Every high-level German officer knew of them. Those plans were never seriously considered during World War II but neither were they canceled. The 1899 plan called for a landing of German troops on Long Island where they would establish a large bridgehead, bring in massive reinforcements, invade and conquer New York City and then march south to Washington, DC, and Norfolk, VA. Another option was to march north to Boston.

The 1900 plan called for a huge German armada to sail from Wilhelmshaven and land either at New York or on Cape Cod. In the Cape Cod option, the Cape would become the German staging area from which German troops would march systematically down the Atlantic coast.

Bombing the United States from bases in Europe was given very serious consideration by the Germans, too, and the prototype of a long-range bomber was designed and built for that purpose. This was the Messerschmitt Me 264, a plane that greatly resembled the American-made B-29 bomber developed later in the war to bomb Japan from long-range bases. The Messerschmitt Me 264 was highly touted in the German propaganda directed toward the United States and was called the "Amerika Bomber" or the "New York Bomber." It was never put into production.

The invasions of the United States, visualized in both the German plans of 1899 and 1900, called for the German Navy to have complete control of the North Atlantic so that once German troops landed in the U.S. they could be maintained and supplied. This military necessity was still true in December 1941, and, here again, depended on the outcome in the Soviet Union. German military planners could foresee a time when, after the Soviet Union and England had been defeated, that Axis resources could be redirected and turned towards the United States.

The scenario would go like this: with England defeated, the world's largest navy, the British Navy, would be neutralized. Then, the German Fleet (the world's 7th largest), the Italian Fleet (5th largest), remnants of the captured Soviet Fleet (6th largest), the French Fleet (4th largest), and the Spanish Fleet (8th largest) could unite to outnumber and force the U.S. Fleet (2nd largest) out of the North Atlantic. Such an alliance of naval forces was very possible because it is exactly what the Allies would succeed in doing later in the war. The Allies combined elements of the U.S. Navy, British Navy, Canadian Navy, Free French Navy, and warships and merchant ships from a dozen or more Allied nations to dominate the North Atlantic Ocean. This conglomerate naval force eventually made possible the invasion of Europe in 1944 and the sustenance of Allied troops over supply lines that stretched thousands of miles back to America.

During the first week in December 1941, it was anyone's guess as to who would eventually win control of the North Atlantic. After December 7, 1941, and the beginning of war between the United States and Japan, the prospects for Axis control brightened considerably because now the Americans had to devote a large part of their naval resources to the Pacific.

When the screenwriters were writing the script in the early months of 1942, they didn't go into great detail to explain the world's military situation to their audiences because almost every literate adult understood what was going on.

On the other hand, few people were aware that so much hinged on the battle for Moscow that was taking place during the time frame of the movie. Ironically, the German onslaught at Moscow was stopped at the gates of that city on December 7, 1941. No one knew it at the time, but this was to be Germany's high-water mark in the Soviet Union.

The war on the eastern front dragged on for two more years, eventually bleeding the Germans white. In Berlin, plans for the invasion of England and the United States were shelved, never to be revived.

It was only at the end of the war, when statistics could be studied, that it became clear that Germany had really lost World War II in the Soviet Union. One statistic told the story in a nutshell: out of every ten German soldiers killed in action during World War II, nine were killed on the eastern front.

None of these things were known when *Casablanca* was being produced, so, in viewing the movie, it is important to keep in mind that the war was in its very early stages and that Germany had yet to suffer a serious military defeat. Nazi Germany seemed invincible and its tentacles reached into far-away places like Casablanca. For Rick, Renault, Sam and the others, those were very uncertain and gloomy days.

So, when Strasser questions Rick about who he thinks will win the war, Rick tells it like it was in those days and says:

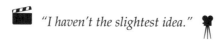 *"I haven't the slightest idea."*

Victor Laszlo's Three Escapes

"Victor Laszlo published the foulest lies in the Prague newspapers until the very day we marched in, and even after that he continued to print scandal sheets in a cellar."
—Strasser to Rick and Renault

The conversation at Strasser's table turns to Victor Laszlo and how he managed to become an enemy of the Reich.

These are the Prague newspapers in which Laszlo might well have printed his "lies" about Germany. This scene is on September 24, 1938, after the Czechoslovakian Government ordered the mobilizations of the nation's armed forces to defend the country against Germany.

Victor Laszlo has managed to escape from the Nazis three times and Strasser is not about to let it happen again. Apparently, Laszlo was a newspaper publisher from Prague, the capital of what used to be Czechoslovakia. In the pursuit of his anti-Nazi activities, he has become an important leader of the Czech Resistance and an enemy of the Reich.

Laszlo's first escape from the Nazis came on March 15, 1939, the day the Germans marched into Prague. If he had not fled, he most certainly would have been arrested.

This was the second phase of the Nazis' takeover of Czechoslovakia, a state that was created after World War I by the victorious Allies. The first phase came as a result of the infamous Munich Conference of September 1938, when the leaders of England and France—Prime Minister Neville Chamberlain and Eduard Daladier—caved in, under a threat of war, to Hitler's demands and allowed him to take the part of Czechoslovakia known as the Sudetenland. The Sudetenland was heavily populated with Germans and Hitler insisted that it should become a part of his Third Reich.

In return, Chamberlain and Daladier received Hitler's promise that he would make no more territorial demands in Europe. That promise soon proved to be worthless.

From his cellar-based printing operation, the fictional Laszlo continued to print illegal newspapers railing against the Nazis—and very possibly against the British and French as well—for having abandoned Czechoslovakia.

March 15, 1939: German troops marched into Prague and occupied the Czech part of Czechoslovakia. The Czechs did not resist. This was the day Laszlo went underground.

Eventually, though, Laszlo was caught and sent to a concentration camp. But, he managed to escape, slipping through the German's fingers a second time.

The third time was when he escaped from the Nazis in occupied Paris after having printed underground newspapers there with the help of the woman to whom he was secretly married, Ilsa Lund.

Czechoslovakia Under Nazi Occupation

Strasser: *"You were a Czechoslovakian. Now you are a subject of the German Reich."*
Laszlo : *"I've never accepted that privilege."*

And so he hadn't. But Strasser is correct from his perspective. In German-controlled Europe, the state of Czechoslovakia no longer existed. In its place were two surviving political entities. The former Czech area had been occupied by the Germans in

Everyone in Germany knew this slogan: "One People, One Reich, One Führer." Now there were seven million Czechs in the German Reich.

the spring of 1939 and renamed The German Protectorate of Bohemia-Moravia. By German law, all Czechs in or out of the protectorate, had been declared subjects of the Third Reich. The Slovak area had become a newly independent state.

The fact that Laszlo and all other Czechs became "subjects" of the German Reich, points out one of the great racial compromises in Nazi ideology. Czechs are of Slavic origin and, therefore, in the eyes of Nazi racial purists *untermenchen* (undermen). Since his first days in politics, Hitler preached that the Third Reich he intended to create would be structured for Germans alone and that all others—especially *untermenchen*—would be expelled.

When the Germans took over Czechoslovakia in March 1939, and created the Protectorate of Bohemia-Moravia, there were suddenly some seven million Czechs within the borders of the Third Reich. This was an uncomfortable thought for the Nazi racial purists who could readily see that the geographically-strategic area was of vital importance to Germany and one day would, and should, become a part of Greater Germany. The question then arose:

What will we do with all these Czechs?

Czechoslovakia had been a manufacturer and exporter of arms since its inception. Rick would have been familiar with Czech weapons because they were used extensively in Ethiopia and Spain. Above is one of the huge Skoda Works in Bohemia. Only Germany's Krupp Works made more arms than Skoda.

The gut reaction of most Nazis was to move them out and replace them with people of Aryan blood. The groundwork for that certainly existed. The Nazi leaders had said many nasty things about the Czechs in the past. Only recently, during the Sudeten crisis, Hermann Goering, Nazidom's number two man, had called the Czechs a "pygmy race."

But, from a practical point of view, replacing seven million people would be a horrendous undertaking, and, when it came to replacing them, the question was: "with whom?" Germany was already facing a manpower shortage with her economy nearing full employment and the armed forces taking tens of thousands of men for military service. Clearly, removal and replacement of the Czechs wasn't practical. The "pygmies" had to stay.

After many discussions and much searching of their evil souls, the Nazi leaders decided that the Czechs could, with time and effort, be Germanized under the guiding hand of the SS. In the long history of the German people, other minorities had been successfully Germanized, so a historical precedent existed to ease the consciences of those Nazis who were uncomfortable with the concept. The Nazi racists could generalize that, even though the Czechs were *untermenchen*, they were very talented *untermenchen*. They knew how to make tanks, bombs, artillery pieces, and many other items Germany would need in the coming years. Furthermore, it just didn't make sense to expel these people and let Germany's enemies gain the benefits of their skills.

A Germanization program was drawn up and finalized on October 9, 1940, in the Prague office of Bohemia-Moravia's Reich Protector, Baron Konstantine von Neurath.

WAFFEN-ϟϟ

EINTRITT NACH VOLLENDETEM 17. LEBENSJAHR

The Waffen SS was the private army of the Nazi Party and fought at the front along side the Regular German Army. Much of the Waffen SS' arms and equipment was made in the Protectorate of Bohemia-Moravia, the former Czechoslovakia.

It was agreed that about half of the Czechs would be Germanized and the other half would be given "special treatment," a Nazi euphemism for elimination. Those Czechs who were racially acceptable and cooperative would be Germanized. Among those to be eliminated would be the nation's intellectuals, individuals with mongoloid features, and the mentally and physically incurables. In the meantime, Czechs would be considered German subjects—not citizens—similar to colonial peoples. Strasser, therefore, used the right word by calling Laszlo a "subject" of the German Reich.

The SS was to be in charge of the Germanization program and, therefore, the Protectorate eventually became something of an SS fiefdom. This turned out to be a bonanza for the SS. The Waffen SS, the Nazi Party's private army, needed weapons like those already being produced in the Protectorate. So, they received first choice of that area's war production. This fit well into German military planning because in Germany the German Army got first choice of German production and the Waffen SS had to take what was left over.

These decisions bode well for the Czech people in the coming war years, because, as useful subjects of the German Reich, they lived almost as well as the Germans. Their neighbors—the Slovaks, Poles and Hungarians—had it much harder.

*Actress
Lida Baarova,
Joseph Goebbels'
Czech mistress.*

Some Czechs became overzealous in their desire to be Germanized because such behavior led to better jobs, more generous rations and other privileges. Those individuals became known within Czech society as "Margarine Germans."

Goebbels' Czech Mistress

Joseph Goebbels, Germany's Minister of Propaganda and movie czar, thought the Germanization of the Czechs was a wonderful idea and was eager to do his part. To this end, he had acquired a Czech mistress. She was Lida Baarova, a beautiful actress then working in Germany. Goebbels' cozy relationship with Baarova was common knowledge throughout Germany despite the fact that nothing about it had ever been printed or broadcasted. After all, Goebbels controlled the media.

Unfortunately for Goebbels, he was married and had four children. Furthermore, he and his wife, Magda, had been held up before the German people for years as a shining example of a perfect Nazi family.

Nazi Polygamy?

In the highest echelons of the Nazi Party, serious consideration was being given to the possibility of allowing the German people to practice polygamy after the final German victory so as to rapidly replenish Germany's human losses. There was a precedent for this in German history: After the Thirty Years War, polygamy was practiced in some parts of Germany for the same reason.

As the war dragged on and Germany's losses on the eastern front mounted, the prospect of practicing postwar polygamy increased. So, good Nazi wives had to accept the idea of their husbands taking a second wife. Having a mistress was, therefore, the first step in this program. The wives were given assurances, though, that they would remain wife No. 1 and have a higher status than wife No. 2.

Joseph and Magda Goebbels and their children in 1939 soon after his break-up with lida Baarove. The Goebbels family was touted by the German media as the perfect Nazi family. They would, in the end, live up to this image. In the last days of the war, rather than be captured by the advancing Red Army, Goebbels and Magda would commit suicide in the Berlin bunker, but not before poisoning their five children.

Magda Goebbels knew of her husband's liaison with Baarova and had, at first, tolerated it. But, eventually she reached the point where she got fed up and threatened divorce. When Hitler heard of this, he was furious and feared that an ugly scandal within the highest ranks of the Nazi Party would hurt his regime. He interceded in the affair, and ordered Goebbels to give up his mistress and go back to his wife. Goebbels, always the loyal Nazi, did as his Führer commanded. Lida was shipped off to Bohemia-Moravia and worked for the rest of the war in the small Czech film industry there. All of her films were banned in Germany. Goebbels went back to his wife, and, in 1940, she presented him with their fifth child.

Shortages in French North Africa

As Captain Renault points out to Laszlo and Ilsa, gasoline is in very short supply in French North Africa. The French Empire, despite its great size, had no major source of petroleum at this point in time and had to rely on foreign sources. In peacetime, France's primary supplier of petroleum products was the United States but that had ended with the establishment of the British naval blockade. The Vichy Government was forced to search for petroleum sources wherever they could be found. The gasoline shortage was so acute in France and French North Africa that some automobile owners went to the trouble and expense of converting their vehicles to use alternative fuels.

Some items were still coming to French North Africa from America, though—primarily food, humanitarian supplies and consumer items. This was being done with the approval of the British in an effort to maintain relatively good relations between the Vichy French authorities in North Africa and the Americans. The British saw this as beneficial to their war effort and allowed the American supplies through their blockade. One of the commodities delivered by the Americans to French North Africa was English tea. It was a staple in the diet of the Moroccans and, of course, put a few Moroccan francs into the British treasury.

As Time Goes By

 "Play it, Sam. Play 'As Time Goes By.'"
—Ilsa to Sam

"As Time Goes By" first appeared in the Depression-era play, *Everybody's Welcome,* starring Frances Williams. Written by Herman Hupfeld, the song caught on and Rudy Vallee, one of the famous band leaders of the day, recorded and sang it, as did Miss Williams.

At Cornell University in upstate New York, a college boy named Murray Burnett fell in love with the song, bought Frances Williams' recording and played it over and over again in his fraternity house. Several years later, Burnett, by then a high school teacher in New York City, tried his hand, with his colleague Joan Alison, at writing a play. The song "As Time Goes By" was written into the *Everybody Come to Rick's,* romantically linking the leading man and leading lady. This play, of course, became the basis for *Casablanca,* and the song became its main musical theme.

Sam sings only the melody for us in the movie, but here are the complete lyrics.

This day and age we're living in,
Gives cause for apprehension,
With speed and new inventions,
And things like third dimension.

Yet we get a trifle weary,
With Mr. Einstein's Theory,
So we must get down to earth at times,
Relax, relieve the tension.

No matter what the progress,
Of what may yet be proved,
The simple facts of life are such,
They cannot be removed.

You must remember this,
A kiss is still a kiss,
A sigh is just a sigh,

The fundamental things apply
As time goes by.

And when two lovers woo,
They still say, I love you,
On that you can rely;
No matter what the future brings
As time goes by.

Moonlight and love songs, never out of date,
Hearts full of passion, jealously and hate,
Woman need man, and man must have his mate,
That no one can deny.

It's still the some old story,
A fight for love and glory,
A case of do or die.
The world will always welcome lovers
As time goes by.

This is a scene at the Demarcation Line between occupied France and unoccupied France near Moulins. The automobile has been converted to use a substitute fuel.

English tea is not consumed by Rick or the other principal characters in the movie, but, at both Rick's and the Blue Parrot, waiters are seen serving a beverage in small pots and cups. Could this be English tea?

Under the American-Vichy food arrangement, four Vichy merchant ships were allowed to sail back and forth between Casablanca and New York City. Two ships would be in each port at the same time and depart at the same time. They would cross paths in mid-ocean. The ships in New York were thoroughly inspected by British representatives before leaving to see that they were not carrying contraband. Once cleared, the ships' captains were given certificates, called Navicerts, showing that the ships' cargoes had been inspected and approved for passage through the British blockade. Navicerts were used in case the ships were stopped on the high seas by British warships enforcing the blockade.

It is very possible that some of the food and beverages Rick offered in his Cafe Americain, came on those ships.

Chapter Four

The Paris Flashback

War Comes to Paris

On June 3, 1940, the Germans bombed Paris for the first time. Rick and Ilsa almost certainly experienced it. Some 200 bombers dropped in excess of 1,000 bombs and incendiaries, mainly on industrial targets, killing 254 and injuring 652 people.

On June 5, the Germans launched their expected offensive southward towards Paris. Because French defenses were weak, the Germans broke through them and began to advance into the heartland of France.

On that day, a relatively unknown French Army officer, just recently promoted from colonel to a one-star general, was brought into the Government in Paris as Undersecretary to The Minister of National Defense. He was Charles De Gaulle, a specialist on armored units and tank warfare. This was his first government position. He would serve in the Government for only 18 days.

The Germans advanced steadily southward. On June 9, German forces crossed the Somme River and encircled the French 10th Army. Other German forces crossed the Oise River and prepared to march on to Paris from the east.

On June 10, Italy declared war on France and Italian forces invaded southeastern France. German forces fought their way into the suburbs of Rouen, just 70 miles west of Paris, and crossed the Seine, cutting off Paris from the sea. In Paris, the French Government of Paul Reynaud fled to the city of Tours. Thousands of Parisians began to flee, too, choking the roads leading south out of town. The Germans treated the long columns of refugees leaving Paris as legitimate military targets and often attacked them from the air.

The next day, Reynaud's government completed its evacuation of Paris and the city was declared an Open City, meaning that the French Army would not attempt to defend it. The Germans quickly responded by radio, announcing that they would not attack the city as long as the French honored their Open City pledge. There was some rejoicing in Paris as it became reasonably certain that the city would not become a battleground.

French refugees take cover from marauding German aircraft.

That afternoon, June 11, 1940, Rick and Ilsa are in an outdoor cafe in the Montmarte district of Paris. A man is selling newspapers on the corner to a crowd of people. There is excitement. The papers are dated June 11, 1940 and the headlines read "Paris, Open City: Order of Evacuation", "Advice for the Population", "Aggression Unleashed: Italy Declares War on Us."

Rick buys a newspaper and begins to read. A loudspeaker truck nearby makes a public announcement.

Rick, still reading the newspaper, says…

"Nothing can stop them now! Wednesday [June 12], *Thursday* [June 13] *at the latest they'll be in Paris."*

Rick was one day off on his prediction. The Germans entered Paris on Friday June 14, 1940.

The loudspeaker trucks in these scenes are accurate representations of the way fast-breaking news was announced in Europe at that time. Not everyone owned a radio and loudspeaker trucks were used extensively to inform large numbers of people quickly about such news events.

By June 12, the city of Reims, 80 miles northeast of Paris, was in German hands and their march towards Paris continued. Later that day, German troops took the town of Chalons-sur-Marne, 80 miles east of the capital. The German plan was to take Paris from the east and northeast. German forces northwest of Paris bypassed the city and headed for the Cherbourg and Brittany Peninsulas to prevent them from becoming Allied military redoubts (fortresses). By nightfall on June 12, advance elements of the German Army were only twelve miles east of Paris.

The flood of refugees out of the city turned into a torrent. Before it was over, two-thirds of the population of Paris would flee.

This is the newspaper Rick bought telling of the German advance towards Paris and that Paris was an Open City. To the right of the front page is a photo of President Roosevelt and a report of the statement he made the day before about Italy's attack on France, "The hand that held the dagger has struck it into the back of its neighbor." That statement became one of the most famous statements of the war.

The activities of Rick and Ilsa are not shown on this day, June 12, but it turns out to be a monumental day for Ilsa. Sometime during the day, she got word that her husband, Victor Laszlo, was not dead but had just escaped from a concentration camp. Furthermore, he was on his way to Paris to return to her and to report to the Czechoslovakian Government-in-Exile which had established its headquarters in Paris in late 1939. Ilsa was shocked with disbelief. Now she was in love with another man, and, all of a sudden, her husband is to reappear. She now faced the dilemma of having to choose between her husband and her lover.

The audience is not witness to Ilsa's anguish, but her decision was a foregone conclusion in 1942 Hollywood. She would remain true to her marriage vows and choose her husband over her lover. The Hays Office, the keeper of Hollywood's moral code, would insist upon it.

At this point, Ilsa becomes a true heroine of the resistance movement in her own right. Rather than running away with Rick to safety, she chooses to be with her husband and face, with him, a very uncertain future in German-occupied Paris.

Rick, The Gunrunner

When Rick identifies the artillery fire as a German 77 about 35 miles away, he gives the viewing audience a big hint as to what he's been up to in Paris. Only a person very familiar with modern weapons could identify the caliber of an artillery piece

Germans often brought their own loudspeaker trucks into newly occupied towns and cities to give instructions to the populace.

and its distance by the sound of its being fired. Since Rick demonstrates that he has that ability, it is very likely he is still up to his old tricks—dealing in arms.

There's one slight historical error in Rick's statement, though. At no time during World War II did the Germans have a 77 mm artillery piece.

The Germans Enter Paris

On the morning of Friday, June 14, 1940, the first German troops entered Paris. There was no resistance. This was one of the greatest victories so far in the war for the Germans and they wanted to celebrate it in grand style. To show their new mastery over the capital of France, the Germans marched into the heart of the city in ceremonial formations complete with a marching band.

The German Army imposed military rule on the city and the Gestapo arrived on the heels of the German soldiers to impose law and order and to search for enemies of the Reich. General Otto von Stuelpnagel, the German Military commander of the city, set up his headquarters in the fashionable Crillon Hotel directly across from the American Embassy. In this way, the Americans were reminded, every minute of the day, of who was in charge in Paris. Von Stuelpnagel took for his personal quarters the hotel's Prince of Wales Suite. German troops were garrisoned outside the city and instructed not to wear their uniforms in the city unless they were on official Army business. A great many of the German soldiers wanted to see Paris, and, for the rest of the summer the French tour operators experienced a flourishing business as the German soldiers turned into tourists.

Left: German troops enter the heart of Paris in formations led by a band. They marched around the Arc de Triomphe rather than through it so as to not overly agitate the French.

Within hours of their occupation of Paris, the Germans plastered the town with propaganda posters such as this one. It reads "Abandoned people, put your trust in the German soldier."

Jean Chiappe, Paris' Prefect of Police, was appointed civil governor of Paris and worked closely with the Germans to maintain order. The movie's Prefect of Police, Captain Renault, would act in a similar manner after the defeat of France and worked collaboratively with the German Armistice Commission and Major Strasser.

On June 15, Paul Reynaud's Government arrived in Bordeaux. Its members were by now polarized as to whether or not to ask the Germans for an armistice. After hours of heated debate, Reynaud concluded that his Government was hopelessly deadlocked on the issue. Around midnight June 16/17, Renaud resigned and recommended that World War I hero and elder statesman, Marshal Henri Petain, should be appointed as his replacement and that Petain form a new Government. President Albert Lebrun agreed and the last Government of the French Third Republic was formed with Petain as Premier. The Marshal was determined to save what he could of France before the entire country was overrun. Within a few hours of his appointment he asked the Germans for an Armistice. They agreed and the fighting in France ended soon afterwards.

Later on June 17, the British Government announced that it would continue the struggle alone against Germany and Italy. On June 18, General Charles De Gaulle announced from London that he intended to ignore Petain's surrender and continue the

Hollywood Laments Loss Of Paris

The loss of Paris and the fall of France had a dramatic effect on Hollywood. Movies with French themes had been popular in America and the events in France mandated that the trend continue but, of course, in touch with this new and dynamic turn of events in France. Such movies would, as dictated by the sentiments of the American public, be sympathetic to the French people but, now, not necessarily to the French Government. *Casablanca* would be one of those movies, but before Burnett and Alison's play was discovered by Warner Bros., there were other movies with French themes already playing on American screens. When France fell, Warner Bros. had, purely by coincidence, a movie in circulation with a combination American and French theme. It was *The Fighting 69th* (1940), starring James Cagney and Pat O'Brien and detailed the exploits of the famous American infantry division in France during World War I.

By 1942, movies referring to German-occupied Paris began to appear. Warner Bros. had one of the first. They produced *This Was Paris* (1941) in their British studio starring Ben Lyon and Ann Dvorak. This was a spy story centered in Paris just before the German occupation. That same year, Universal Studios released *Paris Calling* starring Elisabeth Bergner and Basil Rathbone as a married couple in Paris under the occupation. During the course of the movie, the wife discovers that her husband has become a traitor.

Movies made in 1941 and released in 1942 include RKO's *Joan of Paris* starring Paul Henreid (*Casablanca*'s Laszlo) and Michele Morgan. In this film, Henreid plays a French resistance leader who sacrifices himself so that Allied flyers can escape to England. MGM's *Reunion in France*, with John Wayne and Joan Crawford, had Crawford, a Paris *couturiére* (fashion designer), hiding a downed American flyer (Wayne) while having to contend with the advances of a German admirer. Twentieth Century-Fox produced *The Pied Piper* (1942) starring Monty Wolley and Anne Baxter. Based on a novel by Nevil Shute, the movie was about an old man who, despite his dislike for children, finds himself smuggling youngsters out of occupied France. Republic's offering that year was *Spy Smasher* with Kane Richard and Marguerite Chapman telling of a U.S. spy in France who was captured by the Nazis while trying to unmask "The Mask," a movie serial character of the times.

The British produced *Pimpernel Smith* (1941) with Leslie Howard—Humphrey Bogart's good friend and mentor—and Mary Morris. This was a follow-up to Howard's great success *The Scarlet Pimpernel* (1934) in which he plays a British aristocrat who rescues French aristocrats from the horrors of the French Revolution. In *Pimpernel Smith*, Howard rescues refugees from occupied France.

In the literary world, author Elliot Paul produced a best-selling book entitled *The Last Time I Saw Paris* and in the music field Oscar Hammerstein II and Jerome Kern wrote the ever-popular song by the same name.

It was during this time, late 1940-early 1941, that Murray Burnett and Joan Alison were writing their play. They were very much aware of the tragedy that had befallen France.

fight. He asked Frenchmen all over the world to join him. Later that day, British Prime Minister Winston Churchill made one of the most memorable speeches of his life in an effort to rouse the spirits of the British people. In it, he made one of the most famous remarks of the war: "Let us brace ourselves to our duties, and so bear ourselves that if the British Empire and its Commonwealths last for a thousand years, men will say, 'This was their finest hour.'"

On June 20, at Germany's insistence, France asked Italy for armistice terms. German troops were still driving deep into France and captured Lyons and Vichy.

On the 22th, representatives of the French and German Governments signed the armistice documents in the same railroad car that Germany had surrendered to France 22 years earlier at the end of World War I.

On the 24th, France and Italy signed their armistice documents at the Villa Inlisa near Rome.

German troops continued their march into France and occupied the entire French Atlantic coast from Belgium to Spain. Petain's Government fled Bordeaux into unoccupied southern France.

On the 25th, the German-French Armistice conditions went into effect and the Germans withdrew from the cities of Lyons and Vichy in southern France. The Germans told Petain that his government could return to Paris if it wished, but Petain chose to remain in Unoccupied France where he and his Government would have more freedom of action. In looking for a place to establish itself, the Petain Government chose Vichy.

Rick's Arrival In Casablanca

It is not known when Rick and Sam arrived in Casablanca, but it was probably around the first week in July 1940. Their route was a fairly easy one. When their train reached Marseilles, there were plenty of commercial vessels to take them on to one of the major ports in Algeria. There was some naval activity in the western Mediterranean Sea between the British and Italian navies during the latter part of June, but it did not interrupt commercial traffic. The commercial vessels heading from southern France to Algeria were crowded with refugees as were the trains and buses to Casablanca, but, with persistence, individuals could get through.

Upon arriving in Casablanca, Rick and Sam found a modern thriving city untouched by the war, but filled with European refugees and very few Americans. At this time, there were less than 200 American living in all of French Morocco. Virtually all of the refugees in Casablanca harbored dreams of going to America. Rick surely noticed this and realized that the refugees who had made it this far, and had plans to go further, likely had money. Those without money had no real need to go to Casablanca and, in all likelihood, had accepted refuge somewhere along the refugee route.

Rick undoubtedly learned quickly of the exit visa scam that plagued the refugees and the fact that the local Prefect of Police was heavily involved in it. He surely learned, too, of the black market and of its top man, Ferrari.

Furthermore, Rick would have discovered the relatively good feeling in Casablanca towards Americans and the United States. The United States had maintained diplomatic relations with the new French regime in Vichy and had expressed great concern for the French people in their time of need and had even offered to send aid. The native Moroccans had good feelings towards the United States because America had been a valuable trading partner with many American items of quality available in Moroccan stores. Furthermore, American foreign policy had consistently, over the years, supported political independence at the earliest possible moment for colonial countries like Morocco.

Obviously, Rick surveyed the scene before him and saw a very positive atmosphere for things American. He saw refugees with money and a black market where he could get things from America. In addition, in his friend, Sam, he had a black musician who could sing and play all of the latest American songs. Sam, having worked in night clubs for years, would have some knowledge of the night club business. Putting these things together, Rick discovered a unique business opportunity: a need for an American-style night club in Casablanca. And not the least, with a corrupt Prefect of Police, he could ensure the success of his establishment by putting in a gambling room and offering the Prefect a piece of the action.

This is what Rick did. He decided to forsake the arms business and become a saloon keeper. How Rick went about it is not told, but whatever he did, he did it fast. The next time Rick is seen after Paris, it's only 17 months later. He is a well-known and highly respected Casablanca businessman—on a first name basis with both the Prefect of Police and the head of the black market.

Casablanca In Danger

There was little chance that German Armies would, in the near future, invade French Morocco, but there were dangers from other quarters, especially from the British and Spanish. After the Mers el Kebir incident of July 4, 1940, no one could be certain that such an attack wouldn't happen again. Casablanca could well be the next target. There were rumors that the British would invade French Morocco and turn it over to De Gaulle's Free French as a base of operations from which to invade Algeria. Those rumors gave rise to other rumors that the Germans would send troops into French Morocco to guard against such an invasion. None of these things happened, but such concerns and fears persisted.

Another, and perhaps greater, threat came from Spanish Morocco to the north. Spain had long-standing territorial claims to areas of French Morocco as far south as Casablanca, and in Algeria as far east as Oran. If Spain entered the war on the side of the Axis, part of her compensation from Germany and Italy might be their approval for Spain to make good on these territorial claims. And, if the French chose to fight, French Morocco could become a battleground.

Spain had already rattled its saber when, on June 14, 1940, the day before the Germans entered Paris, Spanish troops arbitrarily took control of the international city of

Tangier on the south shore of the Strait of Gibraltar. Up to then, France had been one of the several parties that governed that city.

Seven days later, on June 21, the Spanish Foreign Minister in Madrid suggested to the French Ambassador, Count de la Baume, that France turn over to Spain the tribal territories of the Beni-Zeroual in western French Morocco and those of the Beni-Snassen in eastern French Morocco. Two days later, after the German and French Armistice had been signed, the Spanish Ambassador to France, Jose Felix de Lequerira, made the same request to the Petain Government in Vichy. To the French, these "requests" were seen as a threat of possible Spanish military action if France refused. The French reaction was to avoid saying "no" and to stall for time. Surely, Hitler would have a say in this matter and the French needed time to establish their new political relationship with him.

The French were right. The Spanish "requests" were the beginning of much bigger things as far as Spain was concerned. On June 19, two days before the first request was made to the French Ambassador in Madrid, the Spanish government sent a memo to Berlin indicating that Spain was ready to enter the war on the side of the Axis. Madrid's conditions were that Spain receive all of French Morocco, Gibraltar, the Department of Oran in Algeria and other minor territorial adjustments in sub-Saharan Africa at the expense of the British and French. The Spanish also asked for substantial German military aid in accomplishing these goals.

This memo was received with mixed emotions by Hitler who was, at that time, meeting with Mussolini in Munich. Hitler discussed the Spanish proposal with Mussolini and both men agreed that they would welcome Spain as an active ally and liked the idea of capturing Gibraltar from the British. And, that after the final Axis victory, Spain could, indeed, have all of French Morocco and the Department of Oran. But for the moment, Hitler had no desire to see the war spread to another part of Africa where only Spain would benefit and Germany would be committed to sustaining Spain's military operations. He feared that he might eventually have to send in German troops. After all, it was only recently that Hitler had to send General Rommel and the Afrika Corps to Libya and Egypt to salvage Italy's military operations. He didn't want to have to do it again for Spain. But Hitler could see considerable advantages to Spain's entering the war and, with German help, capturing Gibraltar.

So, Hitler's reply to Madrid was, "Let's talk." These talks developed favorably and on November 12, 1940, Hitler issued Directive #18, ordering German military planners to create a plan whereby Germany would assist Spain in the conquest of Gibraltar and the securing of the entire Iberian peninsula. That plan was named "Operation Felix." A group of 50 German officers went to Spain to work with Spanish military leaders and, while at Jura, special German assault troops began training for the attack on Gibraltar. The target date for implementing "Operation Felix" was to be the first week in January 1941.

Once Gibraltar was taken, "Operation Felix" called for German troops to be stationed on both sides of the Strait of Gibraltar to deny its use to the Allies. This would

Hitler (left) and Franco (right) met for the first time at Hendaye, France to discuss Spain's entry into World War II as an Axis Ally. Hitler and Franco, though, developed an instant dislike for each other. This and other events postponed, indefinitely, Spain's entry into the war.

mean, of course, that German troops would be stationed in Spanish Morocco. Spain's territorial claims in French Morocco and Algeria would be dealt with in future discussions. This was Hitler's way of dangling the carrot before the Spanish to make sure they pulled their own weight during "Operation Felix."

The French could clearly see the Spanish and British threats to French Morocco, and, as a part of their defensive strategy, sent their new, but as yet uncompleted, battleship, "Jean Bart," to take up station at Casablanca. The "Jean Bart" was not operational for sea duty, but her guns were in place and could be used effectively to defend the city against air and sea attacks.

The "Jean Bart" arrived at Casablanca, along with other French warships, on June 22, 1940, and dropped anchor in the harbor. Their officers and crew began making preparation for a long stay. Those ships would still be there two years and five months later when the Americans invaded French Morocco in November 1942. At that time, the "Jean Bart" and the other French warships did as they were originally ordered: do battle against any invader.

Between June 1940, and November 1942, the French naval officers and crewmen at Casablanca had little to do and were given generous shore leave. In the movie, some of them are seen frequenting Rick's. The first French seaman to appear in Casablanca is when the front door of Rick's Cafe is first seen. One of the individuals entering Rick's that Tuesday night is a French naval officer with the rank of lieutenant.

A French sailor, an enlisted man, is at the Blue Parrot in the scene where Rick comes to pick up his supplies that have just arrived by bus. Here is another bit of historical accuracy in the movie. Officers were more likely to frequent an upscale establishment like Rick's while enlisted men felt more at home in a place like the Blue Parrot.

During August 1940, about the time Rick's Cafe Americain first opened for business, the Spanish began increasing their troop strength along the Spanish Moroccan-French Moroccan border, a move the French viewed with alarm. The Spanish forces grew in strength to 150,000 troops, poised to invade French Morocco upon Madrid's command. The Spaniards began a propaganda campaign in North Africa, primarily by radio, supporting their territorial demands. Broadcasts were made in both French and Arabic. About this same time, the Germans began propaganda broadcasts to French North Africa, but the German broadcasts did not threaten the French in North Africa with invasion. Rather, they preached their conventional anti-British and anti-Semitic themes along with the theme that the war was almost over and that the Axis-dominated

American Tramp Replaced By Norwegian Heroine

In *Everybody Comes To Rick's*, the leading lady was Lois Meredith, an unmarried American woman of loose morals who sleeps with three different men during the course of the play. For the Warner Bros. screenwriters, her character was a problem from the beginning because such behavior was not to be shown in American movies and almost certainly wouldn't have been approved by the Hays Office, the keeper of Hollywood's Production Code.

When it was learned that Swedish beauty Ingrid Bergman had been engaged for the role of leading lady, new possibilities opened up for the writers. She proved ideal for their need to clean up Lois' act. Bergman was a bright new star on the American scene with an impeccable reputation and a delightful Scandinavian accent. So, it was easy to change the movie's leading lady into a fine and honorable European woman who is loyal to her husband until she believes him dead; then loyal to her new lover, Rick; then loyal again to her husband when he reappears. Thus Lois Meredith became Ilsa Lund.

As for Ilsa's nationality, there was really only one logical choice—Norwegian. This was for several reasons. First of all, most of the other Scandinavian countries were not in political favor at the time. This included Bergman's native country, Sweden, which was a neutral nation but was actively trading with the Axis nations. The Swedes were selling the Germans high-grade iron ore, precision ball-bearings used in aircraft engines and other war-related items. Because of this, Sweden was getting a considerable amount of bad press in the west. Denmark was out of the question because when the Germans invaded that country in April, 1940, the Danish Army offered only token resistance and the Danish Government and King Christian chose to remain in Copenhagen and were eventually forced to submit to the will to the Nazis.

Ilsa could not have been Finnish because Finland was at war with The Soviet Union and Britain, and Finnish troops were actively cooperating with the Germans inside the Soviet Union, particularly with regards to the Siege of Leningrad (St. Petersburg).

Ilsa might have been Icelandic, another Scandinavian nation, because Iceland had, by roundabout means, become an Allied nation. At the beginning of the war, Iceland was a possession of Denmark, but, under strong diplomatic pressure from Britain and the United States, proclaimed its independence and joined the Allies. But, all told, the American public knew little of Iceland and its people.

On the other hand, the Americans and other westerners had a strong love-hate relationship with Norway. The hate factor centered around one man, Vidkun Quisling. Quisling had been the leader of the small pre-war Norwegian Nazi Party known as the "Nasjonal Samling." When the Germans occupied Norway, Quisling sold his soul to the Germans in order to become Norway's top political leader. His cavorting with the enemy was so blatant and outrageous that he was vilified time and again in the western press to the point where his name became synonymous with "traitor." Throughout the war, the word "quisling" was used to describe others who betrayed their countries. That word came into such universal use that it survived the war and appears today in most English language dictionaries. It still means traitor.

As for the love part of the equation, there was plenty. Americans had long admired the Norwegians as being peace-loving, democratic, hardworking, clean and honorable people. When the Germans attacked their country in April, 1940,

Vidkun Quisling, the German's top puppet political leader in Norway. His name became a synonym for "traitor."

their small army put up a heroic, but futile attempt to save the nation. The Government of King Haakon VII refused to surrender and fled to England to carry on the fight as a Government-in-exile. Rallying to that Government came the magnificent Norwegian merchant fleet, one of the largest in the world. That fleet, which consisted of more than 1,800 vessels, became a vital part of the Allies worldwide sea-going transportation operations. A considerable number of Norwegian ships were sunk by enemy action during the war and many Norwegian merchant seamen gave their lives for the Allied cause.

Furthermore, the Norwegians had an unofficial, but very attractive ambassador in Holly

Sonja Henie won three gold medals in figure skating at the 1936 Winter Olympics in Germany. Here, she is being personally congratulated by Hitler. Soon afterwards, Henie went to America and became a popular movie star.

wood during the time *Casablanca* was coming into being. She was ice skating champion Sonja Henie, an Olympic gold-medalist-turned-movie star. Henie appeared in a series of movies centered around ice skating, romance and popular music and became something of a darling daughter to everyone. In 1939, she was Hollywood's third-ranked star after Shirley Temple and Clark Gable.

Sonja Henie also had a popular ice show in which she starred and toured the nation.

In 1942, the British-made movie shown in the United States under the title *The Avengers*, enjoyed some considerable success. This movie told the story of Norwegian resistance fighters who destroy a German submarine base with the help of British Commandos.

Warner Bros.' rivals, Twentieth Century-Fox and Columbia, were currently working on Norwegian films that would run concurrently with *Casablanca*. Twentieth Century-Fox's film was entitled *The Moon is Down* (1943) and was based on John Steinbeck's best-selling novel of the same name which related the story of a Norwegian town that resists the Nazis. Columbia's film was *First Comes Courage* (1943) that told the story of a Norwegian girl who appears to be a quisling but, in reality, is a spy for the Allies.

Furthermore, Warner Bros. had their own Norwegian film in the making entitled *Edge of Darkness*. This film, starring Errol Flynn and Ann Sheridan, told a story much like Twentieth Century-Fox's *The Moon is Down* about a Norwegian village fighting the Nazis. Helmut Dantine (*Casablanca*'s Jan) was also in the film.

Given these conditions, could Ilsa, with her Scandinavian accent and wholesomeness, be anything other than Norwegian?

The Warner Bros. writers also slipped another Norwegian into the script. He is Berger, the Free French operative who reveals himself to Laszlo early in the movie by means of his ring which bears the Cross of Lorraine. Berger, could have been any of several nationalities, and most likely should have been French. But, the Norwegian appeal was so strong in Hollywood that Norway won out again.

After *Casablanca* was released, Jack Warner was asked if the movie was beneficial in any way to the war effort. In reply, he cited the Ilsa character in the movie as promoting international understanding as a courageous Norwegian woman and a reminder of the suffering of the Norwegian people.

New Order was here to stay. The German broadcasts also supported the French political right, the most supportive element of the Vichy Government. These broadcasts had very little effect on the people of North Africa because the Germans continued to hold some 60,000 North African prisoners of war, most of them natives, to use as political bargaining chips with the Vichy Government. This, and the fact that stories of maltreatment of prisoners of war in the German camps filtered back to North Africa.

The prospect of Spain's entry into the war on the side of the Axis resulted in a meeting between Hitler and Spain's Generalissimo Franco on October 23, 1940, at Hendaye, France, on the Spanish-French border. By then, Franco had increased his price for Spain's joining the Axis and was losing faith, to some degree, in a German victory because Britain had not yet surrendered. Similarly, Hitler was beginning to lose interest in Spain because he was, by then, committed to invading the Soviet Union and would need virtually all of the Germany's military forces for that undertaking. To complicate matters further, Hitler and Franco developed an instant dislike for each other at the meeting.

The meeting, though, proceeded cordially but Hitler backed down from supporting Spain's territorial ambitions in French North Africa and Franco correspondingly lost interest in joining the Axis. An agreement was made, though, to continue to study ways by which Spain might still join the Axis. From Hitler's point of view, any future venture into the Iberian Peninsula would have to be shelved until the Soviet Union was eliminated.

Five days after the Hendaye meeting, Italy invaded Greece, and, before the year was out, Hitler had to send substantial numbers of German troops into the Balkans to rescue the Italians once again. This all but killed any chance that German resources would be available to carry out military operations with Spain.

The Vichy French, of course, did not know of Hitler's plans to attack the Soviet Union, so for them the threat of a Spanish incursions into North Africa, with German backing, continued. It was not until June 22, 1941, when German troops invaded the Soviet Union, that the Vichy French could see that the greater part of Germany's armed might was committed in the east and that the threat from Spain had, for the time being at least, diminished.

Chapter Five

Money, Or Influence, Or Luck

It is now the morning of Wednesday December 3, 1940. Captain Renault and Major Strasser will soon be seen in Renault's office waiting for Victor and Ilsa. But first, the historic events of this historic day will be reviewed.

• **MOSCOW**: On the Moscow front, German troops begin pulling back from the city's suburbs, suffering badly from the winter weather which, at times, has reached -38°C. Strong Arctic winds have made survival in the Russian winter even more perilous. Some German units report that 40 percent of their troops are suffering from frostbite and some battalions are down to 100 men or less.

• **NORTH AFRICA**: In eastern North Africa, a fierce and confusing battle rages around Tobruk, Libya, where the British, who are holding the city, are surrounded by Rommel's Afrika Corps and Italian forces. The British-led 4th Indian Division launches a counter-attack in an effort to break through to relieve Tobruk but it has not yet succeeded. Maneuvering by both sides draws the lines of battle deep into the Sahara Desert.

• **WESTERN PACIFIC**: The Japanese naval strike force continues its course towards Pearl Harbor, Hawaii. It is sailing in the vast emptiness of the Northern Pacific and maintaining absolute radio silence so as not to be detected by the Americans. Japanese spies in Hawaii report that the Americans appear to know nothing of the approaching naval force.

• **SOUTH ATLANTIC**: The American merchant ship "Sagadahoc" is torpedoed and sunk by a German submarine. America is still a neutral country and such sinkings have become increasingly more frequent, driving the American Government and people closer to war.

Americans in Berlin

 "Well we mustn't underestimate American blundering. I was with them when they blundered into Berlin in 1918."

—Renault to Strasser

Renault's comment about the Americans blundering into Berlin would seem to indicate that the Americans captured that city during World War I.

This was not the case.

No Allied army captured Berlin, but the Americans did enter Berlin under other circumstances. Renault could very well have been with them but he had the year wrong.

Here's how it came about.

Soon after the Armistice ending World War I was signed on November 11, 1918, the new and democratic German Government in Berlin responsible for ending the war began to have serious problems when the various political factions within the government began squabbling amongst themselves.

The Government was a broad coalition of many political parties, and the leftist elements, led by the newly emerged Communist-oriented Spartacus League, were pressing for immediate and radical social reforms throughout Germany. The political moderates and conservatives in the Government opposed such quick and radical changes and successfully blocked the efforts of the leftists. In December, the Spartacus League and other leftist radicals broke away from the Government and organized themselves into the German Communist Party. Their political agenda was to create a Soviet-style Government in Germany as soon as possible and by any means necessary, including revolution. This was the tactic the Bolsheviks had used in Russia and it was responsible for that country becoming locked in a bloody civil war that was then raging. The great majority of Germans wanted no such thing to happen inside Germany, nor did the victorious Allies.

But the German Communists pressed on, holding rallies, marches and protest meetings. These events often turned into street fights and riots, especially in Berlin. This situation persisted all through December 1918. In January 1919, conditions deteriorated in Berlin to the point where law and order began to break down and the city was approaching a state of anarchy. With this, the Allies concluded it was time to restore order in Berlin and protect the hard-pressed German Government. This task was assigned to the Americans, because, in the eyes of the Germans, the Americans were the most politically acceptable of all the former enemy forces.

Thus it was that the Americans "blundered" into Berlin to serve as a large and neutral police force to restore law and order. As is common in military operations of this sort, the French, British and other Allies sent liaison and support units to assist the Americans while serving under American command. It must have been in one of these support units that Captain Renault, most likely a young French soldier, entered Berlin "with" the Americans. The date was January 1919, and not 1918 as Renault remembered it.

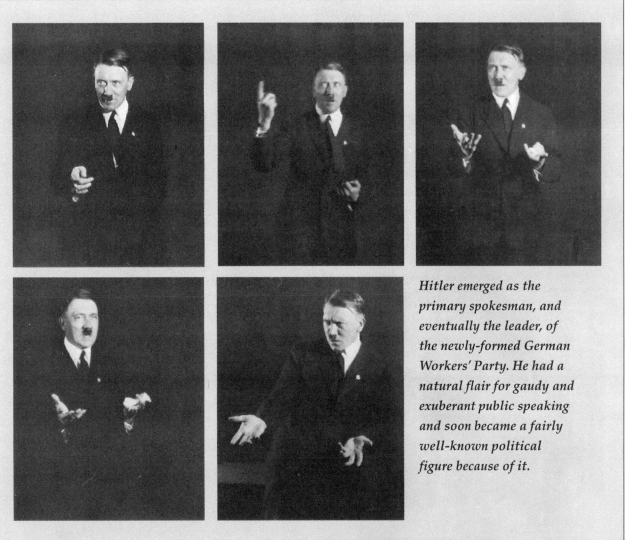

Hitler emerged as the primary spokesman, and eventually the leader, of the newly-formed German Workers' Party. He had a natural flair for gaudy and exuberant public speaking and soon became a fairly well-known political figure because of it.

Hitler Compared Himself To A Film Star

Late in World War II, Hitler's close friend, Albert Speer, Germany's Minister of Armaments and Munitions, asked Hitler why he never married. Hitler had been asked this question before and his standard answer was that he was married to Germany and he that felt there was a lack of time to be a proper German husband and father. However, on this occasion, he gave Speer a different answer. Hitler compared himself to a film star saying, "Lots of women are attracted to me because I am unmarried. That was especially useful during our days of struggle [the 1920s, when Hitler was in his 30s]. It's the same with a film star: when he marries, he loses a certain something for the women who adore him. Then he is no longer their idol as he was before."

"Mickey Mouse" Takes Over The German Film Industry

In January 1933, the Nazis came to power in Germany and one of the first things they did was to take control of all of Germany's media, information and entertainment sources. This included the entire German film industry. Hitler appointed his Minister of Public Enlightenment and Propa-

Dr. Joseph Goebbels, Reich Minister of Public Enlightenment and Propaganda and Germany's film Czar. Note his club foot. Goebbels was very sensitive about this and usually stood behind his desk to hide it when he greeted people in his office. Those visiting Goebbels were advised never to look at his feet.

WHAT IS AN "ARYAN"?
HE IS HANDSOME
AS GOEBBELS

REPRODUCED FROM SOVIET WAR POSTER 1941 · BY RUSSIAN WAR RELIEF INC

Goebbels was given the nickname "Mickey Mouse" by those in the German film industry who didn't like him. This poster, first produced in the Soviet Union and then Americanized for distribution in the U.S., makes use of that nickname.

ganda, Dr. Joseph Goebbels, to oversee this effort which resulted in Goebbels becoming Germany's movie Czar.

Goebbels, like Hitler, loved movies, and realized that they could become a major avenue of Nazi-style enlightenment for the people. But, before he could begin this process, Goebbels ordered the entire film industry cleansed of Jews. This order applied to every foreign film maker and dis-

Hitler with his favorite movie people. Left to right: Else Elster, Leni Marenbach, Hitler, Lilian Harvey, Karin Hardt, Dinah Grace, Willi Fritsch, Leni Riefenstahl (director), and Dinah Grace's sister.

tributor operating in Germany, including Warner Bros. Warner Bros. and the other American film companies, who had good markets established in Germany, reluctantly complied. It was an omen, though, of worse things to come.

Goebbels ferreted out the handful of individuals in the German film industry who had Nazi sympathies and put them in dominant positions along with some appointees of his own. Goebbels then pressed his mark on the industry in a very personal way. He personally reviewed scripts, made casting decisions and previewed every movie before it was released. Furthermore, he sought out the company of movie stars and others prominent in the industry and tried to make personal friends of them. A few responded; most did not. Rumors spread that a starlet could greatly advance her career by bestowing her favors on the good doctor. And, if the good doctor had his eye on a particular young lady she would, sooner or later, receive an invitation to meet with him, alone, in his office.

Behind his back, though, Goebbels was despised by most of the people in the industry and

was made the butt of numerous jokes. The movie crowd gave him a nickname: "Mickey Mouse."

Hitler liked to associate with young actresses, too, but there was never any indication of his taking advantage of his position such as Dr. Goebbels did. Hitler's relationship with the actresses appeared to be truly platonic. One of his favorite ploys was to ask Magda Goebbels, Dr. Goebbels's wife, to invite a number of actresses to tea. He would then show up with flowers and chocolates, turn on the charm and revel in the attention they gave him.

With "Mickey Mouse" now in charge of the German film industry, hundreds of people left the industry and some fled Germany. They usually went to western Europe, hoping that Hitler's regime wouldn't last and that they could return relatively soon. After a while, though, most of them gave up this hope and moved on, hoping to make new lives for themselves in Europe or America.

Conrad Veidt (Strasser) was one of those who fled. Veidt hated the Nazis and was married to a Jewish woman. Since he was such a well-regarded actor (so the Hollywood story goes),

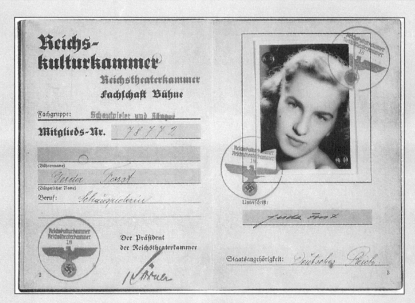

Everyone in the theater in Germany was required to join one of seven state-sponsored guilds or "Chambers" and carry a membership pass such as this one for actress Gerda Forst. It showed that she was a member of the State Theater Chamber. The pass carried a photo of the member, personal information for identification purposes, the rules and regulations of the Chamber and a record of dues payments.

Goebbels tried personally to dissuade him from leaving and gave his personal assurances of safety to him and his wife. The Veidts, however, didn't trust Goebbels and left for England in April 1933. He did not leave until arrangements were made for his former wife, their daughter, and his current wife's family to get out of Germany and safely into Switzerland. In England, Veidt readily found work with Gaumont British Studios.

Veidt then did a very risky thing. He returned to Germany in 1934 to fulfill a previous commitment. While he was in Germany, his British studio announced that he would play the lead in a forthcoming movie entitled *Jud Suss*, a film complimentary to the Jews. When Goebbels learned of this, he ordered Veidt, who was still a German citizen, to decline the role. Veidt had already done one movie in England sympathetic to the Jews, *The Wandering Jew* (1934). In the movie he played the lead role as a Jew condemned to live forever but who dies during the Spanish Inquisition. Veidt refused to comply with Goebbels' order so Goebbels had Veidt put under house arrest, claiming he was ill and couldn't travel. His studio doubted Goebbels' word and sent a team of British doctors to examine Veidt. He was ill, but not too ill to travel. With this, Goebbels backed down

A poster for the Nazis' 1940 production of **Jud Suss**, *a violently anti-Semitic film. Conrad Veidt (Strasser) starred in the British-made version in 1934 which was sympathetic to the Jews.*

and let Veidt leave rather than cause an international incident. To protect himself in the future from such occurences, Veidt became a British citizen in 1939.

Upon returning to England Veidt played the role he was offered in *Jud Suss*, about a Wurttemberg Jew who gains power to help his people only to discover that he is a gentile. In 1940, the Germans would produce a movie with the same title about a Wurttemberg Jew who was an enemy of the German people.

Peter Lorre (Ugarte) fled Germany at about this time because he was a Jew and had done anti-Nazi satirical skits in Berlin. Like Veidt, a Hollywood story later evolved, claiming that Hitler personally asked Lorre to stay on in Germany with guarantees of his safety. This story is, almost certainly, Hollywood hype. Given the extreme anti-Semitic position of the Nazis, it seems highly unlikely that they would ask a Jewish actor to stay in Germany at a time when they were expelling Jewish scientists, engineers and doctors.

It is very likely that two members of *Casablanca*'s cast—Conrad Veidt (Strasser) and Curt Bois (pickpocket)—were in Berlin at this time and witnessed the American effort to restore order.

Nazi Slaughter

 "Even Nazis can't kill that fast."

—Laszlo to Strasser in Renault's office

This statement might be construed by today's audiences as a reference to the Holocaust and the wholesale slaughter of the Jews in the concentration camps. However, Laszlo's comments could not have been related to the Holocaust because the systematic and willful extermination of concentration camp inmates in the gas chambers was, at the time of the story, just beginning and not yet known to the outside world. Ironically, the first mass gassing of Jews in a concentration camp was being planned at the very moment Strasser and Laszlo spoke. It was carried out later that month, December 1941, at Chelmno. This great horror of World War II was formalized as Nazi policy the next month, January 1942, at the infamous Wannsee Conference. Mass exterminations began soon afterwards and were kept as secret as possible—even from the German people. Almost certainly the screenwriters knew nothing of the mass extermination program as they wrote the movie script in early 1942.

The statement about the Nazis killing fast, though, was quite valid. They had viciously eliminated their political opponents in Germany, killed thousands of people with their *blitzkrieg* war tactics, euthanized tens of thousands of their own handicapped and insane, and allowed the mass slaughter and mass starvation of Soviet prisoners of war. All of these things were true and reports of them had reached the West, so the screenwriters had plenty of reason to condemn the Nazis for being able to kill fast.

The Petain Government moved to Vichy, France, because it had adequate hotel space to house the thousands of people associated with the Government. Petain established his headquarters in the hotels Parc et Majestic. Here, Petain is seen at the Hotel Parc's front door with dignitaries of the Catholic Church. Left to right: Marshal Henri Petain, French Chief of State and dictator of France; Cardinal Celestin Suhard, Archbishop of Paris; Cardinal Pierre-Marie Gerlier, Archbishop of Lyon; and Pierre Laval, Premier of France.

The Vichy Government. What Is It?

 "Rick, have you got those letters of transit?
"Louis, are you pro-Vichy or pro-Free French?"
—Exchange between Rick and Renault

This is the first time "Vichy" is mentioned in the movie. Vichy was then, as it is now, a very nice town in east-central France where natural springs produce a steady supply of mineral waters that, for centuries, have been believed to possess healing powers. Over the years, Vichy grew into an upscale spa resort with many fine hotels and other amenities accommodating those who came to take the waters.

When World War II began, tourist activities at Vichy, a city of about 20,000 permanent residents, greatly declined and it became a town with very little business and lots of empty hotels. When the French Government fled Paris they needed a place to go that could accommodate thousands of Government officials, their families, servants, pets, diplomats, media personnel and others. Vichy met this need admirably. It had plenty of available accommodations ready for immediate occupancy.

In searching for a more permanent place to settle in unoccupied France, the Petain Government discovered Vichy. They moved there en masse during July 1940, and Vichy became the capital of France. Petain established his headquarters in the posh Hotels Parc et Majestic and the French Assembly set up shop in the Vichy casino.

The American Embassy followed the Petain Government to Vichy as did the embassies of the other nations that still maintained diplomatic relations with the Petain Government. Upon arrival at Vichy, American Ambassador William Bullitt couldn't find adequate space for himself and his staff so he established the American embassy in a hotel in the small town of La Bourboule, a few miles away. A short time later, a villa in Vichy, owned by Mrs. Jay Gould, an American millionaire, was offered to Bullitt and he moved the embassy there.

Yvonne's Second Front

As Rick and Renault talk Yvonne (played by Madeleine Lebeau), Rick's recently jilted girl friend, walks in with a new gentleman friend, a German officer. The band is playing a swing version of "You Must Have Been a Beautiful Baby". Both Rick and Renault notice their arrival. As Yvonne and her German friend walk past Rick's table she turns and looks down her nose at Rick. Rick comments to Renault that Yvonne has gone over to the enemy. Renault responds by saying...

 "Who knows? In her own way she may constitute an entire second front."

Madeleine Lebeau and Marcel Dalio Flee The Nazis

Madeleine Lebeau (Yvonne) was born in Paris, France June 10, 1923 into a upper middle-class family. Marcel Dalio, her husband who played Rick's croupier, was born Israel Mosche Blauschild in France on July 17, 1900, of Jewish-Rumanian immigrant parents. LeBeau met her future husband, Marcel Dalio during the run of Les Trichers, and they married in April 1939. She was 16; he was 39.

In June 1940, as the Germans approached Paris, she fled to the south alone, carrying what belonging she could with her. Dalio was in the French Army at the time. After three weeks on the road, she reached the Spanish border, and, for the next six weeks, trekked through Spain to Lisbon. There Dalio joined her. Lebeau said of this time, "We were somewhat like those poor unfortunate refugees in Casablanca…We tried in every way we

knew to get to America, but there were so many others…"

After two months in Lisbon, they acquired entry visas to Chile and passage on the Portuguese freighter, "Quanza." When the freighter stopped in Mexico, they discovered that their visas had been fraudulently issued. Some 200 other people had the same problem. They remained on the ship which eventually docked at Norfolk, VA. There, the American newspapers picked up their story, publicized their plight and they were able to obtain Canadian passports and go to Montreal. Lebeau worked briefly there on the stage and then she and her husband got quota numbers to enter the United States.

At one time during the war the Nazis used a photograph of Dalio in a propaganda piece to show what a typical Jew looked like.

French 75

This drink, ordered by Yvonne's German boyfried, is named after a famous French artillery weapon, the 75 mm cannon, and is still served today. To make it, here is the recipe: shake 1/4 oz. of lemon juice, a dash of sugar syrup, a dash of grenadine and 3/4 oz. of gin over ice cubes in a shaker. Strain it into a Champagne flute and fill with Champagne.

The original "French 75" was this 75 mm field gun first produced in 1897.

The Second Front

When Renault refers to Yvonne as an entire second front, he is using a very common World War II phrase. "Second Front" was particularly prominent in the news during 1942 when the screenwriters were creating the movie script. It referred to the announced intention of the Western Powers, and pleadings from Moscow, for the Western Allies to open a second military front against the Axis Powers somewhere in the west in order to relieve Axis military pressure on the Soviet Union in the east.

Actually, for Renault to use the phrase during the first week of December 1941, was premature. With Britain standing alone in the west, and being threatened herself with an invasion, there was little chance that she could, with her limited resources, open a second front. But, after December 7, 1941, when the United States and a host of other nations entered the war, a second front became much more feasible. It was then that the Soviets began pressing for a second front and the phrase came into regular use. The Western leaders promised Moscow that it would happen but for months the British and American leaders couldn't reach an agreement on when or where the second front should be, or how strong their respective forces had to be to ensure a military success.

During the summer of 1942, the British and American leaders finally reached agreement on a second front and in November 1942, that front came into being with the invasion of French North Africa. Washington and London proudly announced that they had lived up to their promise to Moscow and opened a second front. The Soviets, though, weren't impressed and were even scornful that their Western Allies should call an operation against a weakened and neutral power like Vichy France a second front.

The man at the microphone was Renault's boss in Vichy and the man who made the current winds blow. He was Pierre Pucheu, Minister of the Interior, and was in charge of French police operations throughout the French Empire. Behind him, seated at the table in the center of the picture, is Marshal Petain, Chief of State. This photograph was taken at a meeting of over 100 Prefects of Police at Vichy. Renault might well have been there.

Then, in July 1943, the Americans and British invaded Sicily and eventually Italy and announced again that a second front existed. Again the Soviets weren't impressed because it was well known that Italy was one of the weakest members of the Axis Alliance.

It wasn't until massive American and Allied forces landed at Normandy in June 1944, that the Soviets were satisfied that their Western Allies had lived up to their promise and opened a second front.

Blowin' In The Wind

 "I blow with the wind. And the prevailing wind happens to be from Vichy."
—Renault to Strasser

Renault's comment that he will "blow with the wind" is not a spur-of-the-moment comment or a whim of the screenwriters. This was the traditional way French civil servants, such as Renault, kept their jobs in the turbulent world of French politics. It must be remembered that between 1930 and 1940 the French Government in Paris changed, on average, three times a year. Under such conditions, civil servants throughout the Empire had to "blow with the wind" from Paris, and now Vichy.

Howard Koch, one of Casablanca's main screenwriters, says in his book, The 50th Anniversary Edition: Casablanca—Script and Legend, that Renault was appointed Prefect of Police by the Vichy regime.

The Free French in North Africa

Strasser expounds on the shaky stability of Vichy's control over French Africe by telling Renault…

"We know that every French province in Africa is honeycombed with traitors waiting for their chance, waiting, perhaps, for a leader."

With this statement, the screenwriters came about as close as wartime censorship would allow in telling the audiences of 1943 of the true nature of French politics in Africa, especially North Africa. The use of the word "waiting" implies that the French colonial leaders were not willing to follow General Charles De Gaulle in London as an alternative leader to Petain in Vichy and were waiting for someone more acceptable than either De Gaulle or Petain to lead them. This was the actual truth which, at the time, was kept from the American public.

The Allied leaders knew that De Gaulle had some serious shortcomings and could not win over the North African French but, at this time—late 1941 and early 1942—he was all they had. With the war news being so dismal during the last half of 1941 and first half of 1942, the defection of De Gaulle to the Allied cause was one of the few bits of good news for the peoples of the Allied nations. So, De Gaulle and his Free French were give a heroic image and plenty of positive publicity, especially in the United States.

Behind the scenes, though, the Allied leaders were very disappointed with the entire French nation in that not one individual of a higher status than De Gaulle had come forward to carry on the fight against the Axis. Out of an army with several hundred generals, ranking as high as five stars, what the Allies got in De Gaulle was an unknown, recently-promoted one-star general who happened to have served in the French Government for a few days just before it surrendered. Furthermore, De Gaulle had a cantankerous personality and was often uncooperative with Churchill and Roosevelt which further complicated his relationship with those Allied leaders.

It wasn't only the pro-Allied Frenchmen of North Africa who were waiting for a powerful leader, as Strasser tells us, the Allied leaders in Washington and London were doing the same.

In French Africa, De Gaulle's star had plummeted to almost nothing after the Mers el Kebir incident, and also in a second incident at Dakar, in French West Africa, where De Gaulle, with British help, attempted unsuccessfully to win over that vital city to the cause of the Free French. After his failure at Dakar, De Gaulle was looked upon, more than ever, by the French authorities in North Africa, as a political opportunist and an incompetent lackey of the British. The men at Vichy knew, of course, that the great majority of those Frenchmen in Africa who would, under the right circumstances, switch over to the Allied cause were, as Strasser says, waiting for a leader. To prevent this from happening, Vichy had sacked a number of high officials in North Africa—such as General Weygand—whose loyalty was in question and who might have, when conditions were right, stepped forward to lead an anti-Vichy crusade. As a result of Vichy's weeding-out process, most of the men in power in French North Africa were, like Renault, loyal to Vichy.

The Allies saw this problem too, so when the British and Americans invaded French North Africa in November 1942, De Gaulle and his Free French were not invited to take part in the invasion. In De Gaulle's place, the Allies had found another potential pro-Allied French leader, General Henri Giraud. Giraud was a capable military leader who had been captured by the Germans early in the war, escaped from a German prisoner-of-war camp and made his way to Gibraltar. Giraud was untainted by any serious association with Vichy and the Allied leaders put their hopes on him that he could rally the North African French to the Allied cause. But, Giraud turned out to be a very weak political leader and a big disappointment to the Allies. In the political void created after the British and Americans had militarily secured French North Africa, De Gaulle was able to step in, and, with Giraud's tacit cooperation, gain political dominance and eventually rally the North African French to the Allied cause.

Tsar Boris III of Bulgaria

"We come from Bulgaria. Oh, things are very bad there, monsieur. The devil has the people by the throat. So Jan and I we—we don't want our children to grow up in such a country."

—Annina to Rick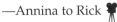

The "devil" that Annina speaks of was Tsar Boris III. He was the absolute ruler of that Balkan country and firmly in cahoots with Hitler.

Bulgaria had been an ally of Germany during World War I, and, like Germany, was one of the losers. The country struggled with democracy during the 1920s and early 1930s, but, in 1934 became a Fascist-like dictatorship after a political coup d'état. In 1935, the leaders of the coup came into conflict with Tsar Boris, so he ousted them from power and took control of the regime they had created. Boris remained Bulgaria's absolute dictator until his mysterious death in 1943.

Because of their common political philosophies, Boris became a friend of both Hitler and Mussolini—more so of Hitler because of his German heritage. Boris had close ties to Mussolini, though, because his wife, the Tsarina, was the daughter of King Victor Emmanuel III of Italy.

Boris did not surround himself with Fascist-like trappings and was not necessarily anti-Semitic, but his rule was dictatorial and, at times, cruel.

Boris' subjects, though, were Slavs and had long-standing ties with their fellow Slavs in Russia, a traditional protector of Bulgarian independence. Boris' dictatorial reign brought political stability and a measure of prosperity to Bulgaria, including a substantial increase in trade with Germany so his people were correspondingly supportive of him.

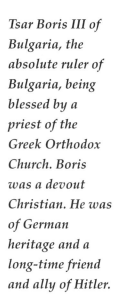

Tsar Boris III of Bulgaria, the absolute ruler of Bulgaria, being blessed by a priest of the Greek Orthodox Church. Boris was a devout Christian. He was of German heritage and a long-time friend and ally of Hitler.

In early 1939, Hitler pressured Boris to enact several anti-Semitic laws. These were relatively mild compared to those in Germany and were all but ignored by the Bulgarian people. Anti-Semitism was not strong in Bulgaria and the country's Jewish community was small—less that 50,000 people. Boris enacted additional anti-Semitic measures, always as a sop to Hitler, but official enforcement was weak. Bulgarian Jews were not rounded up and sent off to German concentration camps as happened elsewhere. However, they were eventually required to wear the yellow Star of David, forbidden to live in Sofia, the nation's capital, and some were placed in Bulgarian concentration camps. Despite these and other harassments, Bulgaria was one of the safer places for Jews in Europe during the war.

In late 1940, distressing events were happening in the Balkans and Bulgaria was very much involved. This was the time when Murray Burnett and Joan Alison were writing the first draft of their play. It can only be surmised what influence these events had on Burnett and Alison to include a Bulgarian couple in their play. Whatever the case may be, the Bulgarian couple had a much larger role in the play than in the movie. The screenwriters reduced their role but retained the main theme that Jan and Annina wanted to flee Bulgaria and go to America and Rick helped them get there.

In October 1940, as has already been related, Italy invaded Greece from its Balkan possession of Albania. But, by the end of the year the combined Greek and British forces in Greece had not only halted the Italian invasion but driven the Italians back into

Albania. Hitler saw no other choice but to come to the aid of the Italians, help conquer Greece, and chase the British out of the Balkans. To do this, German troops had to pass through both Yugoslavia and Bulgaria. So, Hitler began to woo the leaders of both countries, hoping to gain their cooperation in the conquest of Greece.

Tsar Boris proved to be most receptive to Hitler's overtures because Hitler promised him that, in return for his cooperation, Bulgaria could regain the area of Thrace, in easternmost Greece, which had been taken from her after World War I.

As a counter-concession to Hitler, Boris created a state-controlled labor organization patterned after the German Kraft durch Freude and a youth organization, the Brannik (Defender), after Germany's Hitler Youth. Boris also promulgated a new round of anti-Semitic laws and took measures against the Free Masons, Rotary Clubs and other organizations with ties to the west.

Eventually, both Bulgaria and Yugoslavia agreed to cooperate in the planned German attack on Greece and in March 1941, both signed the Tripartite Pact in Vienna making them full-fledged members of the Axis Alliance. The upcoming attack on Greece was kept secret by all parties concerned, but their political and military maneuverings were so obviously directed against Greece that their plans were evident to all. As a result, every action taken by Germany and the Balkan countries was widely reported in the world's press. Burnett and Alison were certainly familiar with these events as they were writing their play.

Jan and Annina, as young unmarried adults, were certainly living through these traumatic times in Bulgaria. They married during the first week of October 1941, and fled the country soon afterwards. It is not known why they left Bulgaria. Perhaps they were Jews, or political dissidents, or perhaps Jan was a draft-dodger. Or, perhaps it was just as Annina said: they didn't want their children to grow up in such a country.

Annina's "devil" remained Bulgaria's absolute dictator until his mysterious death on August 28, 1943. Tsar Boris died at the age of 49 of what was officially labeled a heart attack after having done some strenuous hiking the day before. Few believed this, including Hitler. He sent a team of German doctors to examine the body who reported that Boris had been poisoned and that the Tsarina was the most likely suspect. Others reported that this was just a cover-up for the fact that Boris had been killed by German secret agents for not bringing Bulgaria into the war against the Soviet Union. Still other reports said that Boris had been shot to death by a pro-Russian extremist.

Immigration During World War II

What were Annina and Jan's chances of getting to America, really? The answer is "not good." There is no mention in Casablanca of their having acquired the necessary immigration documents to enter America, so it must be presumed that they had none. If this were the case, they would need to apply for them, obtain a sponsor in America, and meet the yearly quota. Unfortunately for them, Bulgaria was one of the countries discriminated against in the U.S. immigration laws and had been given only the minimum quota of 100 people per year. Small quotas, such as Bulgaria's, were often filled and backed up for years. The U. S. Immigration quotas in effect in December 1941 were as follows:

Afghanistan	100	Ireland	17,853
Albania	100	Italy	5,802
Australia	100	Japan	100
Belgium	1,304	Luxembourg	100
Bulgaria	100	Morocco (French, Spanish,	
China	100	and Tangier)	100
Czechoslovakia	2,874	Netherlands	3,153
Denmark	1,181	Norway	2,377
Egypt	100	Poland	6,524
Ethiopia	100	Portugal	440
Finland	569	Romania	377
France	3,086	Spain	252
Germany (and Austria)	27,370	Sweden	3,314
Great Britain and		Switzerland	1,707
Northern Ireland	65,721	Turkey	226
Greece	307	Union of Soviet	
Hungary	869	Socialist Republics	2712
India	100	Yugoslavia	845

Annina and Jan could go other places, but the longer they waited the more difficult that became. This was the case, not just for Bulgarians, but for all refugees and especially Jews.

Around the world, immigration laws varied widely from nation to nation and were ever-changing. Generally as the war progressed more and more refugees were created as immigration policies of the various nations tended to become more restrictive. The immigration policy of the United States was one of the most consistent throughout the war because the American Government adhered closely to the quota system created by the immigration law of 1924.

The reasons for tightening immigration policies were varied. Some countries, such as Switzerland, simply became overwhelmed with refugees and closed their borders to halt the influx. By the end of 1940, this nation of 4.7 million people had some 400,000 refugees within its borders—many of them dependents of the state. The populations of Basil and Geneva were, at various times, estimated to be nearly 40 percent refugees.

Other countries simply didn't want Jews. For one thing, no national leader wanted to see European-style Jewish ghettos emerge in their major cities. The general fear was that ghettos could emerge if large numbers of Jews were allowed to enter. Some countries still had open frontiers and wanted immigrants who would migrate to the land and not to the cities, as was generally believed would be the case with Jews.

In this respect, a Ukrainian farmer who would be willing to homestead virgin land on the frontier was a more desirable immigrant than a Jewish watchmaker who would probably migrate to a large city. This feeling was especially strong in South American countries such as Brazil, Chile and Paraguay which had existing frontiers and whose major cities were crowded, short of housing and had public services stretched to the limits.

Latin America remained one of the best hopes for refugees, especially if they couldn't get into the United States right away. The United States had no quota system for Latin American countries. Immigration from those countries into the United States was based on other considerations and it was often easier to get into the U.S. from a Latin American country than directly from Europe. In this respect, many hopeful immigrants went to Mexico and took up residence along the U.S-Mexican border, waiting for the first opportunity to get into the United States. This was such a well-known phenomenon during the war that Paramount Studios made a movie about it entitled *Hold Back the Dawn* (1941) starring Charles Boyer and Olivia de Havilland. Boyer portrayed a would-be immigrant who married an American school teacher he didn't love so he could get into the United States as her spouse. Madeleine LeBeau (*Casablanca*'s Yvonne) and Curt Bois (the man shot in the opening scenes) both had roles in that film.

Michael Curtiz, Casablanca's director, had two brothers who went to Mexico in anticipation of entering the U.S. They waited there for about a year before they could enter the U.S.

Eventually, though, Mexico tightened restrictions in an effort to discourage immigrants from using their country as a waiting room for admission to the United States. Instead, those who would take up permanent residence and work towards Mexican citizenship were favored. This fell heaviest on the European Jews because they were, by far, the largest segment of immigrants hoping to get into the United States via Mexico.

Almost all Latin American countries took some immigrants. Paraguay welcomed Czechs and Germans, but not Jews. The Dominican Republic had one of the most generous immigration policies of all. This small Caribbean country began taking Spanish Loyalist refugees in the late 1930s and eventually developed eight internal colonies for those people. By 1940, the number of Spanish Loyalists had declined so the Dominican Republic opened its doors to all European refugees, including Jews. Initial plans called for the acceptance of up to 100,000 refugees to be settled on 26,000 acres of land near Sosua. In 1941, another 50,000 acres was set aside for the immigrants. Most of those accepting the Dominican Republic's offer were European Jews.

The Dominican Republic's neighbor, Cuba, was not nearly so compassionate. Cuba had very restrictive immigration policies that were dramatized in a much-publicized incident of June 1939, when the Cuban Government ordered a ship with over 900 Jews aboard to leave Havana Harbor after refusing its passengers entry into the country.

Guatemala took a considerable number of refugees for its size, but, in 1939, discovered that a disproportionate number of small businesses in the country were being owned and operated by the new immigrants thereby reducing business opportunities for Guatemalan citizens. The Guatemalan Government then closed its door abruptly.

British Guiana, on the northeastern coast of South America, opened its doors to European refugees and encouraged them to settle in the country's jungle-like interior. But, after about 5,000 settlers were moved in, it was discovered that the jungles and the European lifestyle were not compatible because of the Europeans' susceptibility to tropical diseases.

Brazil took 22,688 immigrants in 1939 and 21,259 in 1940. The Government opened its state of Santa Catharina to unlimited immigration by Portuguese and people from English-speaking North America because there was a disproportionate number of German-speaking immigrants in that state who showed little inclination to assimilate. To encourage such people to come to Brazil, the Government offered free land of up to 75 acres in the state's cattle, grain and cotton-growing areas. On the other hand, Brazil discouraged Jewish immigration because it was believed that they would migrate to the big cities, most of which were already overcrowded. In 1941, though, Brazil changed its immigration policy drastically to discourage unskilled, low-skilled and impoverished immigrants in favor of skilled and educated people, people from North America, and people who could bring into the country $20,000 or more in capital. There was one exception to this: agricultural workers were still accepted. Eleanor Roosevelt, the wife of the American President, was not hesitant when it came to speaking out on any important social issue and she began stating publicly that European refugees might be settled in Brazil's Amazon region. The Brazilians went quietly to Eleanor and pointed out that the area was utterly primitive and to begin building even a minimal infrastructure of roads, railroads, cities, utilities, schools and the like would be beyond the financial capability of the Brazilian Government. Eleanor got the message and dropped the subject.

Chile accepted immigrants, Jewish or not, on the condition that they move to the sparsely-settled southern part of the country. Chile was another of the several Latin American countries that welcomed refugees from the Spanish Civil War. Other South American countries not at all receptive to immigrants were Bolivia, Argentina, Ecuador and Peru. Those countries had severe internal political or military problems. Ecuador and Peru, for example, were involved in a border war in 1940-41.

Panama took a small number of immigrants, but a new constitution of 1941 forbade the immigration of Africans and Asians.

Great Britain accepted some refugees although it was well known that Britain had not been a traditional haven for refugees as France had been. In 1929, eleven years after the end of World War I, Britain had only 250,000 aliens while France still had some 3 million. British immigration policy was based on a per-case basis and the tone of this process was usually negative. Prospective immigrants were often advised to try some other part of the British Empire.

Between 1933 and 1939, as the Nazi terror generated hundreds of thousands of new refugees on the Continent, Britain took only about 50,000 Germans and 6,000

Czechs, or a little less than 11,000 a year. There was in Parliament a determined and vocal right-wing political minority that constantly opposed large-scale immigration. They often had their say.

After World War II started in September 1939, the British Government grew very paranoid about its alien population, fearing that it was riddled with enemy agents and spies. The Government set up 120 special tribunals across the nation and reviewed the status and loyalty of every alien. A relatively large number of them were determined to be security risks and sent to internment camps. As the war progressed, Britain's paranoia subsided and three-quarters of those interned were released.

After the fall of France in June 1940, the British paranoia returned, aliens were closely scrutinized again, and more were interned.

In July 1938, a world conference on the placement of Jews was held at Evian-les-Bains, France. It was not very successful and it showed how unwanted the Jews were around the world. For example, the British Government stated that it had no territory anywhere in the Empire suitable for the settlement of large numbers of Jews. The Australian delegate said, "We have no real racial problem, we are not desirous of importing one." New Zealand took the same line. France and Argentina claimed that they had reached the saturation point and would not accept large numbers of refugees. Canada, Columbia, Venezuela and Uruguay announced that they would accept only farmers. Nicaragua, Costa Rica, Honduras and Panama announced jointly that they would accept only "traders and intellectuals."

On the positive side, Denmark and the Netherlands announced that they would accept Jews without qualification. The United States announced that it would continue to honor its yearly quota of 27,370 immigrants from Germany and Austria and abide by its immigration law of 1924 which did have some limited restrictions on Jews. Unfortunately, though, the U.S. quotas for 1938 and 1939 were already filled.

Out of the Evian Conference grew the InterGovernmental Committee supported by 32 nations charged with the responsibility of finding places around the world for Jews. This Committee, often working with other agencies and organizations, had some success and placed Jews in Northern Rhodesia, Kenya, Tanganyika, Nyasaland, the Belgian Congo, Mauritius, Surinam, Cyprus, the Dutch East Indies, the Philippines and Japan.

Soon after the Evian Conference, influential movie people in Hollywood started the "European Film Fund" whose purpose was to help movie people from Europe get to America. The Fund sought sponsors and jobs for those who came. Michael Curtiz (director), Paul Henreid (Laszlo) and Peter Lorre (Ugarte) contributed to the Fund and the Epstein twins (two of *Casablanca*'s screenwriters) served as sponsors for several people. The refugees were frequently given one-year contracts by the various studios and a salary of $100-a-week which satisfied the Government's requirement that they be self-supporting. During that year, most of those so employed were given little to do, but were encouraged by the studios to learn English and look for something more permanent. Five of *Casablanca*'s cast members were helped, in one way or another, by the Fund. They were Curt Bois (pickpocket), Lotte Palfi (woman selling jewelry), Paul

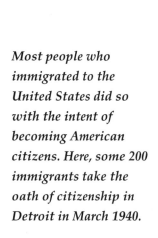

Most people who immigrated to the United States did so with the intent of becoming American citizens. Here, some 200 immigrants take the oath of citizenship in Detroit in March 1940.

Andor (man shot in opening scenes), and Ilka Gruning and Ludwig Stossel (the German couple on their way to America). A number of non-speaking extras on the movie were also helped.

As stated previously, the United States remained committed to its quota system throughout the war. This resulted in a fairly large number of immigrants coming to America—more so than in the 1930s when quotas often went unfilled. Once in America, many of the immigrants eagerly sought U.S. citizenship, but between the time they arrived and the time they became citizens they were classified as aliens. By the end of 1940, the U.S. had 4.9 million aliens in the country out of a total population of 131.7 million.

Throughout the war, the "immigrant question" remained a political football in the U.S. The U.S. Government opened the Virgin Islands in 1940 for the settlement of immigrants who could be self-supporting. And, in July 1940, the State Department announced that an unlimited number of the refugees' children could be admitted as "visitors" outside the quota.

In June 1941, however, the U.S. Government passed the "Russell Bill" that instructed the State Department to ban the entry of refugees with relatives in Germany and German-occupied territories. This was modified in December 1941, with the new wording stating that refugees whose presence in the United States was deemed prejudicial to the interest of the country would be denied entry. In July 1941, the State Department took steps to reduce overall immigration to the United States by tightening restrictions on those coming from Latin America.

It wasn't until mid-1944 that the United States accepted genuine refugees outside of the immigration quotas. Several thousand people, mostly European Jews, were brought to the United States and sent to the vacant U.S. Army facility of Ft. Ontario near Oswego, New York, and housed there until the end of the war. They were returned to Europe.

The Price Of An Exit Visa

Rick takes pity on Aninna, goes to the gambling room, and allows her husband Jan to win at roulette. From the amount of money Jan wins at the roulette table, a "couple of thousand" as the croupier had said, a hint is given as to what Renault charges for an exit visa—1,000 francs ($30) apiece. This figure seems too low. Could the screenwriters be using easy-sounding numbers again?

Helmut Dantine Sent To Dachau

Helmut Dantine (Jan) was born in Vienna October 7, 1917, into an upper middle class Austrian family. At the age of 21, he acquired a position with the Austrian Government as a consular official in London. When Hitler began intensifying his pressure on Austria to agree to the "Anschluss" (political union with Germany), Dantine left his post in London and returned to Vienna to help organize an anti-Nazi youth movement.

When the "Anschluss" occurred in March 1938, Dantine was one of the first individuals rounded up by the Nazis and put into a concentration camp. With the help of a uncle, who was a Vice President in the Consolidated Aircraft Co., an American company, Dantine was released from the camp, after serving three months, with the understanding that he would leave Austria.

Dantine went to Los Angeles, California and enrolled in The University of California at Los Angeles (UCLA) to complete his education. While at UCLA he became a member of the Pasadena Community Players, a local theatrical group. When World War II started and Warner Bros. began searching for good-looking young men with acting abilities and German accents to portray German roles in their movies, they found Dantine. This was 1941. Dantine's first movie was Warner Bros.' *Inter-*

This is Dachau Concentration Camp in June 1933, about the time Helmut Dantine was released.

national Squadron (1941) starring Ronald Reagan. Dantine had a minor supporting role. In 1942, MGM gave him a good role in *Mrs. Miniver* as the German airman who parachutes down into Mrs. Miniver's back yard. Following that, he went back to Warner Bros. to play Jan, the Bulgarian man, who hits it big on number 22 at Rick's Roulette table.

Chapter Six

The Beginning Of A Beautiful Friendship

The Singing Of The Marseillaise

Oh, what a glorious scene! This was the brainstorm of Murray Burnett and Joan Alison, but they wrote it somewhat differently. Their version offers an interesting comparison.

In the stage play, two German officers who have been drinking at the bar force Sam to play the "Horst Wessel," a Nazi Party song. They sing the song and within a few seconds everything else in the cafe goes silent. The customers look daggers at the officers and at Sam. When they finish singing, there is a dead silence. The two German officers return to the bar, their boots loudly clicking on the floor. Rick comes up to Sam and whispers in his ear. Sam shakes his head violently. There is still dead silence in the room. Laszlo steps forward and asks Sam if he knows "La Marseillaise." Sam, reluctantly says "They like swing here, sir!" Laszlo says in a more commanding voice, "Play La Marseillaise." Sam looks at him uncertainly, but Rick nods his head "yes." Sam starts to play and Laszlo starts singing the words. Everyone in the cafe begins to join in. A French officer steps forward to stand beside Laszlo and sing with him. Everyone at the bar moves away, leaving the two German officers standing there alone. The music swells to a high triumphant finish and there is dead silence again. Laszlo then shouts, "Drinks for everybody." The customers roar their approval, and return to their seats.

Strasser, who is in the cafe but not seen, does not use this as an excuse to shut down the cafe. It is Rinaldo (Renault in the movie) who shuts down the cafe a few scenes later after he makes a pass at Annina and gets into a fight with Jan, during which the lights go out. In the darkness, Jan and Annina disappear—thanks to Rick who hides them behind a secret partition. When the lights come on again, Rinaldo can't find Jan and Annina, and orders the cafe closed until they are found.

Victor Laslo leading the patrons at Rick's in the singing of **La Marseillaise.**

In the movie version, though, Strasser is outraged at the embarrassment Laszlo has caused him. He jumps to his feet and orders Renault to shut down Rick's Cafe Americain. Which Renault does, somewhat reluctantly.

German Guarantees

After La Marseillese is sung, Strasser goes up to Ilsa and tells her that Laszlo must return to Occupied France under safe conduct from him. Ilsa questions the validity of his guarantee. She is absolutely right. German guarantees have been of little value in the past. The most outstanding example of this, one that virtually every adult American was aware of in 1943, was the guarantee Hitler gave at the infamous Munich Conference in September 1938. Just prior to that occasion, Hitler had been demanding that the westernmost area of Czechoslovakia, known as the Sudetenland, be ceded to Germany because about half of its inhabitants were German. Hitler further threatened to take the area by military force if necessary. Britain and France, who had military alliance pacts with Czechoslovakia, did not want to go to war with Germany over the Sudetenland. So, Hitler; Britain's Prime Minister, Neville Chamberlain; France's Premier, Eduard Daladier; and Italy's dictator, Benito Mussolini, acting as a moderator, met in Munich during the last days of September to try to prevent a European war from erupting over Czechoslovakia. The Czechs were not invited.

It was at this time that Hitler gave his famous, and soon to be proven worthless, guarantee that if Germany was given the Sudetenland that it would be his last territorial demand in Europe. Chamberlain, Daladier, and Mussolini took Hitler at his word and an agreement was reached that Britain and France would not honor their prom-

Chamberlain displays the piece of paper to the crowd at the airport bearing Hitler's promise and signature. This was the apex of the "appeasement" era.

ise to protect Czechoslovakia and, instead, let Hitler have what he wanted. The next day, German troops marched into the Sudetenland. The Czechs, unable to fight Germany alone, did not resist.

Chamberlain and Daladier, following this policy of appeasement, believed they had prevented a second European war and the phrase "peace in our time" grew out of this triumph and spread around the world. Chamberlain returned to London and upon landing at the airport displayed the piece of paper bearing Hitler's promise and signature.

For a few days Chamberlain and Daladier were hailed as heroes, Mussolini received international laurels for his role as mediator, and millions of people around the world honestly believed that Hitler's aggressive behavior had come to an end.

Hitler, though, had no intention of living up to his promise. Soon after Chamberlain left Munich, Hitler joked to his colleagues that Chamberlain was such a "nice old man" he thought he'd give him his "autograph."

Within days, Hitler publicly reneged on his promise and began making demands on Poland to return land taken from Germany after World War I. Again, Hitler threatened to use military force if his demands were not met. It was at this time that the entire world learned the value of German guarantees.

The British and French Governments did not back down now. There was no second Munich-type meeting. On September 1, 1939, Hitler carried out his threat and invaded Poland. Britain and France honored their military commitments to Poland, declared war on Germany, and World War II began.

Ironically, Hitler often bragged how he kept his promises. But, he had two kinds of promises: ones he made to the German people, which he did try to keep; and promises he made to foreigners which were just a part of the game of politics.

No Concentration Camps
In French North Africa

Strasser's threat that the French authorities would find a reason to put Laszlo in a concentration camp in French North Africa doesn't hold water since there were no concentration camps, or death camps, as the world came to know them, in French Morocco. The phrase "concentration camp," however, was used rather loosely to refer to other types of camps: internment camps, refugee camps, relocation camps and work camps.

The French did have internment camps, refugee camps and work camps in French Morocco and Algeria plus more camps in metropolitan France. Being sent to any one of these could mean incarceration for the duration of the war, which is the point Strasser was trying to make.

Ilsa's Story

In the stage play, Laszlo, who is much more of a rascal than he is in the movie, suggests that Lois (Ilsa) sleep with Rick in order to get the letters of transit. Rick finds out about this from Rinaldo (Renault) after he and Lois have spent the night together, gets angry, and accuses Laszlo of pimping. Rick then does a bit of pimping of his own and suggests to Lois that she sleep with Rinaldo and try to get exit visas.

All this talk of sleeping around was permitted on the stage in the 1940s where it was presumed that the audiences were mostly adults. But, for Hollywood, it was unacceptable.

In the movie, Ilsa goes to see Rick in his office a second time after Laslo has left their hotel for an underground meeting and tries to get the letters of transit. When Rick refuses to help her, she pulls out a gun, but this doesn't work either. Finally, she breaks down and tells him that she still loves him. Rick takes her in his arms and they kiss. Time passes and the audience is left to imagine what happens next. In the next scene, Ilsa finally tells Rick the truth about her marriage.

Laszlo and Ilsa were secretly married in late 1938 or early 1939 and Laszlo went back to Prague soon afterwards. There, he became involved in the publishing business again and became an outspoken opponent of the Nazis.

When the Germans marched into the remainder of Czechoslovakia on March 15, 1939, and proclaimed it the new German Protectorate of Bohemia-Moravia, Laszlo went underground. He continued to print clandestine newspapers in a cellar, but was eventually caught and sent to a concentration camp.

When the screenwriters changed the nature of the Laszlo character from the play's rich playboy publisher to a dedicated resistance leader, they might have been inspired by a real life individual who very closely fits the Laszlo mold. He was Vojtech Pressig, an American of Czech heritage who was in Czechoslovakia at the time of the Nazi takeover. Pressig went into hiding and was responsible for printing an underground anti-

An underground newspaper from wartime France of the type that Laszlo might have printed.

Nazi newspaper called V boj. Pressig was eventually captured, sent to Dachau Concentration Camp, and died there in 1944.

Before Ilsa met Rick in Paris, she had been told that her husband was sent to a concentration camp and was shot while trying to escape. That word probably came to Ilsa in late 1939 or early 1940 after she had spent months trying to get information. By that time, Rick had been back from Spain for about a year.

On the day before she was supposed to go to Marseilles with Rick, she found out that Laszlo was in a freightcar just outside Paris, weak and sick. She had to go and help him and didn't want to tell Rick because he might not have left Paris and the Gestapo would have caught him.

So, Ilsa stayed behind with Victor while Rick left Paris with Sam, hurt, angry, and not knowing why Ilsa had suddenly left him.

Laszlo and Ilsa went into hiding. Laszlo eventually recovered, and, as Strasser has already told us, continued his underground activities in Paris fighting with the French resistance and printing underground newspapers.

In World War II, as in any war, there are great sacrifices. Many of them are made by women. The audience has seen Ilsa sacrifice herself once before for Laszlo and his cause. Annina was willing to sacrifice herself for Jan. And now, Ilsa is willing to sacrifice herself again by consenting to a life-long adulterous and common law relationship with Rick. But, it will be a loving relationship. She'll be with the other man she loves and they'll both live out their lives in Casablanca and die there.

Is Ilsa being truthful or is she pretending? Once Laszlo is safe, might she not dump Rick again and make her way to Lisbon and then on to join Laszlo? This would have satisfied the Hays Office.

While Rick and Ilsa are re-pledging their love to each other in Rick's apartment Laszlo and Carl suddenly enter the empty and darkened cafe. Rick hears their voices and goes to investigate. Laszlo and Carl's underground meeting was broken up and they had come to the cafe to escape the police.

Rick summons Carl to the apartment to perform a minor task. When Carl walks into the apartment he sees Ilsa and Rick whispers to him to take her back to her hotel. Rick then goes downstairs to talk with, and stall, Laszlo. In their conversation Laszlo suggests to Rick that he use the letters of transit to take Ilsa to safety while he remains in Casablanca to take his chances. Rick is impressed with Laszlo's willingness to sacrifice himself for Ilsa, just as she is willing to sacrifice for Laszlo

Moments later there is a crashing sound at the door and several French policemen rush in and arrest Laszlo. He asks what the charge is and is told that Renault will discuss it with him in the morning.

December 4, 1941

Another day passes in Casablanca and it is December 4, 1941. America is three days away from entering the war.

• **NORTHWESTERN PACIFIC OCEAN**: The Japanese naval strike force crosses the International Date Line, still undetected by the Americans. The Japanese pilots aboard the aircraft carriers, who will carry out the air attacks on Pearl Harbor, have been briefed and are eager to attack.

• **SOUTHEAST ASIA**: Japanese transport ships loaded with soldiers and landing craft, leave Hainan Island heading south. Their mission is to invade the British colony of Malaya and southern Thailand, and advance on Singapore, Britain's most powerful naval base in Southeast Asia.

• **TOKYO**: The Japanese Government announces that, as a member of the Axis Alliance with Germany, it now considers the Netherlands Government-in-Exile in London to be an enemy because, in retaliation for recent threatening Japanese military moves in Southeast Asia, that government has cut off all shipments of oil and other vital materials to Japan. The announcement states that Japan will henceforth treat the Dutch as if a state of war exists between them.

• **SOVIET UNION**: The battle for Moscow continues to take its horrible toll of life and suffering—and the issue is still in doubt. The weather is horrible for the men in the field. Food in cans and water in canteen freeze solid, guns won't work and wounded men die before they can be treated.

• **WASHINGTON, DC**: The talks between Secretary of State Cordell Hull and the Japanese envoys continues, but stalemate is still the order of the day.

• **BRITAIN**: Parliament passes a bill allowing for the conscription of women for war-related labor service.

Morning in Casablanca

It's morning in Casablanca. Rick has had time to think things out and has formulated a plan. It is a noble plan, one that will add him to the list of those willing to make sacrifices.

Here, the movie plot gets a little ridiculous and, at times, hard to follow. It reflects the problems the Warner Bros. writers had in coming up with an ending that was entertaining, dramatic, yet plausible. All indications are, at this point in the story, that Rick has decided to let Laszlo and Ilsa have the letters of transit and escape to Lisbon. The most logical course of action, then, would be for him to simply give, or sell, the letters to Laszlo and Ilsa, and let them be on their way. By doing this, he would avoid a confrontation with Renault and a life-threatening shoot-out with Strasser. In the play, Rick gives one of the letters to the Bulgarian couple (the play's letters of transit had space for two names) and lets them go on their way. He gives the other one to Laszlo and Lois under circumstances similar to those in the movie, and is then arrested by Strasser.

For the movie, though, the powers at Warner Bros. deemed that the ending would have to be more exciting and the writers came through. The ending subsequently produced is, indeed, entertaining and dramatic—but not very plausible.

Rick and Renault are talking in Renault's office. Rick is trying to talk Renault into letting Laszlo go. Rick tells Renault that he has the letters of transit and that he intends to use them for himself tonight, taking the last plane to Lisbon—with Ilsa Lund. Because he's stealing away with Laszlo's wife, Rick wants Laszlo put away for good—or so he tells Renault.

By revealing to Renault that he has the letters of transit, Renault could have arrested Rick on the spot for possession of stolen property. This, and the recovery of the stolen letters of transit, would have put the police chief in good favor with Strasser and his superiors in Vichy. But, Renault was probably very reluctant to arrest his friend.

Rick offers Renault a deal that would put Laszlo in a concentration camp for years and, at the same time, make Renault look good. Rick then lays out his plan. He'll arrange to have Laszlo at his cafe a half hour before the Lisbon plane leaves. Renault will be there ahead of time and hiding. When Laszlo comes in ,Rick will give him the stolen letters of transit, Renault can then arrest him and recover the letters of transit.

Here is one of the inconsistencies in the storyline and possibly the revelation of a very deep subplot that has not yet been mentioned. If Rick and Ilsa were going to fly off to Lisbon that night, Renault would have had to provide them with exit visas and there is no mention of this having been the case. It is possible that Rick might have acquired exit visas from someone else, possibly Ferrari, but there is no mention of this either. The only other option would be for Rick to take the letters of transit back from Renault. That is unlikely because Renault would have wanted to return them to Strasser.

As shall be seen, Renault charges Laszlo with being an accessory to the murder of the German couriers. So, here is a new facet to the story, and, an as yet unmentioned, subplot. Apparently Ugarte and Laszlo were in cahoots from the beginning. Laszlo either helped Ugarte plan the murders of the couriers or, at least, consented to them. For Laszlo, though, the killing of two Germans wasn't murder because Germans serving the Nazi cause anywhere are his enemies. In the eyes of the neutral Vichy Government, though, such an act, carried out on French soil, was murder.

Renault agrees to Rick's plan. He'd be foolish not too. He'll catch the big fish Strasser wants caught, recover the letters of transit and win 10,000 francs ($300) from Rick. He'll have to turn his back, though, and let the two smaller fish, Rick and Ilsa, go.

Rick Sets His Plan In Motion

Rick starts to tie up some loose ends. He goes to the Blue Parrot and sells his bar to Ferrari who assures him that Sam, Carl, Sacha and Abdul will stay on under their present arrangements.

Rick then goes back to his office. There's a knock at the door. It's Renault. The sound of a car is heard outside Rick's front door and Renault waits out of sight. It's Laszlo and Ilsa arriving by taxi. While Laszlo pays the driver, Ilsa rushes in ahead of him. "As Time Goes By" is heard again. She has just enough time to tell Rick that Laszlo still thinks she's leaving with him. Rick assures her that everything is all right and that they'll tell him at the airport. Laszlo walks in, thanks Rick profusely and offers to give him the money they spoke of for the letters. Rick refuses, saying that they can use it better in America. Rick asks if they'll have any troubles in Lisbon but Laszlo says that everything has been arranged.

Undoubtedly it was. There are cases on record of the Allies sending military aircraft to Lisbon to pick up VIPs coming out of neutral or Axis territory. It's not mentioned whether or not Laszlo rated such treatment. It must be remembered, too, that Laszlo might have flown on to London, where the Czechoslovak Government-in-Exile was located, rather than to America.

Rick hands Laszlo the letters, explaining that all he needs to do is to fill in the names. At that moment Renault appears and arrests Laszlo as an accessory to the murder of the couriers. Laszlo and Ilsa look at Rick with anger. As Renault takes the letters from Laszlo, he is startled when Rick points a gun at him. Rick orders Renault to phone the airport and tell them to expect two letters of transit on the Lisbon plane. He pretends to do so, but unbeknownst to Rick, dials Strasser's number. Strasser is sitting at a desk in the office of the Armistice Commission in the Miramar Hotel in Fedala and answers the phone. On the wall is a portrait of Adolph Hitler, the last of the three real-life people to appear or be mentioned in the movie. Renault pretends to be talking to the airport, and, when Renault hangs up, Strasser realizes there is trouble and orders his car. Strasser then calls the office of the Prefect of Police and orders a squad of policemen to meet him at the airport as soon as possible. He hangs up, grabs his hat, and hurries out the door.

At the airport, the Lisbon airplane can be seen through the hangar door in a light fog with maintenance men attending it. An orderly comes to the phone in the hangar, dials the tower and reports on weather conditions.

The airplane is an American-made Lockheed 12A Electra twin-engine transport plane, a popular export model during the late 1930s. A subsequent close-up of the plane reveals a flying seahorse in a circle. This was the emblem, at the time, of the French national airline, Air France.

Captain Renault tells one of his police officers to put Laszlo's luggage on the Lisbon plane. Rick, who has a gun in his pocket, is in control of the situation.

Rick, Renault, Laszlo and Ilsa arrive at the airport in a 1940 Buick phaeton with a red, white and blue bull's-eye emblem on the front windshield, similar to that used on French military aircraft, indicating, apparently, that this is a Government vehicle.

It may seem a bit strange that Rick and his party would be in an American-made automobile in Casablanca, but this is not beyond the realm of possibility. By 1940, the major European powers were at war and all of the major European automobile manufacturers had stopped making cars and switched over to war work. That left the United States as one of the few places in the world where new cars could be purchased.

When Strasser arrives, he will also be driving a new car, a 1940 two-door Buick convertible. Perhaps these are part of a fleet of cars the French purchased from the United States in 1940. When Strasser came to Casablanca, the French authorities might well have loaned, or leased, the two-door convertible to Strasser during his stay. In early 1942, all automobile production in America stopped, too, and wasn't resumed until 1946.

Rick is wearing a trench coat and hat and keeping his right hand in his pocket on his gun. This is a typical Bogart trademark worked into every Bogart script wherever possible.

Once out of the car, Rick orders Renault to get Laszlo's luggage and put it on the plane. A policeman takes Laszlo's luggage and walks off towards the plane. Laszlo follows.

Rick hands Renault the letters of transit and tells him to fill in the names Mr. and Mrs. Victor Laszlo so that it will look more official.

Ilsa is bewildered and reminds him of what they said last night but Rick insists that she belongs on the plane with Laszlo and that if she stayed, she would regret it.

 "Maybe not today, maybe not tomorrow, but soon, and for the rest of your life."
Ilsa then asks, "But what about us?"
Rick replies, "We'll always have Paris. We didn't have it, we'd lost it, until you came to Casablanca. We got it back last night."

Rick then tells Ilsa that he has a job to do and that she can't follow him. He concludes his speech with one of the movie's most famous lines:

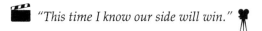 *"I'm no good at being noble, but it doesn't take much to see that the problems of three little people don't amount to a hill of beans in this crazy world. Someday you'll understand that. Not now. Here's looking at you, kid."*

At that moment, Laszlo returns and says that everything is in order. Rick then tells him of Ilsa's visit and that she tried desperately to get the letters of transit, but nothing worked. She pretended she was still in love with him, and he let her pretend.

As Rick hands him the letters of transit, Laszlo thanks him and welcomes him back to the fight, saying:

"This time I know our side will win."

"As Time Goes By" gives way to martial music. The engines of the airplane start up. Laszlo asks Ilsa if she's ready. She says she is. She looks compassionately at Rick and says:

 *"Good-bye, Rick. God bless you."*

Rick tells them to hurry. "As Time Goes By" is heard again as Laszlo and Ilsa walk off towards the plane.

Renault tells Rick he'll have to arrest him but Rick replies that it won't happen until the plane leaves.

A workman closes the airplane door. Beside the closed door is a sign on the plane reading "Lisbonne, Tangier, Casablanca."

As the plane begins to taxi down the runway for takeoff, Strasser arrives alone.

It's amazing that Strasser got to the airport so quickly from the Miramar Hotel in Fedala, a distance of 24 miles, and beat the squad of police who had only six miles to go.

Strasser jumps out of his car and walks briskly towards Renault, asking for an explanation of the strange phone call. Renault tells him that Laszlo is on the plane and nods in its direction. Strasser asks angrily why he didn't stop him. Renault tells him to ask Rick. Strasser looks briefly at Rick, then walks briskly to the telephone just inside the hangar door. Rick pulls his revolver out of his coat pocket and orders Strasser to get away from the phone. Strasser sees the gun and stops momentarily, telling Rick not to interfere. Rick then says:

 "I was willing to shoot Captain Renault, and I'm willing to shoot you."

Strasser runs towards the phone and grabs the receiver. "Deutschland Uber Alles" is heard in the background. Rick orders Strasser to put the phone down but he refuses and asks the party on the other line to get him the radio tower.

Laszlo and Ilsa are not safe yet. Strasser could, in all likelihood, order the plane to return. Or, since the plane landed in Spanish-controlled Tangier, he could radio ahead and ask the Axis-friendly Spanish authorities to take Laszlo and Ilsa off the plane and hold them.

Rick orders Strasser again to put the phone down. He doesn't. Martial music is heard. Strasser reaches into his coat pocket, pulls out a pistol, and shoots at Rick. The shot misses. Rick shoots back and hits Strasser who crumples to the floor, dead. In the background, "Deutschland Uber Alles" gives way to "La Marseillaise."

At that moment, the squad of four policemen arrive. One of them runs up to Renault to report. In the distance, the plane is turning onto the runway. Renault tells the policeman that Strasser's been shot. He looks at Rick, pauses, and says to the policeman:

 "Round up the usual suspects."

Rick looks at Renault with a half smile as the policemen pick up Strasser's body and carry it away.

Rick and Renault stand there, glancing at each other, neither of them speaking. Two of the policemen drive off in the police car and two in Strasser's car. Renault turns, walks over to a stand-up desk and reaches for a bottle of Vichy water. "La Marseillaise" begins playing in the background. He looks at the label on the Vichy water bottle, a look of disgust comes over his face as he throws the bottle into the waste basket and kicks it over. Martial music surges back.

Rick and Renault stand together, watching the plane get airborne and disappear into the darkness. They say nothing.

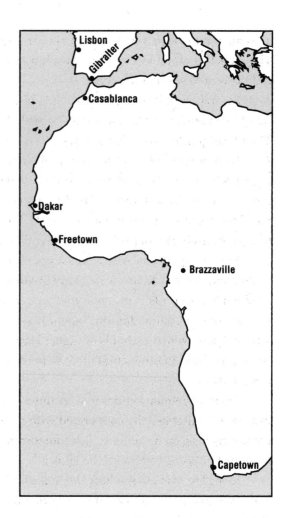

Africa in late 1941. Brazzaville, French Equatorial Africa, was the capital of General Charles De Gaulle's Free French movement.

As they begin to walk away, Renault tells Rick that it might be a good idea if he left Casablanca for a while and suggests going to the Free French garrison over at Brazzaville.

Brazzaville

Brazzaville is 3,000 miles southeast of Casablanca on the Congo River in the heart of Africa. It was, at that time, the capital of French Equatorial Africa, a huge colonial holding that sprawled through the heart of Africa from the Belgian Congo northward to the southern edge of the Sahara Desert.

When General De Gaulle defied the Petain Government in June 1940, and vowed to continue the struggle against Germany under the banner of the Free French, French Equatorial Africa was the largest French colony to join him. De Gaulle soon journeyed there and proclaimed Brazzaville as his capital.

As a world capital, Brazzaville was pretty pathetic. Aside from the few government buildings, churches, missionary schools and homes belonging to Europeans, it was pretty much a shanty town, directly across the Congo River from the town of Leopoldville, the capital of the Belgian Congo, a colony firmly in the Allied camp. This was a factor in French Equatorial Africa's siding with De Gaulle. Also, a substantial amount of the colony's trade was carried on with British-controlled Nigeria to the west. The French colonial leaders, the French business community, and many tribal chiefs didn't want to see that disrupted.

Even though Brazzaville was his capital, De Gaulle continued to operate out of London where he and his closest aides could be in close contact with the other Allies. Their headquarters were located at #4 Carlton Gardens.

During September, October and November 1940, a mini civil war in the adjoining French colony of Gabon, which had sided with Vichy, took place between Pro-Vichy forces and Free French forces. The Free French won and Gabon was brought into the Free French camp. That war ended when Gabon's pro-Vichy Governor General Masson hanged himself. His deputies then surrendered to the Free French.

French Equatorial Africa was a poor and primitive land with an estimated 3.5 million inhabitants. Roads were made of dirt, or at best, gravel, and the only railroads ran from the sea ports to the areas that produced lumber, rubber and gold. The colony's schools could accommodate only about 11,000 children from grade school through high school. There were no schools of higher learning in the colony. Tropical diseases were widespread and in some areas up to 40 percent of the population suffered from trypanosomiasis.

There were many tribes that, at times, were in conflict with one another, plus a mulatto elite that usually cooperated with the French. There was also an all-black petite bourgeoisie community which sometimes cooperated with the French and sometimes did not cooperate with the French.

In the United States, where De Gaulle and the Free French were receiving frequent and favorable press, Brazzaville was often mentioned and American movie-goers in 1943 were familiar with the name.

"La Marseillaise" is still playing. Rick tells Renault that he could use a little trip. But, he adds:

 "It doesn't make any difference about our bet. You still owe me 10,000 francs."
Renault replies, "And that 10,000 francs should pay our expenses."
Rick is very surprised and asks, "Our expenses?"
Renault replies, "Uh huh."
Then, as they walk off into the mist, Rick says, "Louis, I think this is the beginning of a beautiful friendship." 🎥

Chapter Seven

Making The Movie Under Wartime Conditions

Japan Declares War

On Monday morning, December 8, 1941, the talk in every office, factory, store and workplace in America was of the events of the previous day. The Japanese had attacked America's naval and air bases at Pearl Harbor, Hawaii—an outright act of war—and it was a certainty now that the United States would be drawn into World War II. On everyone's mind was a concern for the future—for the safety of their families and themselves, their homes, their jobs, their cities and their nation. The future held one goal now and only one: winning this war as soon as possible. Losing it was unthinkable.

Minutes after the attack began, the Japanese envoys who had been negotiating with Secretary of State Cordell Hull in Washington, DC, handed him Japan's formal declaration of war upon the United States. For Hull, this was not totally unexpected. He knew from American intelligence reports that such a move by the Japanese was very possible. He, nevertheless, expressed anger and disgust with the Japanese Government and ordered the envoys out of his office.

It was 11 a.m. Sunday morning, December 7, 1941, when news of the attack broke on the west coast of the United States.

In Canada, Britain, Australia, New Zealand and South Africa, Japanese diplomats were also handing declarations of war to the Government officials of those countries.

On Monday morning, December 8, at 10 a.m. Washington, DC, time, President Franklin D. Roosevelt addressed a special joint session of Congress and outlined the

President Franklin D. Roosevelt signs America's declaration of war on Japan on December 8, 1941. It was 1:10 p.m. in Hollywood.

events of the previous day. His address was broadcast nationwide by radio. In his speech to Congress and the nation, he called Sunday, December 7, 1941, "A day which will live in infamy" and asked Congress to declare war on Japan.

In Hollywood, it was 7 a.m. Monday when the President began his address to Congress . Most of the Warner Bros. employees heard the speech as they finished their breakfasts or on their car radios on the way to work. Three hours and ten minutes later, Congress passed a resolution declaring war on Japan and the President signed it at 4:10 p.m. Washington time. America had entered World War II.

During these traumatic days in December 1941, the world would witness a surge of declarations of war unlike anything ever experienced before. Before it was over, more nations of the world than not would be at war. And, nations would continue to declare war on each other at various times over the next four years. It was, in every sense of the word, a world war.

The United States was not the first country to declare war on Japan after the Pearl Harbor attack. Canada, Costa Rica and Guatemala had all declared war on December 7. And, by coincidence—and concerning issues that had nothing to do with the Pearl Harbor attack—Britain, Canada, New Zealand and India declared war on Finland, Hungary and Romania that same day, seven and a half hours before the Japanese attacked Pearl Harbor

Before the next day—Monday, December 8—had passed into history, Britain, China, The Netherlands Government-in-Exile (London), The Free French National Committee (Brazzaville), The Greek Government-in-Exile (Cairo), Honduras, El Salvador, Panama, Haiti and The Dominican Republic had all declared war on Japan. Manchukuo, Japan's satellite in Manchuria, declared war on the United States.

War Jitters On The West Coast

On that Monday morning, there was not only talk about the events of December 7, but great tension among virtually everyone along the Pacific coast. In some places this tension bordered on near panic—and it was justified. Rumors spread rapidly that the Japanese task force that had attacked Pearl Harbor was continuing eastward and would attack cities along the U.S. Pacific coast and possibly invade the United States at one or more locations. Everyone realized there was nothing to stop the Japanese. America's Pacific Fleet lay in ruins at the bottom of Pearl Harbor. To make matters worse, U.S. military and Government authorities could not deny the possibility of Japanese attacks on the west coast. It was a frightening time for hundreds of thousands of Americans. The Japanese, though, had no intention of attacking or invading the U.S. west coast. The naval task force that attacked Pearl Harbor was returning to Japan. But, the Americans had no way of knowing this.

In Los Angeles the rumors ran wild. There were reports of enemy ships and submarines being seen off the coast, of secret Japanese air fields in the California desert and in Mexico, and there were concerns that spies and saboteurs would soon be at work blowing up bridges, power plants, aircraft factories and poisoning water supplies. And members of the ethnic Japanese community were the prime suspects.

The largest concentration of ethnic Japanese in the Los Angeles area was on Terminal Island in Los Angeles Harbor. This was a community of about 5,000 people who made their living by fishing. Also on Terminal Island were sizable commercial oil facilities and a large naval installation. Rumor had it that Japanese "5th Columnists" (a popular wartime phrase meaning spies and saboteurs stemming from the Spanish Civil War) were sabotaging the oil and naval facilities and that they had used their fishing boats to stash drums of diesel fuel in remote coves along the West Coast and would deliver them to Japanese submarines when they arrived. When Japanese submarines did arrive in west coast waters several days later, these reports became very believable. To clamp down on this nest of enemies within, the Federal Government declared martial law on Terminal Island, the only place along the west coast where such drastic action was taken. Martial law meant that the U.S. Army became responsible for all security measures on Terminal Island and that the civil rights of those living there were suspended.

Other measures were immediately taken against the ethnic Japanese. The FBI began rounding up Japanese nationals suspected of being security risks. By nightfall on Monday, December 8, 736 individuals—mostly from the west coast—had been taken into custody. This was a very small percentage of the estimated 80,000 Japanese nationals known to be in the U.S.

Additional arrests continued for weeks.

Civil Aviation Administration Chairman Robert Hinkey issued an emergency order forbidding Japanese nationals from flying on U.S. commercial airliners and any Japanese national attempting to fly to Mexico was to be arrested immediately.

We'll Fight Them On The Beaches

Soon after the attack on Pearl Harbor, the U.S. Army halted all training operations along the west coast and rushed all available military personnel and mobile guns to pre-selected points along the coast to watch for enemy ships and planes. When they reached the West Coast, the soldiers began to build temporary defensive positions in the hills and sand dunes, and to erect landing craft obstacles and barbed wire barriers on the beaches. Civil Defense personnel, spur-of-the-moment volunteers and the curious flocked to the beaches to watch the sea and the sky for an approaching enemy. Some of them brought guns. Before long, these zealous but woefully inexperienced patriots were seeing enemy airplanes, ships, periscopes, mysterious flashing lights and suspicious individuals, and began reporting these sightings to various Government agencies. This caused chaos in some government offices.

Beginning at sunrise on December 8, 1941, aircraft from several Army Air Force bases along the Pacific coast began sending patrol planes far out to sea in search of approaching ships. They flew only in daylight hours because, at this stage of the war, very few American aircraft were equipped with radar which allowed them to "see" in the dark.

In Los Angeles and elsewhere along the west coast, the phone service was overwhelmed. Government offices and military installations were inundated with people calling in with sightings, questions, offers to volunteer and the like.

Owners and managers of potential military targets—such as power plants, radio stations, dams, harbor, railroad and oil facilities—besieged government and military authorities to send guards and anti-aircraft guns to protect their properties.

Blackouts were ordered in some areas and homeowners were encouraged to accumulate buckets of sand to throw on incendiary bombs in the event they should fall on their property.

Secret Agent Of Japan

Twentieth Century-Fox had a problem. That studio was making a movie entitled *Secret Agent of Japan* and had hired 30 ethnic Japanese for various "Japanese" roles. This was unusual in itself because most studios were reluctant to hire real Japanese in the first place because of the unsavory reputation Japan had made for itself in its war with China (which began in 1937). Furthermore, many ethnic Japanese were reluctant to play Japanese movie roles because those characters were almost always evil and the actors feared they might suffer retribution from members of their own community and cause problems for relatives back in Japan.

There was yet another problem in hiring ethnic Japanese. Many of them were being watched by both the FBI and U.S. Naval Intelligence for suspicious activities even before the attack on Pearl Harbor. This was because virtually all of the original Japanese immigrants still held Japanese citizenship, and their children, the Nisei (the first generation offspring of the original Japanese immigrants), held dual Japanese and American citizenship. Most of the original immigrants, who by now were in their fifties, had never applied for American citizenship and remained aliens. As such, they were required to register with the FBI in compliance with the 1940 Alien Registration Act. This brought the FBI into their lives.

The U. S. Navy was interested in the ethnic Japanese community because it was believed that any Japanese spies or saboteurs operating in the U. S. would be harbored within that community. The Navy, quite understandably, had a need to protect its numerous facilities along the west coast from possible enemy agents. Furthermore, military logic dictated that any future war with Japan would be primarily a naval war pitting the American Navy against the Japanese Navy.

As for the Nisei,, Japan recognized them as Japanese citizens if their parents were Japanese citizens—which was the case more often than not. The U.S. Government also recognized them as American citizens because they were born in the United States. To complicate matters further, about 15 percent of the Nisei had, at one time or another, been sent back to Japan by their parents for a "proper" Japanese education. Upon returning, these people, known as the "Kibei," became something of an elitist group within the Japanese community and it was believed by many American authorities that the loyalty of the Kibei to America was questionable.

When war erupted between the United States and Japan discussion of removing the ethnic Japanese from the west coast began in the news media. Twentieth Century-Fox could see that their Japanese actors might be whisked away at any moment causing a production problem on the movie *Secret Agent of Japan*. Because of this, and because the film had suddenly become very timely, the studio rushed the movie to completion and released it immediately. In the meantime, the studio police were instructed to watch the Japanese actors very closely and not to let them wander off.

Secret Agent of Japan was released early in 1942 and starred Preston Foster and Lynn Bari. It told the story of a female British spy, Bari, operating out of the International Settlement in Japanese-occupied Shanghai, China, who successfully outwits the Japanese occupation authorities. The film was running in American theaters while *Casablanca* was being produced.

On December 9, 1941, two Los Angeles newspapers reported on the events at San Francisco the day before, giving them credibility and scaring the daylights out of thousands of Californians.

War jitters were the worst in the San Francisco Bay area. On December 8, three separate air raid alerts were sounded and reports were received of up to 20 enemy aircraft having flown over San Francisco. Supporting this report came a second report that an enemy aircraft carrier had been seen in the waters off San Francisco. The Army's top west coast commander, Lt. Gen. John L. DeWitt, whose headquarters were at Ft. Mason in San Francisco, was one of those who believed these false reports. After studying them, he stated publicly, "Death and destruction are likely to come to this city at any moment. These planes were over our community for a definite period. They were enemy planes, I mean Japanese planes. They were tracked out to sea. Why bombs were not dropped, I do not know."

In Oakland, schools were closed and that evening a blackout was ordered throughout the Bay area. The next day, December 9, the headlines of the *Los Angeles Times* read "Enemy Planes sighted over California Coast" and the *Los Angeles Herald Express*, the evening newspaper, headlined "Hunt Jap Air Carrier Off Cal."

News From The War Fronts

On the radio and in the newspapers of December 7 and 8 were two reports from the eastern front in the Soviet Union that, if they had come on any other day, would have made headlines of their own. But, because of the events in the Pacific, these reports were relegated to the "other news" reported by radio commentators and to small print headers in the newspapers.

The first report, received on December 7 from Moscow, stated that the German offensive against Moscow had been halted and turned back. The second report, on December 8, received from Berlin, was an admission that the German offensive to take Moscow had failed and would not resume until Spring. This event was every bit as important to the course of World War II as was the Japanese attack on Pearl Harbor, because, for the first time in the war, the German Army had been stopped in Europe and their aura of invincibility shattered. Furthermore, the conquest of the Soviet Union, which Hitler had boasted would be completed by Christmas 1941, would not happen and fighting on the eastern front would now go on for at least another year. This was a blessing of sorts for the western Allies, because, during that time, England would be relatively safe from an invasion and the U.S. would have time to build up its armed forces.

It Came In The Mail

In spite of this new and mind-boggling atmosphere of war, the chores of the workaday world had to go on. So it was with Warner Bros. Their business was making movies and that had to continue. When Stephen Karnot, Warner Bros.' story analyst, finally got to his mail that fateful Monday, he found that a bulky packet had arrived from Warner Bros.' New York office. It contained the script of an unproduced play titled *Everybody Comes to Rick's* written by two unknown playwrights, Murray Burnett

A War Movie + Luck = Big Profits

Warner Bros. had a very successful war movie during World War I just as they would have, years later, in World War II with *Casablanca*. Their World War I movie, entitled *My Four Years in Germany*, was based on a best-selling book by General James W. Gerard, America's ambassador to Germany just before that war. In the book, Gerard described Germany's preparations for World War I. The film was produced in record time and highlighted some of the atrocities committed by the Germans which had been reported regularly throughout the war. By an uncanny stroke of luck, similar to that which would affect *Casablanca* during World War II, world events played nicely into the hands of the brothers. *My*

Four Years in Germany was released in New York City on March 21, 1918, which turned out to be the same day the Germans launched their last major offensive in France towards Paris. By this time, American troops were at the front and taking the brunt of the German attack. The American news media boiled over with news from the front, while, at the same time, *My Four Years in Germany* was showing across the nation in first-run theaters everywhere. It was a hand-in-glove situation. People read the news in the media about of the American Doughboys in France and then flocked to see the movie to see why all this was happening. The brothers grossed over $1 million on the film.

and Joan Alison. In the packet was a brief note from the people in New York suggesting that the play be reviewed for movie possibilities. Karnot began reading the play, but he had other things to do too. It would be four days before he would finish reading it and make his recommendation.

Others at work at the studio that memorable Monday were future *Casablanca* stars Humphrey Bogart and Sidney Greenstreet. They were filming *Across the Pacific* (1942), a story concerning Japanese plans to blow up the Panama Canal. Mary Astor was the female lead and she later said of that day in her memoirs, *A Life on Film*, that it was "a creepy feeling" to have been working on a film about the Japanese planning an attack on an important American installation and then learning of their attack on Pearl Harbor. It was like having the Japanese "practically blueprint our script."

On another part of the lot, Peter Lorre, *Casablanca's* Ugarte, was filming *Arsenic and Old Lace* (not released until 1944).

Just starting filming that day at Warner Bros. was yet another movie, *Yankee Doodle Dandy* (1942) with James Cagney. Its director was Michael Curtiz who would direct *Casablanca*. And the Epstein twins, who would later contribute to *Casablanca*, were the screenwriters for *Yankee Doodle Dandy*.

West Coast Invasion Fears

On December 9, Mexico sent troops via San Diego into the Mexican state of Baja California to protect it from a possible invasion. Mexico was not at war with Japan, but military logic deemed that if the long coastline of that sparsely settled peninsula was not defended, it might provide an area where an invasion force could land easily and advance northward into San Diego and Los Angeles. Teams of American Army officers joined the Mexican forces as liaison officers so as to facilitate communications between the Mexicans and U.S. Army headquarters in California.

During the morning of December 9, reports were received of enemy aircraft spotted over the ocean west of Los Angeles. Hours later came a report of 34 enemy vessels approaching the California coast north of the Los Angeles area. Army Air Force planes were dispatched and discovered that the "enemy vessels" were a group of 14 American fishing boats that had been at sea when they heard about Pearl Harbor, had banded together for mutual safety and were hightailing it to port.

Still later came a report of a Japanese cruiser being sighted 20,000 yards off Catalina Island. Other reports added three Japanese destroyers to this phantom fleet.

Army Air Force and Navy planes were busy all day chasing down sightings and some planes dropped bombs. The targets, though, were whales, or floating logs or shadows that had been mistaken for Japanese submarines by the trigger-happy and inexperienced air crews.

Soldiers with loaded weapons began to appear throughout the Los Angeles area guarding vital installations.

During the day, President Roosevelt broadcast to the American people from the White House that the coming war would be long and hard, and he admitted that the

A U.S. soldier guards an oil well in Los Angeles. Note that the well head has been sand-bagged to deter sabotage.

United States had suffered a "serious setback in Hawaii." He added, though, that the United States "can accept no result, save victory, final and complete."

On the east coast, New York and Boston had their first air raid alerts. On Wall Street, the stock markets dropped sharply.

From Southeast Asia came reports that Japanese troops had landed on Luzon Island, the main island of the American-owned Philippines. Japanese forces had landed at Hong Kong and in southern Thailand and were advancing into British-held Malaya.

And the war continued to spread.

Before Tuesday, December 9, had ended, Australia, New Zealand, South Africa, Cuba and Nicaragua had declared war on Japan, and China declared war on Japan, Germany and Italy.

During December 10 and 11, weather reports disappeared from the newspapers and radio broadcasts lest they aid an invading enemy. The U.S. Coast Guard began contacting local fishermen, asking them to be on the lookout for, and to report on, any strange vessels approaching from the west. The Coast Guard also contacted owners of large seaworthy boats, asking them to volunteer their boats, themselves and their crews for daytime coastal patrol duties. This was the beginning of a nationwide effort to enlist the aid of private boat owners to assist in patrolling America's coasts. The response was gratifying and this part-time armada grew to considerable size and eventually became known as "The Hooligan Navy." Humphrey Bogart, an experienced sailor and member of a Coast Guard auxiliary, would participate.

On the night of December 10, more reports of enemy activity were received and Los Angeles was ordered blacked out for three hours. During this, the city's first blackout, there were 130 auto accidents, one person was killed and seven died of heart attacks. Because of blackouts and the fact that many people were being enlisted as coast

On December 11, 1941, the Los Angeles Times *headlined the blackout of the night before. The other headline, "Bombs Fire Jap Battleship," sounded like good news, but it wasn't. This was a false report, one of many, coming from the western Pacific.*

watchers and sky watchers, the sales of eyesight-improving carrots and carrot juice soared.

By December 11, people who lived near the coast could see, even without the aid of carrot juice, artillery pieces, anti-aircraft guns and searchlights being mounted in place. In other parts of the city, there were barrage balloons floating in the sky. On this day too, the entire U.S. west coast was declared a "theater of war" by the U.S. Army. That was a sobering thought and meant that this area might become a battleground.

The Army had asked for truck owners to volunteer their vehicles and their time to help haul the soldiers and their equipment to the beaches. The movie studios responded by supplying 150 trucks and drivers.

Also on December 11, confirmed reports reached the U.S. west coast that a Japanese submarine had torpedoed and sunk the American merchant ship "Lahaina" halfway between Hawaii and the U.S. west coast. This was proof positive that Japanese submarines were operating in the eastern Pacific and it was reasonable to believe that they were heading for the U.S. west coast—and they were.

Late on the evening of December 11 came yet another alarming report that enemy planes had been spotted over the ocean from Point Loma, in the San Diego area, heading northward, possibly to attack Los Angeles. Army Intelligence speculated that the planes might have come from a secret Japanese air base at Magdalena Bay, Baja California, Mexico. To everyone's relief, though, Los Angeles was not bombed. It was just another false report.

The U.S. Goes To War Against Germany And Italy

The American declaration of war on December 8 was against Japan only. But, on the 11th, Germany and Italy, honoring their military alliances with Japan, declared war on the United States. The U.S. Government was forced to respond and that same day declared war on Germany and Italy. Cuba, Costa Rica, Guatemala, Nicaragua and The Dominican Republic also declared war on Germany and Italy that day. From London came declarations of war against Japan from the Polish and The Netherlands Governments-in-Exile.

Box Office Natural

On Thursday, December 11, Stephen Karnot finished reviewing *Everybody Comes to Rick's* and liked what he had read. He wrote a synopsis, calling it an "excellent melodrama" with a "timely background." He suggested that it could be "a box office natural" for Humphrey Bogart, George Raft or James Cagney. For the female lead he suggested Mary Astor.

Karnot's report went to producer Hal Wallis who liked the play too and wanted to produce it for the studio. There was a problem, though. The studio's production schedule for 1942 was already filled. By manipulating schedules, Wallis felt he could find a slot for *Everybody Comes to Rick's*. He was helped by the fact that in October 1941, Jack Warner had ordered an end to the studio's production of "B" movies designed to fill out double features. This freed up space and personnel for the more profitable main features.

Wallis also knew that Jack Warner had been looking for some time for a follow-up movie for *Algiers* (1938) which had been very profitable and *Everybody Comes to Rick's* appeared to fit the bill. With Wallis' backing, the play was sent around to various people at the studios for their comments. Twin brothers and screenwriters Julius and Philip Epstein were among those who reviewed the play at this early stage. They liked the play's story line, too, and Julius, in typical Hollywoodese, labeled it "Slick Shit."

The process of circulating the play took more than a week. Meanwhile, outside the high walls that surrounded the Warner Bros. studio, there was a war going on.

Invasion Jitters Subside

By the third week in December, it was becoming obvious that if the Japanese were going to attack or invade California something would have happened by now. As each day passed, "invasion jitters" subsided.

Still, the rumor mill continued. At 2:55 a.m. on December 14, the headquarters of the 4th Intercepter Command, the Air Force entity responsible for defending California, announced that a flight of enemy aircraft was approaching Southern California from the Mexican coast. At 4 a.m., 4th Interceptor at Riverside, CA, upgraded the report, saying that a Japanese naval force had been spotted off the Southern California coast and that U. S. coastal defense positions could expect air attacks. At 7:50 a.m., another report was received from Northern California that a Japanese naval force had been spotted off Mendocino. That evening, San Francisco had its fifth air raid alert and its longest blackout so far in the war.

But, once again, enemy attacks did not materialize.

From the other side of the Pacific, there came lots of news—all bad. In the Philippines, the Japanese had landed at additional locations and the American and Filipino troops were in retreat. The island of Guam fell to the Japanese. At Hong Kong, the Japanese took the city of Kowloon on the mainland, forcing the British to retreat to Hong Kong Island. In Malaya, British troops were in retreat and, off shore, the Japanese aircraft and submarines sank two large British warships, the battleship "Prince of Wales" and the cruiser "Repulse," which had been the core of Britain's Far Eastern Fleet. On the December 11, Japanese planes bombed the British air base at Tavoy, Burma, and a small army of Japanese-trained Burmese soldiers invaded Burma from Thailand. On December 16, Japanese forces invaded Borneo and on December 20, they invaded Mindanao, the second largest island in the Philippines.

From Europe came word that Germany's Axis allies—Romania, Hungary and Slovakia—had declared war on the United States and Britain on December 12. On the 13th, Bulgaria followed suit as did Croatia the next day. Then, on the 17th, Italy's satellite, Albania, declared war on the United States. But, the score was evened when Panama, El Salvador, Haiti and Honduras declared war on Germany and Italy on the 12th, Britain declared war on Bulgaria on the 13th, and Nicaragua declared war on Romania, Hungary and Bulgaria on the 20th.

Preparing For Invasion

On the west coast, preparations continued for the invasion that never materialized. The Rose Bowl Committee announced that the famous New Year's Day football classic would be transferred to Durham, NC, and that the Rose Parade was to be canceled at the request of the Army. The Army announced that no more than 5,000 people could gather in one place at one time and that no New Year's Eve celebrations could be held outdoors.

People with station wagons were asked to volunteer themselves and their vehicles as emergency ambulances. This effort was being coordinated by the women's Volunteer Service.

From Seattle came sage advice from Eleanor Roosevelt, wife of the President, who, as Assistant Director of Civil Defense, was on an inspection tour there. She advised west coast parents to teach their small children to make a game of blackouts and air raids.

In Hollywood, the movie moguls got together and agreed among themselves that if any of their productions facilities were put out of action as a result of enemy attacks they would pool their resources to keep every studio operating.

RKO agreed to scrap plans for a movie titled *Call Out the Marines* because it poked fun at the Marines. That studio had already put $425,000 into the project.

Enemy Aliens

When a country goes to war, citizens of the enemy nation(s) automatically become classified as enemy aliens under international law. And, under the Geneva Convention Accords of 1929, that most nations adhered to, these people could be arrested and interned by the host nations for all or part of the war. This situation applied to several future *Casablanca* cast members. One was Paul Henreid (Laszlo) who was an Austrian citizen but classified as a German citizen ever since the German annexation of Austria in 1938. For Henreid, this was the second time he had become an enemy alien. The first time was when he was in England at the start of the war (September 1939) and Britain and Germany went to war.

Other future *Casablanca* personnel were Max Steiner (composer) and Helmut Dantine (Jan, the Bulgarian man)—both Austrians; and Curt Bois (pickpocket) and Lotte Palfi (lady selling her jewelry)—both Germans.

When the United States and Hungary went to war, Peter Lorre (Ugarte), S. Z. Sakall (Carl) and Michael Curtiz (director) had the same problem because they were Hungarian citizens. And, there were other enemy aliens among the cast who had lesser roles as well as some of the movie's extras.

These people had little to fear, though, from the American Government because by December 1941, the Federal Bureau of Investigation (FBI), which was charged with watching aliens, had acquired dossiers on virtually every alien in the country and knew who was a security risk and who wasn't. This was brought about by the Alien Registration Act passed by Congress in 1940. That act required every alien in the country to register with the FBI and give considerable information about themselves and their activities in the United States. All aliens were further required by the Act to report to the FBI periodically. The FBI used this information to classify the aliens into categories according to the degree to which they might become a risk to national security in the event of war. Only a handful were deemed dangerous enough to be arrested immediately in the event of war. A slightly larger number were considered possible security risks and were subject to surveillance or were called in for periodic interviews. The remainder—the great majority of aliens—were identified as harmless and left alone so long as they continued to file the periodic reports required by the Alien Registration Act. Most of the people in Hollywood who were classified as enemy aliens were in the harmless category.

When war actually started between the United States and the Axis nations, only a few enemy aliens were incarcerated. And, many of those were later released or paroled. No one associated with *Casablanca* was arrested or otherwise harassed.

All of the studios made arrangements to make duplicate master copies of their films and send them to secret locations in the midwest for safekeeping.

At Warner Bros., serious consideration was given to camouflaging the entire Burbank studio just as entire aircraft factories were being camouflaged at the time. That idea was rejected but it was decided to build air raid shelters and take other measures. About a year earlier, Harry Warner had been instrumental in forming an internal security organization called "Warvets," a volunteer organization of ex-servicemen who performed guard duty in and around the studio. With the coming of war, others were asked to serve in the Warvets and security around the studio's power plant and fuel depot was increased. All employees were encouraged to learn how to use firearms and were offered the use of the studio's rifle range. Furthermore, they were encouraged to learn how to operate the studio's searchlights which had been used for promotional purposes, but could also be used to spot enemy planes.

Harry Warner continued to be active in war-related activities and eventually became the head of the movie industry's Red Cross organization.

Warner Bros.' Burbank studio was very close to Lockheed Aircraft Company's main plant and there was concern that Japanese bomber pilots might target the studio, thinking it was a part of Lockheed. Accordingly, the story circulated that the studio resolved this problem by painting a huge arrow on the top of their largest sound stage pointing towards the Lockheed plant with the inscription "Lockheed That Way."

On the more practical side, the studio did buy two more ambulances and a fire engine for use on their lot and stationed employees on the roofs of the tallest buildings to serve as aircraft spotters. Many of the employees were given classes on fire-fighting, first-aid and becoming air raid wardens. And, as another security measure, visitor access to the studio was greatly curtailed.

On December 15, Warner Bros. ended night operations because of the problems people had getting around in blackouts.

Because blackouts had become a nationwide phenomena, Paramount changed the name of a movie it was about to release to *Pacific Blackout*. It starred Robert Preston and Martha O'Driscoll and told the story of an inventor who escapes from jail and proves his innocence during a practice blackout.

On December 24, Hollywood got a bit of bad, but not unexpected, news. President Roosevelt had appointed Lowell Mellett, a respected ex-newspaper editor and former presidential assistant, to be the Government's liaison man with the motion picture industry. This meant that Government censorship was coming to Hollywood. President Roosevelt, though, hastened to ease the minds of the movie people by saying, "I want no restrictions placed thereon (movies in general) which will impair the usefulness of the film, other than those very necessary restrictions which the dictates of safety make imperative."

During the week after Christmas, there was a bit a good news, though. Movie attendance, which had dropped sharply across the nation after December 7, had returned to normal.

The Real War Comes To California

On December 17 and 18, 1941, nine of the Japanese Navy's most modern long-range submarines arrived to take up battle stations along the U.S. and Canadian west coasts. Their mission was to sink Allied ships. Submarine I-19 was to work the waters off Los Angeles, I-10 was off San Diego and I-21 was off Morro Bay. The Japanese found slim pickings because days earlier the Coast Guard had ordered commercial ships into port, pending clarification of the war situation. Some ships, though, did venture forth in daylight hours. They sailed alone because there was no convoy system yet in place, and, to minimize the danger of possible submarine attacks, they usually sailed a zig-zag course, stayed close to shore, and, at the end of the day, put in at the nearest port for the night.

Unfortunately for the Japanese, this is not what they had hoped for. The Japanese submarine commanders preferred to patrol at night on the surface of the water where they were faster, more maneuverable and could use their deck guns against smaller targets, thus conserving their limited number of torpedoes for bigger targets. Their favorite tactic was to patrol off a large city using the city's lights to silhouette potential victims as they passed in front of the submarine's torpedo tubes. During the day, the submarine would move out to sea and settle on the bottom while the crew rested. This pattern, though, was not always followed, especially after the Japanese discovered that hunting at night was so unproductive.

The first submarine attack along the U.S. Pacific coast came on December 18 off the coast of Northern California near Cape Mendocino. On that night, submarine I-17 attacked the U.S. freighter "Samoa" which was heading south with a load of lumber for San Diego. I-17 fired its deck gun and one torpedo at the ship, but missed due to very rough seas and a heavy fog that hampered visibility. "Samoa" got away undamaged.

On December 20, I-17 found a second target off Cape Mendocino, the empty U.S. tanker "Emidio." I-17 attacked the ship, killing several crewmen and damaging the ship beyond repair. The ship was abandoned, drifted onto some rocks and was eventually cut up for scrap. This was the first American ship lost to enemy action along the U.S. west coast.

Let's Buy It

By December 22, 1941, enough Warner Bros. people had reviewed *Everybody Come to Rick's* and made enough favorable comments for the studio heads to know that they wanted the story. On that date, Hal Wallis asked the story department to find out the costs of the play's rights. This was done and the studio eventually bought the play for $20,000.

On December 31, Wallis changed the name of the play to *Casablanca*, believing that the name would be more appealing to movie audiences because it was more compatible with the studio's last movie on a similar subject, *Algiers*.

On January 5, 1942, the *Hollywood Reporter* announced that Warner Bros. would produce a movie entitled *Casablanca* starring Ann Sheridan, Ronald Reagan and Dennis Morgan.

Bad News From The Pacific

For the American public, the war news from the Pacific continued to be grim. Wake Island fell to the Japanese on December 23 after a heroic two-week defense by the island's garrison. In the Philippines, General Douglas MacArthur, the American commander there, announced that his forces and the Philippines Government of President Manuel Quezon would retreat to the Bataan Peninsula and Corregidor Island at the mouth of

Roosevelt and Churchill Discuss Casablanca, Too— The Real Casablanca

On the other side of the continent, in Washington, DC, President Roosevelt and Britain's Prime Minister Winston Churchill also had Casablanca on their minds. Churchill had come to the United States on December 22 to discuss military strategy with President Roosevelt and America's top military leaders. This meeting became known as the Arcadia Conference and lasted for several days.

One of the proposals Churchill brought with him was a plan for a joint American and British invasion of French North Africa. That operation envisioned the invasion of the Atlantic coast of French Morocco, a quick capture of Casablanca and other Moroccan coastal cities and then an advance into the interior. At the same time, other forces would invade Algeria, and perhaps Tunisia, from the Mediterranean Sea. Such an operation, Churchill argued, would very likely bring the French back into the war against the Axis and would create a pincers operation against Rommel's Afrika Corps and the Italians already

fighting in Libya and Egypt against the British 8th Army. Once the Axis forces were defeated in North Africa, much of the Mediterranean would come under Allied control and Southern Europe, which Churchill called the continent's "soft underbelly," could then be invaded at any one of a number of points.

Roosevelt and his advisers felt that the plan had merit and agreed to study it. It was given the operational name of "Super Gymnast." On December 26, Churchill addressed a joint session of Congress and said that the Allies would probably launch a victory drive against the Axis in 1943. This was the "second front" that was now beginning to be talked about and was being pushed vigorously by the Soviets to relieve Axis military pressure on their front.

Other military plans and options were discussed and an overall war strategy was agreed to before Churchill returned home by way of Canada. These decisions, of course, were kept absolutely secret from the enemy and the public.

Manila Bay and make a determined stand there against the Japanese invader. This meant that all of the rest of the Philippines was to be abandoned to the Japanese.

That same day, Rangoon, the capital of Burma, was bombed by the Japanese for the first time portending a Japanese invasion of that country. Elsewhere, other Japanese forces landed at Sarawak on the island of Borneo in the East Indies.

On Christmas Day, British forces at Hong Kong surrendered to the Japanese, and the next day Manila, the capital of the Philippines, was declared an open city. Despite this announcement, Japanese planes bombed the city on December 28, killing a number of civilians.

On December 28 and 29, World War II spread a little further and Bulgaria was the target. On December 28, Britain declared war on Bulgaria and on December 29, New Zealand did likewise.

No Ships, No Glory

Off the California coast, the Japanese submarines were still having problems finding American ships to sink. Most of the Japanese submarines had yet to encounter their first potential victim after five or six days of patrolling. Then, on December 22, one sub, I-21, got lucky and had the opportunity to sink four ships within a few hours. That morning, I-21 encountered the first ship, the Standard Oil Company's tanker "H. M. Story," off Point Aguello, 55 miles south of Santa Barbara. The sub attacked with her deck gun and one torpedo, but missed. I-21 was maneuvering for a second torpedo shot when several American bombers appeared, forcing it to dive immediately. Minutes later, the bombers dropped several clusters of depth charges but I-21 escaped unharmed. This attack took place within two miles of shore and several witnesses on the shore saw the entire action.

I-21 stayed in the area and at about 2:30 p.m. encountered a second ship, the American tanker "Larry Doheney," six miles off Cayucas on the north edge of Estero Bay. A few eyewitnesses on the shore also watched this action. The submarine used its deck gun first but was unable to hit the ship. She then fired a torpedo that missed, but exploded a few seconds later beyond the ship. The explosion could be heard in San Luis Obispo. The "Larry Doheney" put on full speed, zig-zagged and made it safely into Estero Bay, forcing the submarine to break off the attack.

About an hour later I-21 spotted its third target, the American tanker "Montebello," carrying gasoline. This ship was not so lucky. A torpedo hit the ship, mercifully in an empty tank. The torpedo's explosion did not start a fire, but did enough damage to stop the ship. The crew got into the lifeboats and the submarine finished off the tanker with her deck gun. After the ship went down, the Japanese took a few shots at the defenseless lifeboats, injuring five crewmen. People on shore in the community of Cambria Pines could see the entire action until a fog rolled in and covered the battle scene.

Before sundown, I-21 spotted its fourth target, another American tanker, the "Idaho." The submarine attacked with her deck gun, hit the ship several times and managed to sink her. This action took place just a few miles from where I-21 had attacked the "Montebello."

On December 24, the shooting war came to Los Angeles in the form of the Japanese submarine I-19. At 6:25 a.m.. I-19 spotted the schooner "Barbara Olson" two miles off Long Beach on her way to San Diego with a load of lumber. The submarine, operating from the submerged position, fired one torpedo which pre-detonated about 100 yards before reaching the ship, doing no damage to the "Barbara Olson." Four miles away at the entrance to Los Angeles Harbor was the U.S. Navy subchaser "Amethyst" on routine patrol. Her crewmen heard the explosion and saw the geyser of water caused by the blast. The "Amethyst" raced to the scene to investigate. The Japanese submarine commander saw the "Amethyst" approaching and departed the area at full speed. After reaching the site of the explosion, the "Amethyst" crewmen had no way of knowing that the explosion had been caused by a Japanese torpedo.

I-19 turned to the north and began patrolling off Point Firmin on the surface. This was a risky thing for a submarine to do in daylight off the coast of a big city. But, I-19 and the other subs had been ordered to leave the U.S. coast that evening and return to the Japanese naval base at Kwajalein Island. I-19's captain and crew were willing to take a bigger risk now because in the eight days they had patrolled off Los Angeles they had not been able to sink a single American ship. And their first and only attack so far, a few hours earlier on the "Barbara Olson," had been a failure. At about 10 a.m., I-19's lookouts spotted a big freighter about five miles north of her position heading towards the submarine. It was the U. S. freighter "Absoroka" bound for San Diego with yet another load of lumber. The Japanese crewmen saw this as their big opportunity and positioned the submarine for an attack.

At about the same time the crewmen of I-19 spotted the "Absoroka," a citizen on shore near Point Firmin spotted the submarine and phoned the Coast Guard. The coastguard who answered the phone had received dozens of such calls by now, all false alarms, and believed this to be another one. He simply told the caller to phone back if anything happened. At about 10:30 a.m., the "Absoroka," hugging the coastline for safety, passed about a mile from shore in front of the waiting submarine. At the right moment, the submarine fired two torpedoes. On board the "Absoroka" an alert seaman saw the sub and shouted out, "There's a goddamn Jap submarine." Other crewmen turned and saw the submarine, too. They also saw two torpedo wakes heading their way but there was no time to react. The first torpedo missed, but the second hit the stern of the ship turning it 90 degrees so that its bow now pointed out to sea.

At the foot of Point Firmin Lighthouse, an Army sergeant manning a machine gun position had been watching the "Absoroka" pass by but did not see the submarine. When the torpedo hit, he saw the geyser of water it produced, watched the ship suddenly turn and lumber fly into the air like matchsticks. The commander of the submarine saw the same thing and believed that the torpedo would sink the ship. He turned about, dove, and sped out of the area. It was the prudent thing to do because minutes later American aircraft arrived and dropped depth charges. Soon afterwards, the

Actress Jane Russell poses in the hole in the side of the freighter "Absoroka" made by a Japanese torpedo during an attack on the ship off the coast of Los Angeles. The poster she holds reads, "A Slip of the Lip May Sink a Ship."

subchaser "Amethyst" that had gone to assist the "Barbara Olson," arrived and dropped more depth charges. I-19 escaped, though, unharmed.

Meanwhile on the "Absoroka," the ship's captain, thinking his ship was sinking, ordered the crew to abandon her. They got off into lifeboats but within a short time the ship stabilized—her load of lumber keeping her afloat. The crew reboarded the ship and she was eventually towed safely to San Pedro.

The attacks on the "Barbara Olson" and "Absoroka," of course, made headlines in Los Angeles. A few days later, actress Jane Russell posed in the gaping hole of the "Absoroka" made by the Japanese torpedo for a propaganda photo. That photo was shown nationwide.

That evening, I-19 and the other Japanese subs departed, as ordered, for Kwajalein. The Americans did not know this, of course, and the I-19 story was not over.

The next day, Christmas Day, at 3:15 p.m., a lookout on Palos Verde spotted a "periscope" about two miles off the pier of Redondo Beach and very close to an old four-masted schooner, the "Kohala," that was anchored in the harbor and being used as a fishing barge. Other reports confirmed the "periscope" sighting and the local military authorities theorized that it might be the submarine that had attacked the "Barbara Olson" and Absoroka" the day before. It was likely that the sub had been damaged in the attacks and was now laying on the bottom in shallow water while the crew attempted to make repairs.

The closest weapon to the scene was a World War I-vintage 75 mm howitzer. The gun's crew was ordered to start firing at the "periscope" which was clearly visible from their position. They opened fire and continued firing at the minuscule target. Meanwhile, at 4:40 p.m., Navy planes appeared and dropped bombs on the "submarine." Then the subchaser "Amethyst' closed in and got close enough to the "periscope" to see what it actually was—a chimney attached to a floating galley roof that had come off of a small fishing boat. The "Amethyst" took the debris in tow but lost it in rough seas before the debris could be brought in.

Unfortunately, though, the luckless "Kohala" was badly damaged in the attack and later sank in a storm. The Japanese captain of I-19, who was miles away at sea by then, never knew it but he had finally made a "kill" in American waters.

The presence of Japanese subs in California's water did a lot to keep the rumor pot boiling. On December 31, 1941, another report circulated of enemy planes coming out of Mexico intending to bomb some unsuspecting California city. This time, the rumor had it, the planes were German.

Wartime Shortages

In December 1941, the United States was about to embark on a nationwide building program the likes of which had never been seen before. All over the country, Army camps, air fields, war plants, depots, hospitals, prisoner-of-war camps, etc. would be built at break-neck speed and all at once. To accomplish this, the Federal Government began to requisition lumber, concrete, paint, bricks, tools, plumbing supplies, electrical supplies and all the other materials it takes to build buildings. Shortages of these things began to show up in late December and affected the movie studios who, traditionally, used a considerable amount of building material in the movie sets. When such shortages became apparent, the studios did like everyone else in the same predicament, they began to conserve. They re-used lumber, saved paint, bricks, and many other things. Nails were one of the first things to disappear from the hardware stores. The Warner Club News commented, "if you want to keep working, save nails."

And the studios tried to re-use entire sets when possible. Some of *Casablanca*'s sets would be those used in previous pictures.

A Subdued New Year

The New Year's Eve celebrations around the country for 1942 were noticeably different than those in previous years. The rejoicing was more quiet and subdued. Everyone knew that 1942 would be a year of hardship and suffering, and before it ended many American boys would be killed and maimed because of this damnable war. It was believed that many civilians too might perish if the enemy came to attack America's cities. Every citizen would be expected to do his or her part.

Shortages In Hollywood

The coming of war meant the conscription of men for the military service, and an upswing in the need for workers in war plants and factories. For the studio heads it meant that their male stars and many of their important behind-the-scenes personnel might be called away for military service or leave for war jobs.

To combat these problems, the studio heads would have to rely more on their older male stars who were beyond draft age. Fortunately for Warner Bros., most of their top male stars were safe from the draft. To keep their behind-the-scenes people, the studios would have to meet the wages their workers could get in the war plants and begin to rely more on women, older men, retirees and new trainees to fill the shoes of those who would be drafted or leave.

President Roosevelt gave the film industry a welcome relief when he declared film-making an "essential" industry. This would aid the studios in getting draft deferments for key personnel and gave them a higher priority over items and services in short supply. Later in the year, the Government agency known as the "Office of Coordinator of Inter-American Affairs" aided the film industry further by helping them find new markets for their films in Latin America to help compensate for the lost European and Asian markets.

Another wartime measure the studios would take was to make production schedules as short as possible so that a film could be completed before those individuals critical to the project were called away. This meant tighter scheduling of production; even starting filming before scripts were completed.

Chapter Eight

Making Movies And Watching The Skies

In wartime Hollywood the fear of a Japanese invasion had subsided, but the fear of Japanese air attacks had not. Every day and night, hundreds of people in the Los Angeles area, both civilian and military, scanned the skies watching for enemy aircraft. Anti-aircraft gun crews, search light crews and crews manning the air raid warning sirens were on alert.

Some of those scanning the skies were on the lot of Warner Bros. Studios in Burbank. By January 1942, there were Warner Bros. employees taking shifts on the rooftops of the studio's buildings watching the skies, while other employees, trained to operate the company's search lights, were available on short notice. "Warvet" members patrolled the studio's property and other employees who had taken studio-sponsored classes in first aid were available at the studio in case of an emergency. Practice air raid drills were carried out and every employee knew where the nearest bomb shelter was located. Still others were trained to put out incendiary bombs. Warner Bros. was ready for war.

Speculative Casting

In spite of the added burden of preparing for war, the business of making movies at Warner Bros. proceeded as usual.

"Speculative casting," the practice of announcing in the early stages of a movie's production who its stars would be, was a publicity device used by all of the studios to draw attention to upcoming films.

Warner Bros. had already announced that Ann Sheridan, Ronald Reagan and Dennis Morgan would be the stars of *Casablanca*, but on January 8, 1942, the studio released a news item stating that those stars would be reassigned and were to appear in *Shadow of the Wings*, later renamed *Wings For the Eagle* (1942). At this point, the casting of *Casablanca* was an open question and a means of building public suspense.

Rewriting The Play

The next day, January 9, producer Hal Wallis assigned the first of several screenwriters to modify *Everybody Comes To Rick's* so that it could be made into a movie. They were Aeneas MacKenzie and Wallis' former brother-in-law, Wally Kline. Kline had been married to Wallis' sister, Juel, who died early in life.

Both writers could see that the play needed some major rewriting to be suitable for the movie cameras as well as the Hays Office. Then too, Government war-related censorship was beginning to appear on the horizon. This form of censorship had not been fully defined, but everyone knew it was coming. In the meantime, screenwriters had to second-guess what might and might not be unacceptable in the near future.

On January 12, 1942, Warner Bros. signed the final contract with Murray Burnett and Joan Alison, the authors of the play, which gave Warner Bros. all rights to *Everybody Comes to Rick's*. Burnett and Alison were given temporary contracts at $1,000 a month each to serve as screenwriters and assist in converting the play into a movie. This didn't last long. Burnett learned to hate Hollywood and returned to New York City at the first opportunity.

About this time, Hal Wallis selected Michael Curtiz to direct the film. That brought the production company for the movie up to two people: Wallis and Curtiz.

Wartime Restrictions

Since all of the U.S. west coast had been declared a war zone by the Army, movie companies had another set of wartime rules to abide by. They were no longer allowed to shoot scenes at many off-studio locations. It was forbidden for anyone, not just the movie studios, to photograph military installations, airports, major bridges, railroad tunnels, rolling stock, harbor facilities, ships, power plants, radio stations, or any other facility or building important to the war effort.

Unavailable now to the movie industry were modern military aircraft, large commercial aircraft, modern tanks, artillery pieces, railroad engines and railroad cars and other types of vehicles and major hardware items.

Movie makers could go to locations further east, outside the war zone, if they wished. And, they could shoot scenes at night in the Los Angeles area, but this proved impractical for fear of a sudden blackout. Many residents objected to their neighborhoods being lit brightly at night, reasoning that somehow it might invite an enemy attack. Also forbidden on location scenes was the use of sirens, vital to most movie chases.

Another problem with location filming, one that continued throughout the entire war, was airplane noise. Los Angeles was the nation's largest center for aircraft manufacturing and each company was turning out warplanes as fast as it could. Each plane had to be flight tested—some several times. So, at almost any time during daylight hours, airplanes could be heard overhead in the Los Angeles area.

Casablanca's Roots

When English teacher Murray Burnett turned 27, he inherited $10,000 from an uncle. The next summer, he and his wife used part of the money to make a dream trip to Europe. This was in August 1938, one of the most politically traumatic summers in Europe prior to World War II. The Burnetts soon discovered that they were in for more excitement than they had bargained for. The Nazis had just taken over Austria and were threatening to start a general European war if they were not given the German-populated region of Czechoslovakia known as the Sudetenland. Refugees were streaming through Europe in record numbers, the Spanish Civil War was raging, the French Government was in nearly constant turmoil, the Depression was still having its international effect and Germany and Italy had recently proclaimed their "Axis" Alliance and their intention to bring about a new Fascist-dominated political order in Europe.

Several of Mrs. Burnett's relatives in Vienna wanted to leave Austria (now a part of Germany), but they were not allowed to take anything of value with them, so the Burnetts agreed to go there as tourists, visit the relatives, and bring out items of value. The trip was facilitated by the fact that Mrs. Burnett spoke German.

Murray Burnett went to the American Consulate in Belgium to get visas to enter Austria and was given a small American flag lapel pin and advised to wear it at all times while in Vienna. He was warned that if they got into trouble in Vienna, there was little the American Government could do for them. Suddenly, the Burnetts' dream vacation had turned into a somewhat frightening adventure in smuggling. They went to Vienna, made

A Jewish boy in Vienna being forced to paint the word "Jew" on the door of his house. It was scenes like this that the Burnetts witnessed on their trip to Vienna in August 1938.

contact with the relatives and learned first-hand what was going on in this newly conquered city.

The Germans had marched into Vienna that March and began implementing Nazi rule at once. The shock to Austrian society was dreadful. In Germany, Nazi rule had come about in stages over the past five years, but in Austria it was being implemented in months. Every day, long lines of people, mostly Jews, formed at various foreign embassies in Vienna hoping to get entrance visas to countries that were accepting immigrants.

Aljean Harmetz, who interviewed Burnett for her book, *Round Up The Usual Suspects*, reports on some of the things the Burnetts saw in Vienna.

"In Vienna, Jews weren't allowed to take taxicabs... They drove past a billboard larger than any I have ever seen… and on the billboard was a caricature of a Jew, and it said in huge letters, MURDERER, THIEF. And we'd sit in the relatives' apartment and hear the marching feet outside."

While in Vienna the Burnetts found out how people were getting out of Austria. One such route led to far-away Casablanca in French Morocco.

When the Burnetts left Vienna, they were wearing jewelry all over their persons and Mrs. Burnett was wearing a fur coat in August. They carried a camera which was illegal even for tourists to have at the time.

The Burnetts successfully completed their smuggling operation and traveled on to southern France to continue their vacation. But their strange adventure wasn't over yet.

The things Murray Burnett saw in Vienna weighed heavily on his mind and, as an amateur writer, he pondered ways to express what he had seen. An answer came to him in southern France in a most unusual place: a night club. The Burnetts visited a popular night club called the La Belle Aurore. It was filled with people, but although it was the height of the tourist season, many of the customers didn't look like tourists. Some of them looked like the refugees his relatives in Vienna had told him about. Over the din of table talk and through the smoke-filled atmosphere, the Burnetts observed tense interactions among some of the people at various tables and, across the room a black man was playing the pi-

ano. After studying the scene before him, Burnett said to his wife: "What a setting for a play!" The seed for *Casablanca* was sown.

The Burnetts returned to New York and resumed their workaday lives, but Murray could not forget what he had seen in Europe. Returning from such an adventure, he couldn't wait to tell his story to his friends and associates. One such friend was Joan Alison who had connections in New York theater circles and was currently working with Burnett on another play.

In the summer of 1940, Burnett and Alison started work on the idea Burnett had come up with at La Belle Aurore. By now, World War II had started. In their first draft, they placed Rick's Cafe Americain on the French Riviera. But, during the next three months, France, Belgium, The Netherlands and Luxembourg were all overrun by the Nazis which cut off most of the escape routes to the west, making the few remaining escape routes, especially the one that led through Casablanca, more important. So, Burnett and Alison shifted the location of Rick's Cafe to Casablanca.

Once their play was completed, they tried to interest various parties on Broadway in producing it, but found no takers so they put the play in the hands of an agent who distributed it to the various studios in Hollywood. Warner Bros. became interested but wanted major changes. Alison accommodated them and changed it three times over an 18-month period. Then, the Japanese attacked Pearl Harbor, America went to war and the whole complexion of American society changed dramatically. The people at Warner Bros. could see that movies in which Americans triumphed over the Axis would become the order of the day and, in that respect, the story line of Burnett and Alison's play fit right in. Warner Bros. decided to buy it.

On The War Fronts

News from the war fronts was mixed. The best news for the Allies came from the eastern front where the Red Army had taken the initiative against the Germans. In repeated attacks, the Soviets had succeeded in forcing the Germans to retreat. But, the Germans retreated in good order and the Soviets were unable to achieve any significant breakthroughs. Fighting in the Russian winter, with only six hours of daylight, was brutal.

Good news came from East Africa, where British and Free-French forces were completing the conquest of Italian East Africa (Ethiopia, Eritrea and Italian Somaliland).

On January 1, 1942, 26 nations met in Washington, DC, and signed the Atlantic Charter, the brainchild of President Roosevelt and Prime Minister Winston Churchill at their meeting in Newfoundland in August 1941. The Atlantic Charter guaranteed political, economic and other freedoms to all nations in the postwar era. It was unanimously agreed by the signatories that the Atlantic Charter would serve as the basis for the creation of a new postwar international organization to be known as The United Nations.

Bad news came from many places, too.

On the U.S. east coast, German submarines had arrived from Europe and were sinking American and Allied ships at an alarming rate—much more so than the Japanese submarines had done recently on the west coast.

In Southeast Asia, the Japanese continued their advance down the Malay Peninsula towards Singapore. Kuala Lampur, the capital of Malaya, fell to the Japanese on January 12. By the end of January, the British were forced to abandon the entire Peninsula and retreat to Singapore Island where they hoped to make a last stand.

In the Philippine Islands, Japanese forces occupied Manila, that nation's capital, on January 2. They then began systematically to occupy all the other islands. The Americans and Filipinos could offer little or no resistance.

On January 11, 1942, Japan formally declared war on The Netherlands, and, that same day, Japanese forces invaded the Dutch East Indies for the first time by taking two small islands, Tarakan and Minahassa. Celebes, one of the major islands, was then invaded and soon occupied.

On the 15th, strong Japanese forces invaded Burma from Thailand.

On the 20th, the most deadly aspect of the Holocaust began. On that date, a secret meeting of high-level Nazi SS leaders was held in Berlin to deal with the "Jewish Question." At that meeting, which would go down in history as the "Wannsee Conference," the SS leaders proposed and adopted a program known as "The Final Solution to the Jewish Problem." The plan called for the secret but systematic annihilation of Europe's Jews in a number of specially-selected concentration camps equipped for that purpose. Hitler approved the plan and SS Colonel Adolph Eichmann was put in charge.

On January 30, 1942, the anniversary of his rise to power in Germany, Hitler gave the world a hint of what was in store for Europe's Jews. Having approved the deci-

The Desert Fox

"Rommel, Rommel, Rommel! What else matters but beating him?" This was Winston Churchill's lament in August 1942, after yet another of Rommel's victories against the British in North Africa. It is generally agreed among historians that Rommel was one of World War II's best generals. Time and again he was able to outwit and out-fight his enemies, even though his forces were often outnumbered. This quality was quickly recognized by both the Axis and Allied leaders which gained him the nickname, "The Desert Fox." In the Axis camp, he was praised as a great hero and on the Allied side his achievements were recorded in the media accurately and with reserved admiration.

Hollywood quickly found that Rommel was a worthy subject, and,

in 1942, Paramount produced *Five Graves to Cairo* in which Rommel, played by Erich von Stroheim, was identified by name. Franchot Tone and Ann Baxter had the other lead roles in a story about British spies trying to blow up one of Rommel's secret desert supply dumps.

This was the first of dozens of movies, books, articles and TV shows on Rommel that would follow during the remaining years of the war and well into the postwar era.

Rommel and his Afrika Crops were no threat to French Morocco and Casablanca in western North Africa. Rommel's objectives were to capture the Nile Valley of Egypt and the Suez Canal in eastern North Africa. He never achieved these goals, but he came close.

General Erwin Rommel, "The Desert Fox," being acclaimed as a war hero in Berlin. He was later promoted to Field Marshal.

sion of the secret Wannsee Conference (January 20), Hitler now told the world in a speech "...We are well aware that this war could end and that they (Europe's Jews) be uprooted from Europe and disappear." Hardly anyone realized how truly ominous this warning was.

In North Africa, Rommel's Afrika Corps began a counter-offensive against the British forces that had, over the last few months, penetrated deep into Libya. Rommel's attacks threw the British into retreat, forcing them to give up a significant amount of territory. The offensive lasted until February 7 and pushed the British back to within 120 miles of the Egyptian border.

In late January, Japanese forces began invading the various island groups in the South Pacific. On the 23rd, they invaded the Solomon Islands which, with the construction of new air fields, would put Japanese bombers within range of northern and eastern Australia.

On the 25th, the United States and Britain acquired another enemy when Thailand declared war on both countries. Thereafter, Thai forces joined the Japanese in the invasion of neighboring Burma. Britain, South Africa and New Zealand subsequently declared war on Thailand. The United States followed suit on February 5.

Work Begins On *Casablanca*

During the first week of February 1942, producer Hal Wallis discussed *Casablanca* with scriptwriters Julius and Philip Epstein. Wallis liked the Epsteins and their work and considered them experts at turning plays into movies. They were well-known in the industry for their humor and wit and for livening up a movie script. "The Boys," as Wallis called them, liked Wallis, so their working relationship was excellent. Plus, they had excellent stars to write for. Julius would later say that the Warner Bros. studio had one of the best casting departments in the business and that it was one of their major strengths in the movie industry.

The Epsteins were anxious to do the *Casablanca* movie script but there was a problem. They were scheduled to leave soon for New York City to work on a series of Government-produced documentary films for the war effort collectively known as the *Why We Fight* series. Hollywood producer Frank Capra, who had recently joined the Army and given the rank of captain, was assigned to produce the series. It was Capra who summoned the Epsteins to New York City.

Hollywood Loses One Of Its Own

On January 16, 1942, a commercial air liner crashed in the mountains west of Las Vegas, killing all aboard. One of the passengers was actress Carole Lombard, wife of Clark Gable. Lombard had been on a war bond drive in the midwest and was returning to Hollywood. Her mother was also on board.

Soon afterwards, Clark Gable broke his movie contract with MGM and joined the Army Air Forces. Gable would later see combat over Europe as a gunner aboard a B-17 bomber.

Lombard was the first Hollywood celebrity to be killed as a result of the war. There would be others.

Why We Fight

Why We Fight was a series of seven films commissioned by the U. S. War Department early in the war to be shown to military trainees, American audiences and the audiences of Allied nations. They were entitled: *Prelude To War, The Nazis Strike, Divide* and *Conquer, The Battle of Britain, The Battle of Russia, The Battle of China* and *War Comes to America*.

The Epsteins contributed significantly to these films which have since become historical classics in their own right.

In their discussions with Wallis, the Epsteins offered to work on the *Casablanca* script in their spare time while in New York and then go to it full time upon their return in March. Wallis agreed. By the time the Epsteins left for New York City, Aeneas MacKenzie and Wally Kline had completed their work on the script so it was given to the Epsteins to take with them to review.

On February 7, arrangements were made for Ann Sheridan and Tamara Toumanova to make screen tests for the female lead in *Casablanca*. The fact that Tamara Toumanova was considered for the female lead is indicative that Wallis, Curtiz and others were, at this early stage of production, seriously considering changing the play's leading lady, Lois Meredith, from an American to a European. If Toumanova had been chosen, Rick's lover would very likely have been a Russian woman.

Ann Sheridan, though, was Wallis' choice for the female lead. As for the male lead, Humphrey Bogart had been Wallis' choice almost from the beginning. On February 14, Wallis wrote to Steve Tilling, casting director, saying, "Will you please figure on Humphrey Bogart and Ann Sheridan for *Casablanca*, which is scheduled to start (filming) the latter part of April."

Wallis checked, too, to see if he could borrow Hedy Lamarr from MGM for the female lead because she had been the female lead in *Algiers*. Her tie-in between the two movies would provide great publicity for *Casablanca*. But, Lamarr's time was scheduled elsewhere and she was not available.

Bogart As Rick?

Thus, as the note to Tilling stated, Wallis wanted Bogart to play the male lead in *Casablanca*. But Wallis' word wasn't final. Jack Warner could overrule him and unforeseen circumstances could alter his plans. Others, such as George Raft, James Cagney, Ronald Reagan and Dennis Morgan, were still being considered. Bogart's position, though, was strong. His star was rising fast at Warner Bros. and he had become one of their best box office draws, due in part, to his recent performance in *The Maltese Falcon* (1941). This rapid rise in popularity gave Bogart an advantage. Later on in the year, Bogart would renew his contract with Warner Bros. for a hefty salary increase to $3,500-

a-week for 40 weeks, up from $550-a-week. He was 42 years old. Bogart's future was not all that secure, though. The studio preferred to engage Bogart on a year-to-year basis because of his argumentative attitude and turbulent home life which became something of a concern during the production of *Casablanca*.

On The War Fronts

They didn't know it in London, but on Friday, February 13, 1942, Hitler gave the British a very welcome gift. He canceled German plans to invade England because he needed all the forces he could muster on the eastern front. This, of course, was top secret at the Führer's headquarters. German propaganda and some diversionary activities continued to keep the British thinking that the invasion could still happen.

In North Africa, Rommel was told he could expect no more significant help from home for the same reason. This was another gift from Hitler to the British.

Only bad news came from the Pacific during February.

On the 14th of February, Japanese troops landed on Sumatra, another of the major islands in the Dutch East Indies.

On the 15th, Singapore fell to the Japanese after a hard fight. There were many civilian casualties due to the intense Japanese bombing and shelling of the city. The photograph below was widely circulated in the United States and made American's blood boil with anger at the Japanese—again.

This photograph was widely circulated in the United States. It shows civilians in Singapore immediately after a Japanese bombing attack. The girl at the left has been injured by bomb fragments, the woman in the center has seen her child killed and the driver of the wrecked ricksha lies dead in a pile of bricks behind the ricksha wheel.

Americans had seen highly publicized photos like this ever since Japan invaded China in 1937 and their cumulative effect was to make the American public very angry with the Japanese. Much of that anger was soon to be vented on America's ethnic Japanese community. A few of the hate-inspiring photos that the Americans saw between 1937 and 1941 are shown on the pages following.

A wounded Chinese soldier is tied to a post and bayoneted to death by a Japanese soldier in what the Japanese labeled "War Games."

On February 19, 1942, President Roosevelt issued Executive Order #9066 that authorized the removal and relocation of any ethnic group in the U.S. deemed dangerous to the war effort. This Order was aimed at the ethnic Japanese on the west coast.

Roosevelt's order was put into effect at once and a Federal agency, the War Relocation Authority (WRA), was established under the direction of Milton Eisenhower, General Dwight Eisenhower's brother, to carry out the task in cooperation with the U.S. Army. At first, the west coast Japanese were asked to relocate on their own but this proved a failure. Experience soon showed that as the Japanese individuals and families fanned out over the western states, they were rejected almost everywhere. No community wanted to take them. People wouldn't rent to them, give them jobs, sell them gasoline or groceries, or allow their children into the local schools. A majority of the ethnic Japanese who had ventured forth in this manner returned to the west coast and

Japanese Relocation

By the time the cry arose on the west coast to do something about the small and mostly un-assimilated ethnic Japanese community, Americans had been prepared for action by photos such as those above.

Calls by public officials for the removal of the ethnic Japanese from the west coast began a few hours after the attack on Pearl Harbor. When the west coast was declared a war zone and Japa-

nese submarines appeared off the coast, those calls became louder, and, when reports came in of ethnic Japanese in other lands cooperating openly and willingly with Japanese invaders, the fate of America's ethnic Japanese was sealed. It was widely believed that the secretive and aloof Japanese community within the United States was riddled with spies, saboteurs, subversives and Fifth Columnists.

During a raid on Chungking, China, a bomb made a direct hit on a bomb shelter filled with civilians. It was claimed at the time that 700 people died in the shelter— mostly women and children. Some of the dead are seen here.

put themselves into the hands of the WRA. The WRA felt that they had no other alternative but to round up the ethnic Japanese and transport them to relocation camps in the interior of the United States. Plans and preparations for this were begun.

The United States was not alone in relocating their ethnic Japanese. Canada relocated theirs and put them in a camp in British Columbia. Mexico relocated theirs to

This is one of the most famous photos from the early stages of the war. A Chinese baby sits injured and abandoned on a railroad track in Shanghai, China, after a Japanese bombing raid. Later in the war, it was revealed that this photo was staged, but, by then it had had its desired effect in convincing the American public that the Japanese were a lowly horde of cruel and heartless barbarians.

a camp near Guadalajara. Several other Latin American countries, such as Peru, Ecuador, Columbia, Venezuela and Panama, sent their ethnic Japanese to the United States, and, under international agreements, these people were interned for the duration of the war in camps in Texas. After the war, some of the Latin American countries wouldn't allow their ethnic Japanese to return.

Japanese Gains in Southeast Asia

Bad news continued to flow from Southeast Asia. On February 16, the Japanese completed their conquest of Sumatra as the British and Dutch defenders retreated to the island of Java. Japanese troops were advancing steadily in Burma, and, on the 19th, Japanese planes bombed Darwin, Australia, sinking 12 Allied warships. The Japanese naval task force that carried out the Darwin raid was the same one that attacked Pearl Harbor. Its appearance near far-away Australia brought some relief to the war jitters on the U.S. west coast.

That same day, Japanese forces invaded the island of Bali in the Dutch East Indies. On the 20th, they invaded and occupied the island of Timor, half of which was owned by The Netherlands, the other by Portugal. Occupying the Portuguese half of the island was a direct act of war, but the Portuguese Government chose only to protest the action.

With Japanese forces on Timor, much of western and northern Australia was now within range of Japanese planes and naval units.

The Battle Of Los Angeles

On February 18, 1942, Japanese submarines appeared again in California waters, and, as in December, they found few targets. So, the commander of submarine I-17 decided to attack a target on land. At the time, the submarine was 80 miles north of Los Angeles off Santa Barbara and the Japanese commander knew of a facility that was vulnerable. On the evening of February 23, I-17 ventured close to shore and began shelling a commercial oil facility on the beach just north of Santa Barbara. The subma-

A Japanese soldier prepares to behead a Chinese civilian accused of being a member of a guerrilla band. This photo was not staged. Beheading was a standard means of execution by the Japanese and photos such as this appeared regularly in the United States throughout the war. Some of the photos showed Americans being beheaded. Such photos convinced a greater part of the American public that the Japanese, no matter where they were in the world, deserved no mercy.

rine fired 25 shells in a period of 15 minutes. This did minimal damage to the oil facility, but made big news the next days in the Los Angeles newspapers. Rumors began to spread that the attack at Santa Barbara was a preliminary to additional and more concentrated enemy attacks. By nightfall on the 24th, many people in the city were nervous and on edge. That night, around midnight, a false report was sent out to anti-aircraft gunners in the hills around Los Angeles that enemy planes had been spotted over the city. The gunners in one section of the city opened fire on the unseen aircraft and their search lights scanned the empty sky. The frenzy spread and other gunners opened fire. Some civilians rushed to shelters while others simply came out of their homes and gazed at the sky. Some people thought they saw planes; others saw parachutes and bombs falling. Spent anti-aircraft shells rained down on rooftops and cars. Santa Monica and Long Beach were the hardest hit. Air raid wardens dashed about, ordering people to take cover and to extinguish lights. Rumors spread that sections of the city were on fire and that a plane had crashed at the intersection of 185th and Vermont Ave. There was a rash of auto accidents as drivers tried to maneuver in darkened streets with their headlights turned off. Several people had heart attacks.

The "battle" went on for over two hours before the guns fell silent. The next morning, headlines in the *Los Angeles Times* screamed "L. A. AREA RAIDED." It was not true but even the newspaper's editors had succumbed to the panic. This incident is now recorded in the history books with the tongue-in-cheek title, "The Battle of Los Angeles." And, virtually all of *Casablanca*'s future cast members were witnesses to the event.

The truth eventually became known that the city had not been attacked and life returned to normal, but an aura of tension persisted for a long time.

After shelling the oil facility at Santa Barbara, I-17 sailed north and on March 1 attacked the U.S. tanker "William H. Berg" 55 miles southwest of San Francisco. The attack was unsuccessful and the ship escaped undamaged. This attack, and the one on the oil facility, nevertheless, served to keep people on edge all along the U.S. west coast.

Two nights after "The Battle of Los Angeles," the annual Academy Awards was held in Hollywood. The affair went pretty much as usual except that there were no search lights and word got around to the women that it would be inappropriate to wear orchids in wartime. That evening Gary Cooper won Best Actor for his portrayal in the World War I drama, *Sergeant York* (1941).

Allied Defeats

Between February 27 and 29, 1942, the first large-scale ship-to-ship naval battle of the war between the Japanese and the Allies took place in the Java Sea in Southeast Asia. It was a disaster for the Allies. The Allied fleet of Dutch, American, British and Australian ships was decimated, and the invasion route to Java, the most important island in the Dutch East Indies, lay open to the Japanese. On March 1, Japanese troops landed simultaneously at three locations on Java and the next day captured the colony's capital, Batavia. That same day, Allied warships retreating to Australia were attacked

The Hooligan Navy

By February 1942, the "Hooligan Navy" of civilian yachtsmen who had volunteered to help the U.S. Coast Guard patrol American coastal waters was operational along many stretches of the U.S. coast line, including the Los Angeles area. Humphrey Bogart owned and operated a large ocean-going yacht, and, as a member of the Coast Guard's Reserve Flotilla #21, became one of the volunteers. There is no record of Bogart ever spotting an enemy submarine, but this was not unusual.

The boats and yachts of the volunteer organization were equipped with radios and authorized to use Coast Guard frequencies to report anything of an unusual nature. The Japanese submarine commanders knew this and when they encountered a small vessel that they suspected was a patrol vessel they would sail out of the area so that their position would not be revealed. This, though, was the main purpose of the "Hooligan Navy" because it kept the submarines on the run and submerged, where they were slower, less maneuverable and unable to use their deck guns.

Submarine commanders would not normally attack the ships of the "Hooligan Navy" because they were of such small military value and because such attacks would reveal the submarine's location.

The "Hooligan Navy" lasted about a year and was eventually phased out as the Coast Guard acquired enough men and ships to carry out the necessary patrols on its own.

The Battling Bogarts

Humphrey Bogart didn't like General MacArthur but his wife, Mayo Methot, did—and they would argue about it. Fighting had become a way of life at the Bogart household by 1942 and was well-known to the public, their neighbors and the people at Warner Bros. Humphrey and Mayo were, at this time, both heavy drinkers. They would get drunk together and fight about almost anything, both in private and in public. The gossip columnists and movie tabloids picked up on this and had a field day reporting their exploits. In the process, Humphrey and Mayo became known as "The Battling Bogarts."

Peter Lorre (Ugarte) was a personal friend of the Bogarts and well-known as a prankster. He boasted to a mutual friend that he knew how to get the Bogarts into an argument and demonstrated his unique talent at a party. Lorre succeeded simply by bringing up the subject of General MacArthur. Humphrey and Mayo took the bait and the guests witnessed one more episode in the saga of "The Battling Bogarts."

again by Japanese aircraft and warships. They were defeated for a second time in a week. The U.S. cruiser "Houston" and two destroyers were lost along with the Australian cruiser "Perth" and a tanker. The Japanese lost four transport ships.

On March 2, Australia declared war on Thailand, and, on the 7th, fighting ended on Java with the Japanese in complete control of that island.

The next day, Japanese forces occupied Rangoon, the capital of Burma. British and Indian forces retreated into the interior of Burma. On the 7th, and again on the 10th, Japanese troops landed on New Guinea, the large half-Dutch-owned and half-British-owned island off the northern coast of Australia.

On the 12th, Dutch forces throughout the Dutch East Indies formally surrendered to the Japanese.

On March 14, the first American troops arrived in Australia and on the 16th came the welcome news that the Americans were beginning to strike back against the Japanese. On that day, U.S. Bombers from Australia attacked Japanese targets in the Philippines.

Between March 11 and 14, General Douglas MacArthur, Commander of Allied forces in the Philippines, and his family, made a daring escape through Japanese-controlled waters in four patrol-torpedo boats from Corregidor to Mindanao, the southernmost island in the Philippines. From Mindanao, they flew to Australia. Upon his arrival, MacArthur made his famous pledge, "I shall return."

Sayonara

During the first week in March 1942, the War Relocation Authority, with the help of the U.S. Army, began moving America's west coast ethnic Japanese into the relocation camps. Virtually no one protested the action and those being evacuated offered no resistance. Most of the ethnic Japanese remained in the camps until early 1945.

Little Tokyo, U.S.A.

As the Japanese families in the Los Angeles area were being loaded onto the Army trucks with their meager belongings, Twentieth Century-Fox cameramen were on hand to record the action. That studio was gathering stock footage for a movie they planned to make on the relocation entitled *Little Tokyo, U.S.A.* (1942), a "B" movie starring Preston Foster as a Los Angeles police detective with the all-American name of Mike Steele, and his lady-love Maris Hanover, a radio announcer, played by Brenda Joyce. The movie was produced concurrently with *Casablanca* but released in the summer of 1942. In keeping with the national temperament of the times, the movie was very critical of the ethnic Japanese.

In the opening scenes, Ho Takimura, the fictional leader of the main Japanese spy ring in Southern California, is seen addressing his followers in Little Tokyo, the main Japanese section of Los Angeles. Takimura tells his men that soon the Empire of Japan will strike its "greatest enemy—the United States of America." He goes on to say that, "On a morning not so far distant the United States shall receive a rude shock—before breakfast." The scene changes and it's early morning on Sunday December 7, 1941. Takimura and his associates are assembled again and Takimura is telling them of the pending attack on Pearl Harbor, saying, "Nothing will go wrong. We have planned long and thoroughly. The first bomb will fall on Pearl Harbor exactly on schedule—four minutes from now... Here in California we will do our part."

Then, detective Mike Steele appears. He has been assigned to investigate a murder in Little Tokyo but knows nothing about the Japanese spy ring. Steele soon discovers that his murder investigation is getting nowhere because the entire ethnic Japanese community is conspiring to thwart his efforts. From this, he begins to suspect that there is more here than just a murder. Oshima, a high school friend of Steele's, comes forward and offers to help, but soon ends up in the city morgue without his head. Steele eventually discovers the spy ring, their conspiracy, an illegal radio transmitter and the ring's leader, Takimura. As can be predicted, Steele breaks up the ring and arrests Takimura, but not before punching him out and uttering the memorable line, "That's for Pearl Harbor, you slant-eyed..."

In the final scenes, the remaining members of Takimura's gang are sent off to the relocation camps. Maris Hanover is seen broadcasting from one of the evacuation centers saying, "And so, in the interests of national safety all Japanese, whether citizens or not, are being evacuated from strategic military zones on the Pacific Coast. Unfortunately, in time of war, the loyal must suffer inconvenience with the disloyal... Be vigilant America!"

By the time Twentieth Century-Fox started filming, virtually all of the ethnic Japanese had been removed from Los Angeles and the studio had to use non-Japanese to play Japanese roles. This would become standard practice in Hollywood for the remainder of the war. In *Little Tokyo, U.S.A.* Takimura was played by character actor Harold Huber, heavily made-up to look Japanese. Oshima was played by Richard Loo, a Chinese-American. With Little Tokyo now a ghost town, street scenes were shot in Los Angeles' Chinatown.

In a curious contrast, there were plenty of ethnic Germans to play German roles and ethnic Italians to play Italian roles in Hollywood throughout the war. Casablanca was a good example of that.

The Epsteins Return

On Monday March 16, 1942, Julius and Philip Epstein returned to Warner Bros. from New York City and began working full-time on the *Casablanca* script according to their agreement with Hal Wallis. The Epsteins' salaries were $1,250 a week, and, from the beginning, they wrote with the idea that Humphrey Bogart would play Rick. Julius Epstein would later say of the script, "It had a lot of juice in it, and we loved Bogart's character."

By the end of the month, they had a completed draft ready for review. They changed Rick from a married lawyer and family man to an unmarried man of mystery who was cynical and worldly yet, at times, displayed a sentimental side.

The Epsteins softened Rick's role and added the fact that Rick couldn't return to America. They tried to come up with a reason, but couldn't, so they left it a mystery.

The role of Laszlo was changed too. He was no longer a wealthy Czech publisher with the Nazis after his money, but an important Czech resistance leader with the Nazis after him personally.

The Epsteins were also responsible for most of the humorous scenes in the movie.

Lois was still Lois and an American at this time, and would leave *Casablanca* with Laszlo at the end of the film.

Captain Rinaldo, the corrupt Prefect of Police, was re-named Captain Renault because the Epsteins and others thought the name "Rinaldo" was too Spanish-sounding and might offend Latin American audiences. The Epsteins built up Renault's relationship with Rick and gave Renault some of his best lines, including the ones about the "Third Reich." They said they chose the name "Renault" because the French-made automobile of the same name was well-known in the United States—and well-known it was, especially in March 1942.

Renault In The News

On March 3, 1942, an event happened in France that might well have influenced the Epsteins. On that day, the British carried out a massive air raid on the huge Renault industrial complex outside Paris because that facility was producing war materials for the Germans. It was a devastating raid and one of the first large-scale air attacks carried out on a non-German target. Some bombs missed their mark and fell on the homes of French civilians. Soon afterwards, the Germans reported that 623 French civilians had been killed and 1,500 injured. These figures were probably exaggerated but they had the desired effect on the Allies. Prominent Allied leaders spoke out against the raid and Gen. Charles De Gaulle, leader of the Free French, publicly condemned it. Those who had ordered and carried out the raid defended it as a necessity of war. Thus a nasty and unwelcome split in the Allied camp was revealed, much to the delight of the Axis Powers. The proponents of such raids, though, would eventually have their way. Many other raids of this type would be carried out by the Allies on French and other non-German targets on the contention that the Axis Powers must have no safe sanctuaries to produce weapons.

French Premier Paul Reynaud (holding a briefcase) and his associates hold an impromptu conference in a doorway. Left to right are General Maxim Weygand, who hated Reynaud; Paul Baudouin, a member of Reynaud's Cabinet; and Marshal Henri Petain, Reynaud's soon-to-be successor.

The British raid was the second raid on the Renault works. The Germans had bombed it in June 1940.

Renault was well-known to Americans in a second way in the person of Paul Reynaud (pronounced "Renault"), a colorful and controversial French politician who had been the Premier of France when the French Government fled from Paris to Bordeaux in June 1940. The reader may recall that Reynaud and his Cabinet were faced with the awesome decision of whether to continue the war against the Germans and Italians under very difficult circumstances, or to seek an armistice.

Behind the scenes of the Reynaud Administration, but yet very visible, was his mistress, The Countess de Portes. The Countess was very outspoken on political issues

The Countess de Portes, mistress of French Premier Paul Reynaud at the time of France's collapse and one of Reynaud's most influential unofficial advisors.

and suspected of having a major influence on Reynaud. At Bordeaux, she was one of the strongest proponents of France's continuing the war.

Despite his mistress' urging, Reynaud and his cabinet were unable to make a decision about the war and he resigned. Marshal Petain succeeded him as Premier and promptly capitulated to the enemy.

Before Reynaud resigned, however, General De Gaulle confided in him that he wanted to go to England rather than accept a surrender. Reynaud was sympathetic to this and gave De Gaulle 100,000 francs ($2,000) out of a secret fund to help him along and pulled strings so that De Gaulle's wife and children could make it to England, too.

The Reynaud story, though, wasn't over. When the Petain Government decided to move to Vichy, Reynaud and the Countess followed. On the way, they became involved in a serious automobile accident during which some loose luggage suddenly flew forward, killing the Countess instantly. Reynaud was injured but recovered and continued on to Vichy alone. There, his wife was waiting for him and let it be known to family and friends that she would welcome his return because now she could exact her revenge.

At Vichy, Reynaud's fortunes went from bad to worse. On September 6, 1940, the Petain Government arrested him and others on charges of treason for allowing the French military to fall into such a decrepit state of affairs before the war that it was unable to prevent France's defeat. Reynaud was also charged with embezzlement and speculation in national currency. He was subsequently tried and convicted on four out of seven counts and sent to prison. Some of his opponents called for his execution, but Reynaud had a savior—a very unlikely savior—Adolph Hitler. Hitler said that his execution wasn't necessary and the Vichy Government acquiesced to the Führer's judgment.

Reynaud was in prison during the time *Casablanca* was being made and shown to the public. He was released at the end of the war and became a leading politician once again in postwar France.

The American public had been exposed to the Renault name in yet another way in 1942, because running in the nation's theaters at the time was a Twentieth Century-Fox movie entitled *Dr. Renault's Secret*. This was a story about a scientist who turns an ape into a semi-human which then runs amok.

War News From America And Abroad

On March 19, 1942, the people at Warner Bros. had something else to worry about. On that date, the Federal Government required that older men, aged 45 to 64, register with their draft boards for possible conscription for non-military duty. Other countries had similar regulations during the war and it was not uncommon for older men with much-needed skills—such as electricians, plumbers, carpenters and machinists—to be called up for wartime service. Fortunately, the U.S. didn't have to resort to drafting older men for such duties, but the concern was ever-present for those involved. The loss of such skilled people for a movie studio could have created a major problem.

In Europe, a week later, on March 26, 1942, under utmost secrecy, the Germans began sending Jews to Auschwitz for extermination.

In America, on March 30, rationing began. Citizens were required to report to registration centers, usually set up in local schools, and sign up to get their ration cards and stamps. Eventually, things such as meat, coffee, sugar, butter, cooking oils, canned milk, shoes, firewood, typewriters, bicycles, farm machinery, gasoline and rubber products would be rationed.

In the Soviet Union, the hard winter fighting had come to a temporary halt because both sides were exhausted and the spring thaw had set in, turning all but the most northerly battlefields into seas of mud. The Soviets had made significant territorial gains during the winter but had failed to accomplish a knock-out blow against the Germans. The Axis armies in the Soviet Union were still strong and Hitler was promising that by the end of 1942, the Soviet Union would be no more.

On April 1, 1942, the Federal Government announced new restrictions on the manufacture of clothing to save cloth. Henceforth, double-breasted coats would be out, ties would be narrower, men's pants cuffs would be eliminated and slacks for women, especially those working in factories, would be "in." They, too, would be cuffless. Dress hats for both men and women were also discouraged. The new trend was labeled the "Victory Style."

These wartime fashion trends were not followed by Warner Bros.' wardrobe department for *Casablanca* because they would not have been historically correct. In the movie, Rick, Laszlo, Ugarte, Rick's croupier, the band members and several of the bit players wore double-breasted coats and wide pre-war ties while Ilsa wore a variety of dress hats. And, of course, Bogart wore his famous fedora in the Paris rail station scenes, at the Blue Parrot and at the airport.

On April 9, 1942, sad news came from the Philippines that the American and Filipino defenders on the Bataan Peninsula had surrendered. They were out of food, ammunition and medical supplies and were facing an overwhelming Japanese force. What was not announced, and what the world did not know until 1944, was that this was the beginning of the infamous "Bataan Death March." Some 76,000 American and Filipino prisoners of war were forced to walk over a hundred miles through the tropical heat without adequate food and water to prisoner-of-war camps. Those who fell behind or complained were beaten by their Japanese guards. Many fell ill and died along the way. Others who fell ill were summarily executed.

There was still some hope for the Americans though. The island-fortress of Corregidor, in Manila Bay, held out.

Lead Roles For *Casablanca* Still In Flux

On April 2, 1942, the Epsteins completed their third draft of the script. They were convinced by now that the female lead should be a European woman with an untarnished reputation rather than the less-than-virtuous American, Lois Meredith. Jack Warner was thinking along the same lines and believed that the newly-arrived Swedish actress, Ingrid Bergman, might be right for the part. The day before, he had asked independent producer David O. Selznick, who held Bergman's contract, if he might send the Epsteins to talk to him at his New York City office about hiring Bergman. Selznick agreed to talk.

Meanwhile, Jack Warner was having some doubts about Humphrey Bogart playing the male lead and suggested actor George Raft. Wallis, however, said he wanted to stay with Bogart and that the script was being tailored for Bogart. Michael Curtiz, who was to direct the film, agreed with Wallis. So, Warner relented and agreed to keep Bogart.

On the 10th, the studio announced to the press that Bogart would play the lead role in *Casablanca* and not Ronald Reagan as had been previously announced. The reason given was that Reagan was going into the Army, which he did soon afterwards.

About this time, the starting date for the filming of *Casablanca* was moved up from late April to early May because of conflicting schedules.

Howard Koch Signed

On April 6, 1942, contract screenwriter Howard Koch was assigned by Wallis to work on *Casablanca*. As was common practice in Hollywood, the Epsteins would continue writing, more or less independently of Koch. Koch went to work on the roles of Jan and Annina, the Bulgarian couple. Their roles had figured prominently in the play but they would be reduced to a sub-plot in the movie.

Koch wrote into the script that Rick and Renault were playing an on-going chess game. The Epsteins didn't like this and wrote it out. Rick then played a one-man chess game on-screen.

Koch worked on Rick's more humane and sentimental nature and wrote in the lines about his having run guns in Ethiopia and fought against the Fascists in Spain. Koch also changed the scene where Rick ejects the man from his gambling room. In the play, the man was an English con-man named Forrester-Smith. Koch changed him to the Deutschebank man.

Ingrid Bergman Made A Movie In Nazi Germany In 1937

Ingrid Bergman attended a rally in Hamburg, Germany in which Dr. Joseph Goebbels (above) was the main speaker.

Soon after David O. Selznick had negotiated a long-term contract with her and promised her the lead in his American version of *Intermezzo*, Bergman went to Germany to fulfill a previous commitment at Germany's Ufa Studio for the film *The Four Companions* (1938). Bergman spoke fluent German, having learned it from her mother. She was also in the early months of a pregnancy. Soon after her arrival, she was informed by her director, Karl Frohlich, that she might get an invitation to tea from Dr. Goebbels, Germany's film Czar, and a man known to have a penchant for young actresses. Frohlich told her that if the invitation came, she absolutely had to go otherwise it would reflect badly on him. This made Bergman's stay in Germany a very tense and unpleasant experience.

She was taken to a Nazi rally in Hamburg where Goebbels was the main speaker. She listened politely and told her German companions that she thought Goebbels was a marvelous speaker. But, when it came time to give the Nazi salute, she refused, which caused considerable embarrassment to those Germans in her party.

Fortunately, the movie was rushed to conclusion because Bergman's pregnancy was beginning to show. And, much to her relief, the invitation to tea from Dr. Goebbels never came. She hurried back to Sweden and told family and friends she would never work in Germany again. *The Four Companions* was the first and only movie she would make for Germany's "Mickey Mouse."

Ethnic Concerns

While the Epsteins and Koch were working on the script, the studio's central office was also checking it out for things that might be offensive to either American or foreign audiences. Special concern was given to the Latin America market, since that market was considered a good potential for the movie.

The question came up about Ugarte's name as possibly being mistaken for a Spanish name. Wallis intervened, saying that he believed it was sufficiently Italian-sounding to be left alone. It was therefore retained.

Señor Martinez, the head of *Casablanca*'s black market in the play, was another matter. That name was very Spanish-sounding and was changed to Ferrari, an Italian name the Americans and Latin Americans would be familiar with because of the Italian sports car of that name.

The pickpocket was not given a name or a nationality. Since he was to be played by a man of dark complexion and dark hair, he was simply referred to as "the dark European." It was hoped that audiences would consider him Italian.

Rick's Latin singer, played by Corinna Mura, was sufficiently Spanish-looking and Spanish-sounding that it would be difficult to mistake her for anything other than Spanish. She was given the name Señorita Androya, but, as things turned out, that name wasn't used.

Strasser and the other German-sounding names were left intact because their nationality was obvious to all.

The central office further saw to it that the movie industry's standard considerations toward Moslems were followed. Hal Wallis called it the "Allah, Allah business." To avoid offending Moslem audiences, no one identified in a movie as a Moslem could be seen drinking, gambling, dancing, flirting or engaging in any other type of neo-sexual activity. Moslem women had to be shown in proper attire and in some Moslem countries it was offensive for a Moslem woman to be seen driving.

In the Blue Parrot scenes, the Moroccan waiters are seen serving tea and coffee, not alcoholic beverages. At one point, Ferrari asks for "the bourbon" but the camera does not reveal who serves it to him. In the early versions of the screenplay, Ferrari was to wear native clothing but this was changed. He is seen in European attire to ensure that he would not be mistaken for a Moslem.

At Rick's, there is a Moroccan waiter in the early scenes of the movie and he, too, is serving tea or coffee. Also, in the first scenes of Rick's gambling room, there is a man with a turban and beard at the roulette table. Presumably he's a Hindu or a Sikh and not a Moslem.

As for the many refugees portrayed in the movie, it was an unwritten law in Hollywood that none of them would be specifically identified as Jews. A large percentage of the world's real refugees were, of course, Jewish, but Hollywood had learned years earlier that movie audiences in America, and many other places around the world, were not very sympathetic to the plight of the Jews.

Screentesting Begins

Since the leading lady had not yet been cast, and Ann Sheridan's chances for the role were fading because of the interest in having a European woman, Michael Curtiz had French actress Michele Morgan screentested on April 10. This fact was made known to David O. Selznick who was still playing coy about loaning Ingrid Bergman. After Morgan's test, Curtiz let it be known that, as far as he was concerned, Morgan had the role. This might well have been a move on the studio's part to urge Selznick to make a decision about Bergman.

On the 17th, French actor Jean-Pierre Aumont was screentested for the role of Laszlo at Wallis' request. Aumont was a handsome war hero-turned-actor, having been awarded the Croix de Guerre by the Free French. Aumont, though, was virtually unknown to American audiences and looked too young for the role.

On the 20th, Curtiz screentested singer Dooley Wilson for the role of Sam. Wilson was under contract with Paramount, but they were willing to loan him out for the role. Wilson did all right, but there were several people who thought that someone better could be found. First of all, Wilson couldn't play the piano so his piano playing would have to be dubbed in. Second, neither Wallis nor Max Steiner (the movie's future musical score director) liked Wilson's voice and about halfway through the movie an attempt was made to have Wilson's voice dubbed. This didn't work out well and the idea was dropped. Wilson kept the part.

Before this, however, Wallis had considered using a black woman in the role. Singers Lena Horn, Hazel Scott and Ella Fitzgerald were all discussed, but replacing Sam with a woman would have complicated the script. Considering the mores of the time, Rick couldn't possibly have been seen traveling from Paris to Casablanca with a black woman. Otherwise, something more than friendship could have been implied and such things simply couldn't be done in the segregated America of the 1940s.

After some debate, and the screen testing of four others for the role, Wilson was given the nod and on May 3 it was announced to the press. Paramount was paid $500 per week for Wilson's services of which Wilson received $350 a week. *Casablanca* was Wilson's fifth movie.

Elliot Carpenter, one of the men tested for Sam's role, was selected to play the piano on the set, but out of sight, as Wilson mimicked playing the piano on camera.

Sam's nationality was never in question. He was an American in the play and remained an American in the movie—the only other American besides Rick.

Tokyo Bombed

On April 18, 1942, Americans had reason to cheer for the first time since the nation went to war. American bombers, led by well-known airman and dare-devil, General Jimmy Doolittle, bombed several cities in Japan including Tokyo, Japan's capital. At last, America had struck a meaningful blow against the hated Japanese. The attack did only minor damage to the Japanese cities, but it proved an enormous morale boost, proving that the Japanese were not invulnerable and that American bombers could strike at the heart of the Japanese homeland.

Hollywood quickly recognized the audience appeal of stories that hit the Japanese in their own land and turned out several movies on the subject. Warner Bros. led the pack by producing, in 1943, *Destination Tokyo*, starring Cary Grant, John Garfield and Alan Hale. This was the fictional story of an American submarine that stealthily made its way into Tokyo Harbor to sink Japanese warships.

The next year, MGM produced *Thirty Seconds Over Tokyo*, a fairly accurate version of the Doolittle Raid from the best-selling book of the same name. That film, starring Spencer Tracy, Van Johnson and Robert Walker, has become a World War II classic.

Japanese Retaliation

Retaliation is one of the unwritten rules of warfare, and, in the eyes of the Japanese, the attack on Tokyo certainly required one or more face-saving strikes on the American homeland.

The American authorities fully realized that the Japanese might attempt retaliatory attacks and that those attacks might fall on the U.S. west coast. One of their great fears was that they would use poison gas against the civilian population as they had done in China. As a precaution, 600,000 additional gas masks were rushed to the west coast.

Meanwhile, in Tokyo, several plans were put forward to retaliate against the Doolittle Raid. Some of them were quite bizarre. The most ambitious was a plan to bomb Washington, DC. This plan, a suicide mission, would utilize the Kawanishi H8K, a long-range sea plane similar in appearance to the Pan American "Clippers." The Japanese had several dozen of these in their inventory and had successfully used them on long-range missions already. The plan called for six of these aircraft to fly to a location off the western coast of Mexico, land on the water, be refueled by a waiting Japanese submarine, then fly on across Mexico (where air defenses were almost non-existent), cross the Rio Grande River and bomb oil fields in Texas. From there, the planes would fly to a ren-dezvous point in the Gulf of Mexico to be refueled by a German submarine. The Germans had been contacted and agreed to cooperate in the project. The Kawanishi H8K's would then fly up the U.S. coast and bomb Washington, DC, and other U.S. cities. They would then fly out into the Atlantic and rendezvous again with German submarines and continue attacking U.S. east coast cities and rendezvousing with German submarines until all of the aircraft and their crews had been destroyed.

A less ambitious plan was advanced to use the same planes to bomb U.S. west coast cities, including Los Angeles. As with the Washington, DC, plan, the planes would rendezvous with Japanese re-fueling submarines off Mexico, carry out their bombing missions along the U.S. west coast, then return to bases in the Marshall Islands.

Neither of these plans were carried out, but the Kawanishi H8K planes remained in the Japanese arsenal throughout the war and the Japanese could have carried out the Washington, DC, plan and/or the west coast bombing plan at any time up to the very last days of the war.

The Japanese leaders did, however, decide on two retaliatory plans. The first was to invade and "liberate" the Hawaiian Islands and the second was to bombard the entire North American Continent with bomb-carrying balloons.

As for the first plan, it was obvious to the Japanese military leaders that the planes that bombed Tokyo had ultimately come from Hawaii. And, if the Americans could do it once, they could do it again. So, the Japanese war planners resurrected a pre-war plan they had on file for conquering the Hawaiian Islands. Up to now, the Japanese had not intended to conquer Hawaii although that option had never been completely ruled out. By occupying the Hawaiian Islands, the Japanese would force the Americans back to the mainland, thereby giving Japan control of the Central Pacific. From the Hawaiian Islands, Japanese ships and planes could carry out regular surveillance of American military activities along the U.S. west coast and launch military attacks against targets there as conditions warranted. In this manner, the Japanese home islands would be protected.

The original plan to occupy Hawaii was updated and put into motion at once with a target date set for early June 1942. This action would result in the famous Battle of Midway.

The Japanese plan called for the occupation of Midway Island, the westernmost island in the Hawaiian chain. From Midway, Japanese planes and ships could attack the rest of the islands. Johnston Island, south of Midway, would then be taken to guard their southern flank while other Japanese troops would invade and conquer the big island of Hawaii. From that island, as well as Midway Island, Japanese ships and planes would besiege, and eventually invade, Oahu Island, the only fortified island in the chain. Once the occupation of the Hawaiian Islands had been completed, the old Hawaiian monarchy would be resurrected, a king or queen put back on the throne, and Hawaii proclaimed an independent nation closely allied with Japan. Japanese farmers and fishermen would then be sent to the islands in large numbers and Hawaii would become a food-

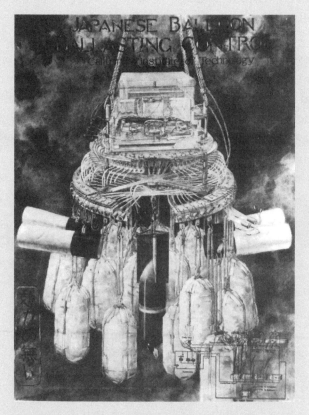

The undercarriage of a Japanese bombing balloon. It consisted of a timing device, ballast bags, incendiary bombs (the horizontal cylindrical objects) and a high explosive bomb in the center. Bombs were released one at a time. The gas bag was 15 meters in diameter and was inflated with hydrogen.

producing nation and a tourist destination within the newly created and Japanese-dominated Asian economic order to be known as "The Greater East-Asian Co-Prosperity Sphere." Hawaii would become the easternmost outpost of the Japanese Empire and a strong Japanese military presence would be maintained at Pearl Harbor to guard against the return of the Americans.

The second plan agreed upon called for the bombing of North America by huge bomb-carrying balloons that would be launched from Japan. The Japanese knew, from actual experiments, that such balloons could be launched from the Japanese home islands, rise into the jet stream, be carried across the Northern Pacific in a matter of a few days, descend over North America and drop a series of time-released incendiary and high explosive bombs as they sailed along.

Since this plan could not be implemented as quickly as the invasion of Hawaii, it did not become operational until the fall of 1944. During the winter of 1944-45, about 10,000 bombing balloons were launched from Japan and most of them made it to North America. They fell as far north as Alaska, as far south as Mexico and as far east as Detroit, MI.

Several balloon bombs or balloons themselves fell in the Los Angeles area. Such objects were discovered and retrieved in the waters off San Pedro, in Ventura, Moorpark and Oxnard. They did no serious damage in the Los Angeles area and caused no injuries. Most Americans weren't aware that the country was being bombarded in this manner because of very tight secrecy measures by the Federal Government.

Chapter Nine

A Story Without An Ending

Desert Training

With the invasion of French North Africa becoming almost a certainty, but still a secret from the public and the enemy, the U.S. Army saw the need to begin training officers and men needed to carry it out. General George S. Patton, Jr. was assigned to command the training operation and instructed to pick a training location. Patton, a native of San Gabriel, CA, a suburb of Los Angeles, was familiar with Southern California and knew that the area east of Los Angeles was a hot and dry desert-like area, very much like that of French Morocco. So, he chose that area and organized it into what was to become known as the California/Arizona Maneuver Area, commonly referred to as The Desert Training Center, the largest training area in the nation. The area covered 18,000 square miles and stretched from the outskirts of Pomona, CA, eastward to within 50 miles of Phoenix, AZ, southward to the outskirts of Yuma, AZ, and northward into the southern tip of Nevada. Temporary army camps, airfields and a command center were established to train the Army's 1st Armored Corps. Training began at the Desert Training Center in April 1942, and continued until August, thus paralleling the filming of *Casablanca* (May 25-August 22, 1942). After the 1st Armored Corps moved out, the 2nd Armored Corps, under General Alvan Gillem, Jr., moved in to begin its training. Following that, several smaller units were trained in the Desert Training Center. In 1944, after the North African campaign had been concluded and the Army had no further need for training troops in desert warfare, the Desert Training Center was closed.

During that time, of course, this vast area, which the Hollywood studios had often used to film westerns, was off limits to the movie companies. Instead of cowboys and Indians, the area swarmed with GIs.

War News Still Bad

In late April 1942, one month before the filming of *Casablanca* was to begin, the news from the war fronts was still bad. The elation the American people felt over the bombing of Tokyo was short-lived. Newspaper headlines and radio news broadcasts soon brought back the harsh reality that the Allies were losing on all fronts, save possibly the eastern front in the Soviet Union where military activity was at a virtual standstill due to the muddy season caused this time by the spring thaw.

On April 20, 1942, Pierre Laval, the pro-Nazi Premier of Vichy France and the number two man in the Vichy Government, announced that a policy of "understanding and true reconciliation with Germany must be loyally carried out." This, and other comments from Laval, was a further indication that Vichy was moving closer to the Axis Powers on political matters and could, under certain circumstances, join the Axis in the war.

This ominous message was, almost certainly, understood by the screenwriters working on Casablanca. The fear that Vichy France might join the Axis was not new, but Laval's comments were the latest and most indicative to date of Vichy's intentions. The general fear of the Vichy Government becoming an Axis partner might well have accounted for some of the pro-German lines given to Captain Renault in the movie and his show of cooperation with Major Strasser. The wind that blew from Vichy during April and May 1942 was definitely pro-German.

On April 21, Generalissimo Franco of Spain offered Hitler a million men to fight with the Axis forces in the Soviet Union provided Germany would equip and supply them. Hitler accepted the offer in part, guaranteeing to equip and supply one division of Spanish volunteers. This resulted in the creation of the all-Spanish "Blue Division" with some 20,000 members, one of the largest divisions of the war. The "Blue Division" fought bravely and honorably on the eastern front for two years and was returned to Spain in 1944. After that, the western Allies viewed the Blue Division and its combat veterans as something of a threat to Spain's ambitions in North Africa.

On April 25, General Rommel resumed his offensive against the British 8th Army in eastern Libya and pushed the British back closer to the Egyptian border.

In Burma, British and Indian forces continued to retreat northward with their backs to the mountains that separate Burma from China and India. On April 29, the city of Lashio fell to the Japanese. This was the southern terminus of the famous "Burma Road," which had been the Allies' only remaining land supply route to Nationalist China. Henceforth, the only way the Allies could get badly-needed war supplies to their Chinese Ally was by air over the Himalaya Mountains. On April 30, Mandalay, Burma's second largest city, fell to the Japanese.

In the Philippines, Japanese forces continued their occupation of that country's many islands. American and Filipino forces were able to offer some resistance on the large southern island of Mindanao, but were unable to stop the Japanese advance. On the tiny but fortified island of Corregidor in Manila Bay, the American and Filipino defenders still held out under frequent and heavy Japanese bombardment. Food, ammunition and other supplies were running dangerously low and re-supply was impossible. It was only a matter of time before Corregidor would be forced to surrender.

In New Guinea, Japanese forces continued to advance along the northern shore of the island. Port Moresby, the capital of Papua (the British half of the island) on the southern coast was in danger of attack. An amphibious assault by the Japanese on Port Moresby was feared.

If all of New Guinea were to be occupied by the Japanese, an invasion of Australia was a very likely next step. Accordingly, areas of Queensland in northern Australia were put on an invasion alert. On April 18, General Douglas MacArthur was appointed Supreme Allied Commander of Allied forces in the Southwest Pacific and charged with the responsibility of stopping the Japanese threat to Australia.

Off the eastern coast of the United States, German submarines continued to ravish commercial shipping. Ships were being sunk at the rate of almost one a day. In early May, ships began being sunk in the Gulf of Mexico, indicating that the German submarines had extended their areas of attack to America's southern coast. For a period of several weeks, German submarines were sinking ships from Nova Scotia to New Orleans.

In Washington, DC, President Roosevelt issued an Executive Order on April 28, freezing retail prices on every major item in the country. This was an effort to curtail inflation caused by rationing and shortages. Roosevelt, in one of his customary radio "Fireside Chats" to the nation, asked all American to accept the coming sacrifices that would be necessary to pursue the war.

In response to the President's call for sacrifices, Hollywood announced that it would do its share. To begin with, limousines routinely used to transport stars and executives were replaced with small buses in which all employees rode alike. The practice of making extra costumes to replace those that got soiled during filming was curtailed. Virtually everyone of importance in Hollywood signed up to buy War Bonds through payroll deductions in order to set an example for the nation.

Warner Bros. eagerly jumped on the band wagon and released photos of their stars saving gasoline and rubber. George Tobias was shown arriving at the studio on horseback. Irene Manning arrived on a bicycle. Ann Sheridan, Dennis Morgan, Michael Curtiz and Arthur Kennedy carpooled in a small bus to and from work with Paramount and Universal employees, all of whom lived in the same area of the San Fernando Valley. During the filming of *Casablanca*, the studio announced that young and healthy Madeleine Lebeau (Yvonne) walked five miles one way to work each day.

Japanese Reprisals

In late April 1942, reports reached the United States from Chungking, capital of Nationalist China, that Chinese civilians were being slaughtered in great numbers in Japanese-occupied eastern China for helping the American flyers who had bombed

Tokyo. After bombing Tokyo, most of General Doolittle's men were forced to land in Japanese-occupied areas of eastern China and were expected to make their way to safety on foot. Some did and some didn't. In any case, the Chinese were very supportive of the American flyers and aided them in their escape efforts. The Japanese, unable to capture all of the Doolittle flyers, took out their wrath on the Chinese. In some cases, the Chungking reports stated, entire villages had been leveled and every man, woman and child executed. The American had yet another reason to hate the Japanese.

Jack Warner Joins The Army
—More Or Less

During April 1942, General Harold "Hap" Arnold, Chief of the U. S. Army Air Forces, summoned Jack Warner to Washington to discuss a recruiting film for the Air Forces. Arnold wanted the film made as quickly as possible because his branch of service was having problems getting enough qualified men to train as pilots. Warner agreed to help Arnold in any way he could, including producing the film at studio expense. In return for his services, Arnold offered Jack Warner a commission of Lt. Colonel in the Army's Signal Corps. Warner was impressed, but asked for more. He wanted to be a general so he could outrank Darryl F. Zanuck, his former employee and now competitor, who had accepted a similar deal and was made a full Colonel. Arnold, though, stood his ground and Warner had to be content with a Lt. Colonel's commission. Warner could gloat, though, because he was one up on David O. Selznick with whom he was currently negotiating for Ingrid Bergman's services in *Casablanca*. Selznick had hoped to get a commission, too, but was rejected because he was overweight, nearsighted and flat-footed.

The movie deal was made and General Arnold arranged for actor Jimmy Stewart, currently in the Air Forces, to be sent back to Hollywood on temporary duty to narrate the film.

Upon his return to the studio, Warner promptly had the wardrobe department make him an Army officer's uniform which he began wearing daily around the studio. He also began signing his name "Col. Jack Warner" and his subordinates, taking the hint, began addressing him as "Colonel."

The script of the recruiting film, titled *Winning Your Wings*, was written in one day by Owen Crump, an experienced screenwriter of movie shorts. Production and filming began immediately and was completed in two weeks—just before the filming of *Casablanca* began. *Winning Your Wings* was released soon afterwards and was a success. The Air Forces said they could trace some 100,000 enlistments directly to the film.

As an Army officer receiving an Army paycheck, the Army began making additional requests of Col. Warner. After a while, he found these intrusions on his time intolerable and eventually resigned his commission. Jack Warner's Army career lasted about six months. During that time, though, *Casablanca* was filmed under the guidance of the "Colonel."

Ingrid Bergman Signed

David O. Selznick was still playing coy. He hadn't yet replied to Wallis' request to borrow Bergman for *Casablanca*, so Wallis sent the Epstein brothers to New York City to meet with Selznick and go over the movie script with him. After hearing the story, it was hoped that Selznick would agree to loan Bergman to Warner Bros. It worked. In their meeting, Selznick liked what he heard of the script and could see that playing opposite Humphrey Bogart, one of the hottest stars in Hollywood, would be a positive move for Bergman's career. Selznick liked Rick's role too and later said Rick reminded him of Rhett Butler, the hero in his own great success, *Gone With the Wind* (1939). Both characters, Selznick pointed out, were cynical individuals and gave up the girl in the end.

An agreement was reached on April 24. Selznick agreed to loan Bergman to Warner Bros. for eight weeks in exchange for eight weeks time from Warner's star, Olivia de Havilland. Selznick had another deal working and ended up loaning de Havilland to RKO for *Government Girl* (1943).

Word of the deal with Warner Bros. was welcome news for Bergman who was then living in Rochester, NY, where her husband was going to medical school. She hadn't worked in a while, had become bored with Rochester and her small town life, and even had fears that her film career might be over.

She received the first draft of the script in late April and began studying it intently. By this time, the female lead had already been changed to a European woman named Ilsa.

Bergman left for Hollywood in early May, alone, leaving her husband and their daughter, Pia, in Rochester. She rented an apartment in Beverly Hills and began preparing for her role in the movie. As a part of her preparation, she went to see Bogart's latest movie *The Maltese Falcon* several times so she could become familiar with his style of acting and, as she later commented, "…so when I met him I wouldn't be so frightened." One of the problems she faced was that of age. She was 26 and Bogart was 43. Also, she was slightly taller than Bogart. This was easily remedied, though, by putting risers in Bogart's shoes.

Paul Henreid Signed

On May 1, 1942, actor Paul Henreid and producer Hal Wallis came to an agreement on Henreid playing the Laszlo role in *Casablanca*. When Henreid first saw one of the early scripts, he showed no interest in the role, calling the movie a "ridiculous fairy tale." But, he changed his mind for a number of reasons. His agent, Lew Wasserman, pointed out to Henreid that since he was an enemy alien (he was an Austrian citizen and Austria was now a part of Germany), taking this anti-Nazi role might help fortify his residency status in America, especially in light of the recent relocation of the ethnic Japanese. Furthermore, Henreid had played Nazis in two of his recent movies, *An Englishman's Home* (1939) and *Night Train* (1940), both of which were made in England.

Wasserman warned against Henreid becoming stereotyped as a Nazi bad guy. Henreid saw the advantages in this argument and began to pursue the role. There was a problem, though. Henreid was currently filming *Now Voyager* (1942) and wouldn't be free until mid-June.

Wallis wanted Henreid badly enough that he agreed to film around his part. So, a deal was eventually struck which included co-star billing for Henreid, a generous seven-year contract with Warner Bros. and an understanding that he would get the girl in this and other movies. It was subsequently announced to the press that Henreid would play the Laszlo character in *Casablanca*.

Production Problems

During the week of May 10, Wallis asked director Mike Curtiz to meet with Studio Art Director, Carl Weyl, and look around the studio for existing sets that could be used for *Casablanca* before attempting to build new ones in face of the current materials shortages.

Another problem that plagued the entire movie industry about this time were reports that movie film, an item for which there was no substitute, might become scarce. In this respect, Warner Bros. had an advantage over its competitors in the person of Jack Warner. Warner, who was known to be frugal, had several pet peeves, one of which was the wasting of film. A big pile of film on the cutting room floor could send him into a rage and everyone at the studio knew it. Fortunately for the movie industry and for Jack Warner, movie film did not become a hard-to-get item during the war. During the filming of *Casablanca*, though, this had not yet become clear so the production company was under pressure to limit retakes and avoid unnecessary shots.

Another problem surfacing was that the screenwriters, the Epsteins and Howard Koch, were off on different tangents. Koch wrote to Wallis on May 11 saying, "They (the Epsteins) apparently see the situations more in terms of their comic possibilities, while my effort has been to legitimize the characters and develop a serious melodrama of present-day significance…" Wallis dealt with this problem by calling in two more screenwriters, Casey Robinson and Lenore Coffee, to read over the composite script and offer suggestions. Robinson was one of the top screenwriters in Hollywood and was known for his ability to adapt plays and books for the screen and for solving censorship problems with the Hays Office. Coffee was well-known both for her ability to write love scenes and to write about all things French.

On May 13, 1942, *Casablanca* was assigned Production No. 410 with a starting date of May 25.

A few days later, Sidney Greenstreet was engaged to play Ferrari.

But, there were still major problems. The roles of Major Strasser, Captain Renault and Ugarte had not yet been assigned and the screenwriters, Howard Koch and the Epsteins, announced that they were having trouble with the movie's ending. Both Koch and the Epsteins had suggested endings, but couldn't agree on which version was best. Wallis and Curtiz weren't impressed with either ending. About the only thing that everyone could agree on at this point was that Ilsa would leave Casablanca with her husband, Laszlo. The problem with the movie's ending was disconcerting to everyone involved, especially to Bogart and Bergman, and it would continue even after filming began.

On May 22, one more problem was resolved. Conrad Veidt, borrowed from MGM, was signed to play Major Strasser. Strasser's role was fairly firm by now. He had been upgraded from the play's young German Army captain attached to the German Consulate in Casablanca to the movie's older, sophisticated and autocratic Gestapo Major who had been sent to Casablanca directly from Germany to apprehend the murderers of the German couriers, recover the letters of transit and keep Laszlo from reaching America.

Veidt had just completed a movie at MGM, *Nazi Agent* (1942), in which he had had the lead. Veidt was born in Germany but had become a naturalized British citizen and hated the Nazis. He didn't mind being stereotyped as a Nazi villain because he looked upon it as something of a patriotic undertaking. Plus it was profitable. Veidt received a major portion of the $5,000 per week MGM received for his services. Good Nazis didn't come cheap in Hollywood.

On the May 20, Casey Robinson reported to Wallis, and wrote, "…my impression about *Casablanca* is that the melodrama is well done, the humor excellent, but the love story deficient." Robinson made suggestions on how to improve the love interests and

Conrad Veidt

Conrad Veidt, who had a very successful movie and stage career going in Germany, was married to a Jewish woman. When the Nazis came to power and took control of the German film industry, he and his wife, Lily, made plans at once to flee the country. The story circulated later that Joseph Goebbels personally asked the Veidts to remain in Germany with his personal guarantees of safety. The Veidts, though, didn't trust the Nazis and fled.

A Jewish man and a non-Jewish woman in Hamburg are forced to wear placards stating that they were living together, a breach of Nazi ideology. With scenes such as this, it is no wonder that the Veidts didn't trust the Nazis.

suggested yet another ending. It was his ending that eventually began the basis for the one used in the film.

Then, on Thursday May 21, four days before filming was to begin, came another unpleasant surprise from Joseph I. Breen, Director of the Production Code Administration—the Hays Office. "Dear Mr. Warner," Breen wrote, "The present material contains certain elements which seem to be unacceptable from the standpoint of the Production Code. Specifically, we cannot approve the present suggestion that Capt. Renault makes a practice of seducing women to whom he grants visas. Any such reference to illicit sex could not be approved in the finished picture." Breen also complained about the suggestion that Ilsa was married when she was having an affair in Paris with Rick. Breen's letter was handed to the writers with Jack Warner's instructions to correct the situation.

By now, just about everyone was working overtime at the studio—even the boss.

On Saturday, May 23, two days before filming was to begin, Jack Warner sent a memo to Curtiz which was something of a pep talk. Warner wrote, "These are turbulent days and I know you will finish *Casablanca* in seven weeks tops. I am depending on you to be the old Curtiz I know you to be, and I am positive you are going to make one great picture."

With the filming deadline so close, *Casablanca* was in about as much trouble as America's war effort.

The Battle of Coral Sea

Between May 2 and 8, a history-making naval battle took place in the Coral Sea off the eastern tip of New Guinea. The battle was the first of its kind because the major warships of each side never had a face-to-face encounter. The bulk of the fighting was done by aircraft. During this on-again-off-again battle, each side lost an aircraft carrier and had a second one damaged. The Americans lost a destroyer and a tanker but the Japanese lost a considerably larger number of aircraft and pilots. Most important of all, the Japanese naval force involved in the battle was an invasion force heading for Port Moresby, New Guinea. Because of its losses and the stiff opposition from the American Navy, that force turned back and the invasion called off. Port Moresby was saved. From the American point of view, the Battle of the Coral Sea proved that the Japanese were not invincible and that their steady string of successful invasions could be stopped.

Other War News

During the Battle of the Coral Sea came the sad news that America's last bastion in the Philippines, Corregidor Island in Manila Bay, had surrendered. Only American and Filipino guerrilla forces now operated in the Philippines against the Japanese.

From Europe came news that the British Royal Air Force (RAF) had carried out a massive air raid on the huge Skoda Works near Pilsen, in German-occupied Czechoslovakia. This was a raid very similar to that on the Renault Works at Paris, France, but this time there were no protests or displays of disunity forthcoming from the Allied camp. As with the Renault Works raid, the Germans announced that large numbers of Czechs had been killed and wounded. Incidents such as this kept Czechoslovakia in the news and served to maintain the feelings of sorrow and respect the American people had for the long-suffering Czech people.

On the eastern front in the Soviet Union, the muddy season was ending and the terrible carnage resumed. The Soviets attacked at Kharkov and the Germans launched an offensive in the Crimean Peninsula. Within days, it became apparent that the Germans had the upper hand. Their offensive in the Crimea forced the Soviets to withdraw after losing 150,000 troops to the Germans as prisoners of war. At Kharkov, the Soviet offensive failed and the Germans launched a successful counter-offensive. By now, it was clear that the major German objectives for the summer of 1942 were to be Stalingrad on the Volga River and the Caucasus region of Southern Russia which was rich with oil.

In Burma, the battle for that British colony came to a halt with the total defeat of the Allied forces there. The survivors of the Allied armies began a grueling trek over the difficult and dangerous mountain passes to safety in India and China. Most made it; many didn't.

From south of the border came the welcome news, on May 22, that Mexico had declared war on Germany, Italy and Japan. This was the direct result of German submarines operating in the Gulf of Mexico and not-so-accidentally sinking several Mexican merchant ships. For the people in Southern California, Mexico's action put an end to rumors that Japan, and possibly Germany, had secret air bases and other forces in Mexico just waiting their chance to march into San Diego and Los Angeles.

Filming Begins

It was a bright and sunny day in Hollywood on Monday May 25, 1942, in Burbank but the people involved in the making of *Casablanca* wouldn't see much of it. They were cooped up most of the day in Warner Bros.' studio 21A. Filming began at 9 a.m. The Paris flashback was the first segment of the movie filmed because that part of the script had been completed and the actors necessary for those scenes were available.

This was the first time Michael Curtiz directed Bergman. He liked her from the start and was courteous and gentle with her throughout the filming. For Bogart, it was his fourth time being directed by Curtiz. The other three movies had been *Kid Galahad* (1937), *Angels With Dirty Faces* (1938) and *Virginia City* (1940).

When filming started, Bogart had three films running in theaters across the country. Some of them had actors who would appear in *Casablanca*. Those films were *All Through the Night* (1942) with Conrad Veidt (Strasser) and Peter Lorre (Ugarte); *The Big Shot* (1942); and *Across the Pacific* (1942) with Sidney Greenstreet (Ferrari).

Curtiz had a bandaged right hand as production started, the result of being hit during a polo match with a mallet by fellow polo player, Sowy Baker. Curtiz, the former cavalry officer in the Austro-Hungarian Army of World War I, was an avid horseman.

The very first scene filmed was the action in La Belle Aurora Cafe in the Montmarte District of Paris. In this scene, it's Thursday June 13, 1940, the day before the Germans marched into Paris. Ilsa has just discovered that her husband, Victor Laszlo, whom she thought dead, is actually alive and on his way to Paris. Rick doesn't know this and she can't tell him. Rick is pouring champagne, making light of the coming German occupation and suggesting that he and Ilsa run off to Marseilles and get married. Sam is playing "As Time Goes By" and Ilsa's anguish is noticeable. It was a "wow" beginning for the first day but, as yet, there was no "wow" ending for the movie.

The Paris flashback scenes were the product of the Warner Bros. writers. There was no Paris flashback in the original play, *Everybody Comes To Rick's*.

That same day, over at the office, Paul Henreid's new contract with Warner Bros., agreed to a few weeks earlier, was formally signed.

At the request of Hal Wallis, Casey Robinson was hired that day as another screenwriter for *Casablanca*. It was expected that Robinson would be on the script for two weeks, but it turned out to be three and a half weeks. At $2,500 per week, Robinson was the highest paid of all the writers.

Robinson was asked to work on the love angle between Rick and Ilsa which Wallis and others thought needed improving. He did this, in part, by increasing the importance of the song, "As Time Goes By," tying it in with the love relationship between Rick and Ilsa. Emphasizing that song was something of a gamble since by then it was all but forgotten and it hadn't been heard very much in the last ten years. Warner Bros. could have substituted one of the many songs they owned in hopes of increasing that song's popularity and their overall profits, but "As Time Goes By" had been written into the original play and seemed to fit, so it was retained.

By promoting "As Time Goes By," Sam's role was enhanced, much to the benefit of Dooley Wilson.

About this time, Casey Robinson, in his efforts to improve the story's love interests, suggested adding the second meeting between Rick and Ilsa in Rick's apartment where Ilsa comes to get the letters of transit at any price. She ends up confessing her love for Rick, and offering to abandon her husband and stay on with him in Casablanca.

Robinson was also assigned to work on the movie's ending which Koch and the Epsteins were likewise pursuing.

At this point, the Epsteins, Howard Koch and Casey Robinson were all writing, more or less independently, and feeding material to Wallis and Curtiz. On Sundays, the four writers would go out to Wallis' ranch in the San Fernando Valley and meet with him. They would spread the pieces of script out on a table and put the story together for the coming week's filming. It really wasn't the best way to make a movie.

Hollywood Hype

As was standard practice at the start of filming, parts of *Casablanca*'s story were given out as publicity by Warner Bros. The public was also informed that American audiences shouldn't expect to see another movie of *Casablanca*'s quality and opulence for the duration of the war. This was partly hype and partly true given the increasing material shortages and the departure of critical personnel for the armed forces and for war work. There was an implied warning that if the Japanese attacked Los Angeles, the Warner Bros. studios might even be blasted to smithereens. The message to the movie-going public was therefore, "You'd better see this one because it might be the last of its kind!"

Warner Bros. also gave out the juicy tidbit that during the first day of filming— as Rick, Ilsa and Sam were waiting in La Belle Aurora Cafe for the Germans to arrive in Paris—one of the extras on the set, a refugee who had lived in Paris, broke down and cried.

The studio's claim that *Casablanca* would be a film of a quality that would not be matched for some time was not necessarily true. A studio memo from Hal Wallis to chief cameraman Arthur Edeson on May 26, the second day of filming, indicated that quality was secondary to other considerations. Wallis complained to Edeson that it took too long to produce the scenes that were made the day before. In his memo Wallis wrote, "You were present at all the meetings we had about all the war emergencies and the necessity of conserving money and material, and I must ask you to sacrifice a little on quality, if necessary, in order not to take these long periods of time for setups. If we continue to move as slowly as we did yesterday, we will run way over our time and money (budget) on the picture."

Lorre and Rains Signed

On Tuesday May 26, filming continued on the Paris flashback at studio 21A. That same day, actors Peter Lorre (borrowed from Universal Studios) and Claude Rains (a freelance actor) were officially engaged to play Ugarte and Renault respectively.

Lorre would be paid $1,750 a week but worked for only six days. Rains received $4,000 a week and would work for seven weeks.

This would be the second time Lorre would appear in a film with Sidney Greenstreet who had been hired earlier to play Ferrari. Their first collaboration had been in *The Maltese Falcon* (1942). Lorre and Greenstreet worked so well together that they were paired time and again in movies throughout the 1940s, usually playing a pair of unsavory characters. So often did they appear together that author Ted Sennett in his book, *Masters of Menace,* called the slightly-built Lorre and the 300-pound Greenstreet, "The Laurel and Hardy of crime."

Greenstreet was paid $3,750 a week for his role in *Casablanca* and was seen on the screen for only five minutes. Due to delays, he worked for a little over three weeks.

Claude Rains, who would play Captain Renault, had been a captain once before in real life—in the British Army During World War I. By 1942, Rains was a veteran actor having been in 31 movies before *Casablanca*. The 52-year-old Rains was a veteran in yet another way. He was on his fourth marriage—he would have six. Almost everyone liked Claude Rains but he could be a bit of a bore on the set at times. He owned a farm in Pennsylvania and loved to talk farming. The Hollywood crowd wasn't much into farming.

Everybody Comes To Rick's—Literally

On May 28, the entire *Casablanca* production company moved to Soundstage 8 on the Warner lot where the set for Rick's Cafe Americain had been constructed. No suitable standing set had been found for Rick's so it was built from scratch, costing the studio $76,565. Some of the props had been rented from local prop suppliers, including the bamboo and rattan chairs.

Some of the supporting actors appeared now for the first time, including Sacha the bartender played by Leonid Kinskey. In an early re-write of the script, Sacha had been the Russian Czar's favorite sword swallower, but this dizzy idea was dropped. Kinskey was paid $750 a week and worked two weeks.

Joy Page, Jack Warner's step-daughter, and the woman who played Annina, the Bulgarian woman, went to work on the film at $100 a week. Due to delays, she was retained for about two months.

Helmut Dantine (Jan, the Bulgarian man) was Joy Page's counterpart and was riding a small wave of popularity at the time. He had appeared in MGM's *Mrs. Miniver* which was showing as *Casablanca* was being produced. Dantine had an important supporting role in the film as the German airman who parachuted down into Mrs. Miniver's back yard during the Battle of Britain. The movie was a smashing success and was Dantine's best role to date. That movie got an additional lift when, after viewing the film, British Prime Minister Winston Churchill wired Louis B. Mayer congratulating him on the film and stating *"Mrs. Miniver* is propaganda worth 100 battleships."

Carl, Rick's head waiter and bookkeeper, to be played by S. Z Sakall, had still not appeared since he had not yet been signed for the movie.

The Second Front

On May 29, 1942, the Soviet Union's Foreign Minister, Vyacheslav Molotov, arrived in the United States for talks with President Roosevelt and top U.S. military leaders. This was the first time such a high-level Soviet official had visited the United States and his arrival was widely covered by all the news media. The timing of Molotov's visit was most fortunate for the Soviet Union because the new German spring offensive on the eastern front was beginning to take hold and the Soviets were suffering severe reversals in the field. American sympathies were definitely with the Soviets and there was a willingness among the American political leaders as well as the American public to help the Russians.

Top priority on Molotov's agenda was to get a commitment from the Western Allies to open a second front somewhere in western Europe in order to reduce the Axis military pressure on the Soviet Union. Molotov mentioned the need for a second front to almost everyone he met in private and in public. Given the developing conditions in the Soviet Union, President Roosevelt had little choice but to give assurances to the Soviets that a second front would soon be forthcoming, but Roosevelt was evasive as to where and when it would take place. He could not give Molotov definite answers because the western leaders had not yet decided these questions among themselves. Two options were being studied, though, both kept secret from Molotov and the general public. One was a cross-channel invasion of France from England and the other was the invasion of French Morocco and Algeria in French North Africa.

Because of Molotov's visit, though, the phrase "second front" was very much in the news and it's not surprising that the *Casablanca* screenwriters picked up on it and used it in the movie.

Script Problems

With *Casablanca* now before the camera, the screenwriters were under extreme pressure to finish the rest of the script. On June 1, 1942, they produced a new version, but there were still unresolved problems, especially with the movie's ending. As filming progressed, the gap between script availability and the needs on the soundstage narrowed. Changes and additions were coming so rapidly that the writers began using different colored paper to identify which segment of script went with which day of production. This gave rise to undue tensions among the people on the lot and there was much arguing and bickering. With fixed costs running about $30,000 a day, it was ulcer time on Soundstage 8.

Chess helped to relieve the tensions for Bogart and Rains. They began a game and played it off-and-on between takes. When Paul Henreid arrived, he would also play chess with Bogart. In addition, Bogart had a solitary chess game set up in his dressing room. Bogart was an avid chess player and had, at times, chess games going on with various people around the country by mail, sending each other their moves by postcard.

An ongoing chess game between Rick and Renault had been written into the script at one point, but then dropped. Rick, though, did play a chess game on screen by himself.

On June 3, filming switched to the Paris train station. This set had been build for *Now Voyager* (1942) and was no longer needed. The filming of *Now Voyager* ended on June 4 and Paul Henreid, the film's male lead, would have been ready to go to work the next day except that he was ill and his doctor had ordered bed-rest. This was another setback for the Casablanca film company. But, now they had a nearly completed script, so they could continue filming around Henreid.

On June 4, Claude Rains (Captain Renault) became available and filming shifted back to Rick's. Conrad Veidt (Major Strasser) became available two days later.

Screenwriter Howard Koch was released from his scriptwriting duties on June 5 and the Epsteins, likewise, on the June 12. They all had done their job well. A few days later, the Hays Office gave its final approval on the script. All the sexual hanky-panky from the original play had been cleaned up and *Casablanca* now met the industry's strict Production Code.

Miracle At Midway

Suddenly there was good news from the Pacific war front—very good news. The Japanese Navy had suffered a stunning defeat at Midway Island, the westernmost island of the Hawaiian chain, and Japan's attempt to invade and occupy the Hawaiian Islands had met with utter defeat. Furthermore, because of that battle the Japanese navy was decimated.

It all started in late May when the Japanese assembled and dispatched a large naval force of warships and troop transports to attack and subsequently occupy Midway as a first step in conquering all of the Hawaiian Islands. Prior to this, though, the Americans had broken a key Japanese code. They knew the Japanese were coming and had a good idea of their strength and plan of attack. The Americans also knew that the Japanese were using four of their eleven aircraft carriers to support the invasion. So, as the Japanese force approached Midway on June 3, the Americans were waiting. During the next three days, the largest naval battle yet in the Pacific war took place in the waters north and west of Midway Island. It was something of a repeat of the Battle of the Coral Sea in that the main weapon used by both sides was the airplane. But, the outcome was considerably different. Thanks to the daring and skill of the American pilots, the superior quality of American planes and to luck. Consequently, the Japanese lost all four of their aircraft carriers, plus over 300 of their best pilots. They also lost a heavy cruiser. The American lost one aircraft carrier, the "Yorktown," a destroyer and about 100 pilots.

Without air cover, the Japanese had no hope of effecting a successful landing on Midway and were forced to retreat. The loss of four of their eleven carriers was a devastating blow to the Japanese Navy. The Japanese had no way to replace those ships in the near future given the size of their industrial base and their shortages of basic materials such as steel. The Americans, on the other hand, with a much larger industrial base and ample materials could build aircraft carriers, and other ships, at an unprecedented rate. From this point on, the Japanese Navy would not only be out-fought by the American Navy but overwhelmed as well by its ever-increasing size.

The Battle of Midway was the turning point of the war in the Pacific. After "Midway," the Japanese Navy was forced to go on the defensive for the rest of the war. The Japanese Army, though, was another matter. It was still strong and, as yet, undefeated. But, it would soon be tested at a place called Guadalcanal.

As the Battle of Midway unfolded, a smaller Japanese force successfully landed Army troops on two undefended islands, Kiska and Attu, in the Aleutian Island chain of Alaska. In the process, Japanese planes bombed Dutch Harbor, Alaska, the only American city on the North American mainland to be bombed during the war. This was a diversionary move by the Japanese to draw American forces away from Hawaii. The Americans couldn't be sure of that, though, and had to consider that the occupation of the Alaskan islands might be a preliminary to further invasions or attacks against Alaska, Canada or the American west coast. So, the Americans sent strong forces to

Alaska to contain the Japanese threat. In the meantime, war jitters along the west coast returned to some degree although not as intensely as during December 1941.

As a part of the new precautions taken along the U.S. west coast, the Federal Government decreed a dusk-to-dawn curfew on all enemy aliens. They had to be in their homes or places of residence each day from 8 p.m. to 6 a.m. This directly affected *Casablanca* members Paul Henreid (German/Austrian), Peter Lorre (Hungarian), Michael Curtiz (Hungarian), S. Z. Sakall (Hungarian), Helmut Dantine (German/Austrian), Curt Bois (German) and several others. Fortunately, the curfew order was soon lifted and didn't contribute significantly to the problems of filming *Casablanca*.

Czechoslovakia Surges Into The News— The Lidice Massacre

While the Battle of Midway was being played out in the Pacific, a small band of Czech partisans assassinated SS General Reinhard Heydrich, Reich Protector of Bohemia-Moravia (Czechoslovakia). Heydrich had been ruling the former Czechoslovakia with a iron hand and used brutal methods to suppress opposition to Germany's plan to Germanize the Czech people. He was universally hated and referred to as "The Hangman." It was not surprising that he would ultimately become the target of an assassination plot.

Heydrich was mortally wounded on May 29, 1942, when hand grenades were thrown into his open car as he and members of his staff drove through the Czech village of Lidice. Heydrich died six days latter.

Hitler was furious with the Czechs for committing such a crime and felt personally betrayed. After all, he had granted them the honor of being Germanized and now they had perpetrated this horrible outrage against the man who was guiding them down that path. Hitler gave the eulogy at Heydrich's funeral and then ordered that

Obergruppenfuhrer Reinhard Heydrich, Reich Protector of Bohemia-Moravia, front row center, shown here at a concert in Prague with associates and his wife, on his right. Heydrich's assassination lead to the tragedy of Lidice.

The Village of Lidice before it was obliterated by the Germans.

40,000 to 50,000 Czechs be shot in reprisal for Heydrich's death. Karl Frank, Heydrich's deputy, convinced Hitler that such a severe reprisal might cause an uprising in the Protectorate and, if not that, a labor shortage and other problems in Czech industry because most of the Czechs were working for the Reich's war effort and their services were essential. Hitler tempered his anger and decreed, instead, that the village of Lidice be obliterated from the face of the earth and its inhabitants punished most severely. In the days that followed, 199 boys over 16 and men from Lidice were summarily executed, 195 women were sent to concentration camps and 98 children were taken from their parents and sent to various camps or orphanages, or put up for adoption by German families to be properly Germanized. Czech patriots in prison for other offenses were executed in reprisal for Heydrich's death and some 3,000 Czech Jews at Mauthhausen and 2,359 at Auschwitz were exterminated. The village of Lidice was completely destroyed, the rubble removed and the ground returned to raw land.

The Germans documented the carnage and destruction at Lidice in newsreels and showed them throughout Czechoslovakia as a warning to others. The Allies, of course, acquired copies of the newsreels and used them in a massive anti-Nazi propaganda campaign throughout the world. The newsreels were so graphic and detailed that they were used after the war as evidence against Nazi leaders at the Nuremberg Trials.

Hollywood quickly made two movies depicting the assassination of Heydrich and the Lidice massacres. Independent producers Arnold Pressburger and Fritz Lang made *Hangmen Also Die* (1943) with Bryan Donlevy and Anna Lee. MGM produced *Hitler's Madmen* (1943) with Patricia Morrison and John Carradine. *Casablanca*'s Ludwig Stossel (the German man on his way to America) had a part in this film.

Both of these films were running in U.S. theaters in 1943 at the same time as *Casablanca*.

During this time, too, Edna St. Vincent Millay wrote a poem entitled "The Murder of Lidice" which became quite popular.

Thus, when the Czech resistance leader, Victor Laszlo, appeared on the screen in *Casablanca* the movie-goers of 1943 were very much aware of his cause and thoroughly understood his need to get to America to carry on the struggle.

Reports From The Fronts

On June 5, 1942, President Roosevelt told the American people that the Japanese had used poison gas again in China. He warned the Japanese that if they didn't stop, the United States would respond in kind. This was frightening news for the people on the U.S. west coast because defenses against poison gas there were almost non-existent. Fortunately for mankind, the Japanese stopped.

In Libya, June 13, 1942, was called "Black Saturday" by the British because, in a masterful maneuver, Rommel's Afrika Corps destroyed 230 of the British 8th Army's 300 tanks. In the days that followed, the Axis troops recaptured the port city of Tobruk and then turned eastward heading for Egypt. The British had virtually nothing with which to stop them and were forced to retreat.

On June 18, Churchill arrived in Washington, DC, for talks again with Roosevelt and American military leaders. Churchill needed help in North Africa but this was not announced to the public. It was announced, though, that high on their agenda were plans for a second front. Two days later, Churchill and Roosevelt secretly agreed that the second front would be the invasion of French Morocco and Algeria in North Africa and that the city of Casablanca would be one of the first objectives captured. By landing in French North Africa, the Allies would create a giant pincers movement able to attack the Germans and Italians in North Africa from both the west and the east. Churchill was promised substantial numbers of American-made Sherman tanks which would be sent to Egypt as soon as possible to replace the British tank losses. These decisions, of course, were top secret.

As Roosevelt and Churchill talked in Washington, General Rommel's forces crossed into Egypt on June 22 and, on the 24th, took the town of Sidi Barrani. The British continued their retreat and Rommel followed them in hot pursuit. Hitler was elated and promoted Rommel to Field Marshal. On the 30th, Rommel's German and Italian forces reached the town of El Alamein, 75 miles west of the major Egyptian city of Alexandria. The British had hastily established a defense line at El Alamein. Rommel's troops attacked the British defenses there but were unable to penetrate them. British resistance had stiffened and Rommel's forces were nearing exhaustion. The fighting died down as both sides rested and brought up reinforcements and supplies.

The Egyptians were frightened though. It looked certain that Rommel's forces would soon march on to Cairo. Thousands fled to Palestine on packed trains, buses, automobiles, animal-drawn carts and on foot. And, the world had yet another mass of refugees to contend with.

On Wednesday July 1, 1942, the British Embassy in Cairo began to burn tons of secret documents, a clear sign that the British too expected to lose the city. Ashes fell all around the area and the local people called it "Ash Wednesday."

Hitler, stimulated by Rommel's success in Egypt, announced that after Egypt was conquered, German troops would march southward from Turkey, with or without Turkey's approval, into the Middle East, forming one arm of a giant pincer movement with Rommel's forces in Egypt forming the other. The objective of the offensive would be to capture the remainder of Egypt, the Suez Canal, Palestine, Transjordan, Syria, Lebanon, as well as oil-rich Iraq and Saudi Arabia.

According to Axis postwar political plans, Egypt was to become an Italian protectorate. So, Italy's dictator, Benito Mussolini, believing that this achievement was close at hand, planned a triumphant entry into Cairo for the first week in July. He had a new marshal's uniform made for himself and sent it to Libya along with his white horse. He then followed to await the fall of Cairo. After the city had been secured, he planned to ride into town on his white horse and in his new marshal's uniform at the head of a magnificent parade.

Back At Warner Bros. . . .

Character actor S. Z. Sakall was signed on June 15 to play Carl, Rick's head waiter and bookkeeper. He played his first scene on the 17th. In an early version of the script, Carl had been identified as a mathematics professor from Leipzig, but this was later dropped.

On the 25th, Paul Henreid was well enough to return to work and the film company returned to Rick's Cafe on Soundstage 8. In the days that followed, most of the scenes with Henreid were filmed, including the inspiring segment showing the singing of "La Marseillaise." Dan Seymour (Abdul) said later that about half of the extras participating in the scene were actually crying by the time it concluded.

700,000 Jews Slaughtered

On June 2, 1942, the British Broadcasting Company (BBC) announced a report from the Polish underground in Warsaw stating that 700,000 Jews had been murdered in Poland by the Nazis. This report did not make big headlines in the United States or other western nations because it was simply unbelievable. It must be remembered that the governments and civilian populations of the western nations had been subjected to a steady stream of false and exaggerated reports for years. It all began in 1935 with the war in Ethiopia. By 1942, a certain skepticism to such things had set in, especially if the reports came from far-away places and had such surprisingly large numbers. Seven hundred thousand Jews might have been relocated—but murdered? Relocating people had oc-

curred many times in the past in this and other wars and was one of the evils of war. After all, the American Government had just completed the relocation of over 100,000 ethnic Japanese. The Germans were the enemy, but they were civilized Europeans, not barbarians who would murder on such a massive scale. The barbarians in this war, people believed, were the Japanese.

Hollywood didn't believe the report either— nor the similar reports that followed. No one in Hollywood made movies during the war showing train-loads of Jews being shipped off to the gas chambers.

No, the BBC's announcement was probably just another exaggerated war report from a far away place and a not-too-reliable source.

Macht Kinder—A Baby For The Führer

While Conrad Veidt was performing his role as Major Strasser on the Warner Bros. lot, his daughter, Viola, who lived in Geneva, Switzerland, was subjected to a humiliating and very unpleasant experience. Viola was Veidt's daughter by his first marriage. Early in the war, she and her mother made it to neutral Switzerland where they lived in relative safety throughout the war. Both were on good terms with Veidt. They corresponded regularly and he sent support money for Viola.

Viola and her mother retained their German citizenship and were thus known to the German Consulate officials in Geneva. Veidt had renounced his German citizenship and had become a British citizen and this, too, was known to the German Consulate in Geneva.

Without warning, Viola, who was 18, received a summons to appear at the German Consulate. Upon arrival, she was ushered in and found herself face to face with the German Consul General himself in his impressive office. She was greeted with "Heil Hitler" to which she replied "Good Day." Moments later, a young German man entered the room, greeted her with a second "Heil Hitler" and remained standing by her chair. The Consul General then began to tell her why she was summoned. As a German citizen, he reminded her, she still had obligations to the Fatherland. And, since her father had disgraced the family name by becoming a British citizen and by performing in anti-German movies she would be given the opportunity to clear the family name and, at the same time, do a great service for Germany.

The young man standing by her chair then produced a thick dossier and handed it to the Consul General. He informed her that it was her dossier. He thumbed through it, making intimidating sounds from time to time, and glancing at Viola.

The Consul General informed her that, according to the dossier, there had been no Jews in her family for five generations and no insanity. This, and other factors, made her of pure Aryan blood. Then he got to the point, saying, "How would you like to return to the Fatherland to promote the German Master Race?"

Viola was being recruited for the "Lebensborn" (Fount of Life) program, an institution of state-run maternity homes in Germany designed to increase the population of postwar Germany by inducing willing young women, married or not, to have babies for the Führer. The Consul General went on to tell her that the young man standing beside her had been selected to father her child if she approved of him. If not, she could choose another or even opt for artificial insemination. Once she became pregnant, she would be eligible to go to a Lebensborn home in Germany where she and her baby's needs would be thoroughly met. And, if she so chose, her participation in the program would be kept secret. Once the baby arrived, she could keep it and if she stayed in Germany she would be given a small allowance. If she chose to give up the child it would be put up for adoption or raised by the State. And, she could make use of the Lebensborn program as many times as she wished.

Viola was stunned. She remained silent for a few moments not knowing what to say. When she regained her composure she blurted out, "I won't! I am not a brood sow! May I go now?" She was allowed to leave without further intimidation. Upon arriving home, she told her mother what had happened, and they both agreed that they would not tell her father because of the anguish it would cause him. According to Viola, Veidt never knew.

The studio's publicity department took special interest in the scene where Berger displays his ring bearing the Cross of Lorraine, the symbol of the Free French, to Laszlo. That ring was touted in the publicity releases for the movie as "a combination ID signet, poison cabinet and microfilm encyclopedia." It was nothing of the sort, having been made in the studio's craft shop specifically for the scene.

Jack Warner still wasn't happy with the movie's ending so on the first day of July he called the Epsteins back to work. By July 6, the Epsteins had what Wallis wanted. In a memo to Curtiz of this date, Wallis wrote, "I think we have successfully licked the big scene between Ilsa and Rick at the airport by bringing Laszlo in at the finish of it."

The next day, on July 7, filming was done at Rick's Cafe again showing Laszlo and Ilsa's arrival and Renault putting Laszlo under arrest.

On Friday, July 10, the film company moved to Van Nuys Airport, then known as Metropolitan Airport. Strasser's arrival was filmed and took a full day. The company then returned to the studio.

Back at the studio, on Saturday, July 11, filming began in Renault's office.

That same day, composer Max Steiner was assigned to write the score for *Casablanca*. As was standard practice, the score was dubbed in after filming had ended.

Steiner was, by 1942, one of Hollywood's most respected composers. He had many years of experience in scoring films, dating back to the silent movie days. His recent accomplishments had been the scoring of *Gone With the Wind* (1939) for which he composed the haunting "Tara Theme." His last work, just before starting on *Casablanca*, had been for *Now Voyager* for which he wrote "It Can't Be Wrong," currently a popular hit.

Steiner didn't like the song "As Time Goes By" and wanted to substitute one of his own, but Jack Warner nixed that idea and Steiner made the most of it.

Hollywood's Airport

By 1942, the Metropolitan Airport in Van Nuys had acquired a movie history of its own. It was built in 1928 and during the 1930s the Hollywood studios made frequent use of it for filming airplane-related scenes. It was also the airport of the stars. Movie people who were pilots in their own right or who owned airplanes utilized the field. Several of those better-known Hollywood types were Howard Hughes, Cecil B. De Mille, Hoot Gibson, Gene Autry and Wallace Beery. Amelia Earhardt set a speed record there in 1929 during an air race.

The *Casablanca* company was one of the last film companies to use the airport during the war because soon afterwards the Army Air Forces (AAF) took it over to use as a military base. It was renamed Van Nuys Army Air Field and filming for movies was no longer permitted. The AAF doubled the size of the field and built many new facilities. In 1949, the field was returned to civilian use and renamed San Fernando Valley Airport. One of the airport's original hangars, which is still in use, has been named "The Casablanca Hangar" because it was used during the filming.

Midgets?

Strangely enough, midgets and other little people were plentiful in the Los Angeles area at this time because of the war. They had been actively recruited by all the aircraft manufacturers, including those in Los Angeles, as assembly workers because they could get into tight spots inside aircraft wings and fuselages to do work that a normal-sized person couldn't do.

President Roosevelt greets two midget aircraft workers at an aircraft plant in Michigan. Midgets and other little people were very valuable and sought-after employees in the aircraft industry because they could get into tight spots inside aircraft wings and fuselages where normal-sized people couldn't go.

On Wednesday, July 15, filming began in Strasser's office, his car and in the waiting room at the jail. By this date, the movie's ending was coming together thanks to the diligent efforts of the Epsteins. The final scenes, which heretofore, were to be played out in Rick's office were moved to the Casablanca Airport. Rick's "hill of beans" speech, in which he tells Ilsa that it's all over between them and that her place is with Laszlo, had been completed.

The next day, the scenes with Bergman and Henreid in the hotel room were filmed and, on Friday, July 17, the company moved to Soundstage #1 for the film's final scenes at the Casablanca Airport.

This was a bad day. It was the 45th day of shooting and people were getting tired and short-tempered. Daytime temperatures in Burbank would reach 100 degrees Fahrenheit at times. Fortunately, Soundstage #1 was air conditioned.

Filming started at 9 a.m. and lasted until 6:14 p.m. The first problems encountered were with the script. The night before, the Epsteins had changed some of the lines and the actors hadn't had enough time to learn them or to discuss how to play them. An internal memo the next day, July 18, between Al Alleborn, Unit Manager, and T.C. Wright, Studio Production Manager relates what happened. Alleborn wrote, "They (Wallis, Curtiz and Bogart) sat around for a long time and argued, finally deciding on how to do the scene."

With time being wasted, money became a concern. Sidney Greenstreet, who was not involved in the airport scenes, was sitting around with nothing to do at the salary rate of $3,750 a week. Alleborn's memo to Wallis on July 20 tells of this problem, too, writing, "We have not been concentrating on Greenstreet, because we have been attempting to finish Claude Rains at $4,000 a week, Conrad Veidt at approximately the same figure, both of which finish in the Airport Sequence we are shooting now."

And, there was another problem, concerning the "airplane" that Ilsa and Laszlo were to board for Lisbon. It was actually an undersize cutout and it looked phony and out of proportion when a normal-sized person stood beside it. These problems were solved in one conventional and one rather unconventional way. The former, the phoniness of the plane, was taken care of by simply moving it further away from the camera and introducing a mist of fog in between. As for the size problem, several midgets were employed as extras to move around the plane and act as airport maintenance personnel.

Casablanca Dodges Censorship "Bullet"

During June 1942, the Federal Government established a new wartime agency called The Office of War Information (OWI) whose purpose was to act as a nationwide censor on all matters concerning the war. In early July, OWI set up an office in Los Angeles near Hollywood Blvd. and Vine St. to work with the motion picture industry. The new office was known as the Bureau of Motion Pictures of the OWI (BMP/OWI) and absorbed the smaller operations established under Lowell Mellett in Hollywood in December 1941.

The BMP/OWI had, almost overnight, become a powerful force in the film industry and had to be accepted by even the most powerful men in the movie industry as a necessity of the times. The BMP/OWI was given the power to censor scripts and scenes, and to issue or deny export licenses for films. The latter was a factor that could make or break a picture financially. This meant that the BMP/OWI was now a second outside force, along with the Hays Office, that could influence film content and distribution.

Politically, the BMP/OWI was strongly influenced by Vice President Henry Wallace who had very liberal views and appeared to some as being—to use the phrase of a later era—"soft on Communism." This was to come back and haunt Hollywood after World War II when the Cold War started and aggressive right-wing senators and congressmen began looking into Communist influences in Hollywood. Ironically, some of those "influences" had come from, or at least been permitted by, one of the Government's own agencies, the BMP/OWI.

The BMP/OWI established a list of six "themes" for movies, one of which a movie had to meet in order to be acceptable. Those themes were:

I. THE ISSUES. Why we fight. What kind of peace will follow victory.

II. THE ENEMY. Whom we fight. The nature of our adversary.

III. THE UNITED NATIONS AND PEOPLES. With whom we are allied in fighting. Our brothers-in-arms.

IV. WORK AND PRODUCTION. How each of us can fight. The war at home.

V. THE HOME FRONT. What we must do. What we must give up to win the fight.

VI. THE FIGHTING FORCES. The job of the fighting man at the front.

Each of the themes had sub-categories.

There was little BMP/OWI could do about movies like Casablanca which were already in production, but such movies were scrutinized anyway. *Casablanca* had no problem meeting BMP/OWI's themes. It qualified under two of them: II-C3 The Enemy, "military;" and III-B The United Nations and People, "conquered nations." There were several adverse comments from BMP/OWI, though. One concerned the character of Captain Renault. They believed that the Vichy Government was portrayed too harshly through him. It was also mentioned that Rick didn't become pro-Allied soon enough.

Nazi Censorship

In June 1933, the Nazis produced their first all-Nazi film titled *SA-Mann Brand* glorifying the exploits of the Nazi Party's paramilitary organization, the SA (*Sturm Arbeiter*, also known as the Brown Shirts). By then, the SA had thousands of members and was a very visible force in Germany. The movie—an amateurish production cast with unknowns—was written, produced and directed by individuals whose credentials were more Nazi than theatrical. A gala premiere was held in Berlin, attended mostly by the SA hierarchy. Thereafter, the German public all but ignored the movie. While it was running in Berlin, Warner Bros.' *I Am a Fugitive From a Chain Gang* (1933) was running and greatly outdrew *SA-Mann Brand*. Goebbels was very annoyed.

Scene from **SA-Mann Brand.** *A young SA man gains his mother's approval.*

Goebbels' reaction was to begin banning American-made movies. The first film banned was *The Prize-Fighter and the Lady* (1933), a story about the boxer Max Baer, a Jew; followed by *The Trial of Mary Dugan* (1933), *My Weakness* (1933), Charlie Chaplin's *The Kid* (1934), and *Tarzan and His Mate* (1935). Many other movies met the same fate. As a result of these actions, American filmmakers, including Warner Bros., closed their offices in Germany. The Warner brothers thereafter became ardent and outspoken Nazi-haters.

Foreign films not pleasing to the Nazis, or that had Jews in them, were likewise banned in Germany. This affected S. Z. Sakall (Carl). Sakall, who was Jewish. He fled Germany in 1933 where he had been popular in comedies and musicals, and returned to his native Hungary. He sought work in the Hungarian film industry but roles for him and other Jews had all but dried up because Germany was a big market for Hungarian films. Sakall stayed in Budapest for three years hoping things would change, but they didn't. In 1935, he moved to Vienna and found adequate work there.

In 1934, Paul Henreid (Laszlo), an Austrian citizen, was working successfully on the Vienna stage, when he received an offer of a good role in an upcoming German film from the German film-maker Ufa. Unaware of the extent to which the Nazis had taken over the German film industry, he traveled to Berlin to sign the contract. When he was told the conditions under which he would work, he backed out of the offer and returned to Vienna. Thereafter, Henreid was blacklisted in Germany on direct orders from Goebbels and his films banned.

In 1935, the ban-happy doctor forbade the showing of many German- and foreign-made pre-Nazi era movies that didn't live up to Nazi standards. With this, the little doctor went too far. A shortage of films developed and both the theater owners and the public began to grumble. To resolve the problem, Goebbels was forced to un-ban some films, including a few American ones.

In December 1935, Goebbels carried his demented controls further by decreeing that critics could no longer say or write negative things about films shown in Germany, films that were, of course, all pre-approved by Goebbels himself. Furthermore, the critics had their name changed. They became "Servants of the Arts." One obedient servant soon wrote, "Only the Party and the state are in a position to determine standards according to the National Socialist (Nazi) concept of culture."

Chapter Ten

Les Jeux Sont Faits– Filming Ends

O n Saturday, August 1, 1942, Bogart finished his last scene and was released from the film company. That same day, Ingrid Bergman, who was still working, got the news she had been hoping for: she had been cast as Marie, the lead role, in Paramount's forthcoming film, *For Whom The Bell Tolls* (1943). Along with the good news came the request that she be ready to leave Monday evening, August 3, for location filming in Sonora, Mexico, after her last scheduled filming day on *Casablanca*. Warner Bros. intervened, saying that they wanted to keep Bergman until Wednesday, August 5, in case any last-minute changes had to be made. Paramount agreed.

On Monday, August 3, the scenes with Ilsa and Laszlo at the Blue Parrot and the Black Market were filmed. Also that day, Curtiz filmed the refugees being herded out of the police wagon and into the police station as well as the refugees looking up at what they believed to be the Lisbon plane.

The film was quickly reviewed by Jack Warner and Hal Wallis and it was determined that Bergman was not needed so she was released. Bergman had her hair cut short for her role in *For Whom The Bell Tolls* and departed for Mexico. At this same time, Paramount put out a considerable amount of publicity on Bergman's accepting the role, going off to Mexico, and cutting her hair.

Essentially, *Casablanca* was completed. It had taken 59 filming days and was eleven days behind schedule. Production costs were $1,039,000, a modest sum in 1942, and the film ran 102 minutes.

Hal Wallis and Jack Warner were not completely satisfied, though, with the ending. It needed a better last line. Two proposals were made: "Louis, I might have known you'd mix your patriotism with a little larceny," and "Louis, I think this is the beginning of a beautiful friendship."

Short Hair Was In

Bergman had her hair cut short primarily for her upcoming role, but there was another reason for it too. With so many women taking jobs in war plants it had been discovered that long hair and spinning equipment were a dangerous combination. So, the Federal Government began a campaign to urge women war workers to cut their hair short and Hollywood was asked to deglamorize long hair to help encourage the new wartime hair style. Hollywood complied and Bergman's hair style in For *Whom The Bell Tolls* was very much in vogue.

In *Casablanca* her hair was not exceptionally long and probably would not have been objectionable. Annina's (the Bulgarian woman) and Corinna Mura's (Spanish singer) hair was longer and wouldn't have conformed to the new wartime style.

The latter was chosen and on August 21 Bogart and Rains were called back to film that scene. They are shown together walking across the air field into the mist as Rick recites the line, making for a wow finish.

The next day, Curtiz made another small addition to the movie by filming the scene in police headquarters showing the French policeman receiving news of the murdered couriers.

In the days that followed, the film was edited and the musical score composed by Max Steiner. By the third week in September it was ready for its first preview.

As *Casablanca* finished, there were six other movies being filmed on the Warner Bros. lot and some of the *Casablanca* cast members went to work on those films or had been working on them at the same time they were working in *Casablanca*. Curt Bois had a part in *Princess O'Rourke* (1943), Helmut Dantine went to work in *Edge of Darkness* (1943), Max Steiner was assigned to score both *Watch on the Rhine* (1943) and *The Adventures of Mark Twain* (1944), and Curt Bois again and Marcel Dalio had roles in *The Desert Song* (1943). None of the *Casablanca* cast worked on the sixth film, *Air Force* (1943). None of these films were based on American war victories, because (except for the Battle of Midway) there had been none.

"Well, That's The Way It Goes. One In And One Out."

This line from the movie, spoken by Rick lamenting Ugarte's demise and Ilsa's arrival, could be applied to two events that actually occurred with regards to *Casablanca*'s cast members. During the filming of the movie, Paul Andor (the man shot in the opening scenes) and Lotte Palfi (the lady selling her jewelry) were courting and later married. On the other hand, husband and wife team, Marcel Dalio and Madeleine Lebeau, filed for divorce during the filming. Their divorce was made final in June 1943. They appeared together again though in 1943 in Twentieth Century-Fox's *Paris After Dark*.

The Cast Moves On

With the ending of the filming of *Casablanca*, the film company was broken up and its members moved on. Bogart had three films lined up: two for Warner Bros. and one for Columbia. For Warner Bros. he did *Action in the North Atlantic* (1943) playing a ship's mate on a cargo ship bound for the Soviet Union that was part of a convoy in

Casablanca Provides Work For Refugees

The filming of *Casablanca* was something of a bonanza for the many real European refugees in Hollywood. Many of these people had been involved in the theater in Europe and had come to Hollywood in hopes of continuing their careers. Many of the 75 individuals who had speaking parts in the movie were refugees and dozens more refugees appeared in the film as non-speaking extras.

Of the actors given screen credits, only Bogart, Wilson, Paul Andor and Joy Page were born in the United States.

Refugees to America gave what they could to help the war effort. Here, actress Elisabeth Bergner, a recent émigrée, christens a new P-40 fighter plane at LaGuardia Airport in New York City during March 1943. Air Force General Willis Taylor looks on. Money for the plane, named "Loyalty," was raised by a 16,000-member refugee organization known as "The Loyalty Committee."

the U-boat-infested waters of the North Atlantic. He then did a cameo performance in *Thank Your Lucky Stars* (1943), a story about singer-comedian Eddy Cantor putting together a star-studded review for the boys in uniform. Bogart played himself as one of the entertainers. S. Z. Sakall (*Casablanca*'s Carl) was also in the film.

Then Bogart was loaned to Columbia Studios to do *Sahara* (1943) and promptly ran into a brick wall erected by the BMP/OWI, the movie industry's Government censor. Based in North Africa, where the real war was still raging, the plot showed how the people of French North Africa remained loyal to their democratic principles despite the fact that their leaders in Vichy—Marshal Henri Petain, Chief of State, and Pierre Laval, Premier—had been corrupted by the Nazis. In the movie, Petain and Laval were identified as themselves and appeared as unsavory characters. Since the American Government was still in the process of trying to entice the Vichy French to the Allied cause, BMP/OWI objected strongly to the negative portrayals of Petain and Laval. Columbia backed down and restructured the movie to a tale about the American commander of the tank "Lullubelle," played by Bogart, who is forced to retreat into the Sahara desert after the capture of Tobruk by Rommel's Afrika Corps. Bogart and his tank crew, a curious assortment of men of mixed nationalities, manage first to find water in the

The Hollywood Canteen

By the summer of 1942, virtually all of the *Casablanca* stars, as well as most of Hollywood's other stars, were doing their bit for the war effort by participating in the Hollywood Canteen. Bette Davis and John Garfield, both Warner Bros. contract stars, had been instrumental in starting the Canteen which was modeled after the famous Stage Door Canteen in New York City. The Hollywood Canteen was a great success and gave the lonely servicemen in the Los Angeles area an entertaining and respectable place to go during their off hours. Singers, dancers and comedians were the most sought-after celebrities because they could stand up and perform. Serious actors were given more mundane jobs but their appearance at the Canteen was nonetheless important. Ingrid Bergman was a regular when she was in town. She handed out sandwiches and cigarettes to the GIs. When Paul Henreid showed up, he was given a job bussing tables. Sidney Greenstreet (Ferrari) worked as a waiter, and beautiful young ladies, such as Joy Page (Annina) and Madeleine Lebeau (Yvonne), danced for hours on end with the soldiers, sailors and marines. S. Z. Sakall (Carl) and Helmut Dantine (Jan) were also regulars.

Both the Stage Door Canteen in New York City and the Hollywood Canteen were good public relations activities of the entertainment industry and Hollywood couldn't let these opportunities pass without blowing their own horn a bit. So, movies were made on each. Producer Sol Lesser acted first and produced *Stage Door Canteen* (1943) with a plethora of celebrities, mostly from the New York stage.

Warner Bros. followed in 1944 with *Hollywood Canteen* in which a host of Warner Bros. contract stars appeared. *Casablanca* cast members who appeared were Paul Henreid, Peter Lorre, S. Z. Sakall and Sydney Greenstreet.

desert and they are then able to snap back and successfully attack the enemy. Columbia found a well-trained group of extras to play Nazis in this film, U.S. Marines waiting to go overseas.

Paul Henreid (Laszlo) stayed on at Warner Bros. and went from *Casablanca* to play a supporting role in *Devotion*. This film, not released until 1946, was about a Yorkshire family in England during Victorian times. Sidney Greenstreet (Ferrari) also appeared in the film.

Peter Lorre (Ugarte) went to work at Universal and had a leading role in their *Invisible Agent* (1942). Lorre, Warner Bros.' ex-Japanese detective Mr. Moto, played a Japanese spy trying to steal the secret of invisibility from its inventor in order to use it for military purposes.

Conrad Veidt (Strasser) went back to MGM and co-starred in their film *Above Suspicion* (1943) in which he again played a Nazi. In this film, Veidt tries to thwart the efforts of Fred MacMurray and Joan Crawford, an Oxford University couple on their honeymoon in Germany, secretly trying to locate a missing British agent.

Dooley Wilson (Sam) got work in the all-black musical *Stormy Weather* (1943) produced by Twentieth Century-Fox and then in RKO's musical *Higher and Higher* (1943), Frank Sinatra's first starring vehicle.

The War Goes On

On the eastern front, the Axis juggernaut was once again rolling over the flat steppes of the Soviet Union. It was summer time, the time that favored the Germans. But the Soviet defenders were better organized and more experienced than they had been the year before. The result was that the Germans were paying a terrible price in lives for the territory they were conquering. On July 3, 1942, the German Army admitted as much by reporting that, up to May, 1942, 7.3 million men had been killed or wounded, or were sick or missing.

On July 12, 1942, the Soviets established what they called "The Stalingrad Front," a line of defense that would be held at all costs. The Germans were equally determined that the city of Stalingrad, on the west bank of the Volga River, would be taken and that Axis troops would capture the oil-rich Caucasus region. From now until the spring of 1943, the word "Stalingrad" and the bloody battles fought in that area would be in American newspapers and on radio news broadcasts almost daily.

Also on the newscasts and in the papers were reports from Moscow pleading with the Western Allies to open a second front in order to relieve some of the Axis military pressures in the Soviet Union. The responses from the Western leaders were positive, but not specific. In Moscow the leader's responses sounded evasive.

During the first week of July, troops of Rommel's Afrika Crops and his Italian allies made several determined, but futile, attempts to break through the British defenses at El Alamein, Egypt. In doing so, they weakened their own strength while the British forces, who were receiving a steady stream of reinforcements and supplies, grew stronger.

Cairo Also In The Movies

With Cairo and Egypt so much in the news, MGM cashed in on the situation and produced a movie named *Cairo* (1942). Robert Young played an American correspondent in Cairo who falls in love with a movie star played by Jeanette MacDonald. Unfortunately, Young's lady-love turns out to be a Nazi spy. *Casablanca*'s Dooley Wilson had a part in this movie.

Back in Libya, Mussolini saw that his triumphant entry into Cairo would not be coming as soon as he had expected. Besides, he was sick with dysentery. On July 10, he returned to Rome. On August 4, Churchill made a surprise visit to Cairo, *sans* white horse and parade, to show the world that the British leadership had faith that the city was not in immediate danger of being captured. The next day, he visited the front at El Alamein, and, with binoculars, peered into Rommel's forward positions.

On August 7, 1942, U.S. Marines landed on several islands in the Solomon Island Group. The main objective was to capture and neutralize an air field being built by the Japanese on the island of Guadalcanal from which Japanese aircraft could reach Australia and attack Allied supply lines coming from North America. The Marines gained their objective within a few days against light opposition, but the Japanese were not about to give up so easily. Tokyo decreed that Guadalcanal must be recaptured at all costs and sent in significant Army reinforcements to accomplish that task. This resulted in a bitter battle that lasted for several months. At home in the U.S.A., the word "Guadalcanal" would appear as frequently in the newspapers and on the radio as did "Stalingrad."

On July 30, 1942, General Patton left the Desert Training Center east of Los Angeles, where his troops were about to complete their training, and went to Washington, DC. There, he met with his superiors and the Army's military planners to discuss the coming invasion of French Morocco. That invasion was now called "Operation Torch" and was planned for late October or early November, or at the latest, before Congressional elections.

On August 8, General Dwight Eisenhower was named the overall commander of Operation Torch and on the 23rd, General Patton was officially named Commander of the Western Invasion Force that would invade French Morocco. An Eastern Invasion Force, comprising both British and American troops, would invade Algeria at the same time Patton's force invaded French Morocco.

On September 1, 1942, German forces entered the suburbs of Stalingrad against fierce Soviet opposition. Stalin had ordered the city defended at all costs and Hitler had ordered it taken at all costs. The result would be one of the longest and bloodiest battles of the war. On September 12, the first snow fell in the Caucasus area, portending an early winter.

On September 20, the top American and British commanders agreed that Allied landings in North Africa would be scheduled for November 8. That would be the day the city of Casablanca would blast into the news.

Exit The Bogey-Man

On Tuesday evening, September 22, 1942, *Casablanca* was previewed in the Los Angeles area for the first time. It was shown at theaters in both Huntington Park and Pasadena. Audience reactions were satisfactory but not outstanding. Julie Epstein thought the movie was a flop and wrote a memo to Wallis telling him so. Wallis saved that memo and through the years used it to his advantage.

Along with the previews, Warner Bros. issued a news release titled "Exit the Bogey-Man" telling of Bogart's transition from a movie villain to a movie lover. This too had satisfactory, but not outstanding, results. The movie magazines and gossip columnists, when they mentioned Bogart, had little interest in touting him as a lover, and preferred to zero in on the latest escapades of the "Battling Bogarts."

Other publicity on the movie followed—some of it quite bizarre and mostly untrue.

It was announced that during the filming of *Casablanca,* Bogart received a letter from a family in Sweden and Ingrid Bergman translated it for him. The letter inquired about the family's son and Bogart was later able to assure them that he was alive and well.

The patriotic Bogart, it was further reported, paid a troop of Sea Scouts to go out and collect scrap metal for the war effort.

Studio publicity directed towards women's magazines stated that Ingrid Bergman refused to appear scantily clad for pinup photos and preferred not to use makeup. It was also said of Bergman that she wore gowns of "Mediterranean Blue" so that they would reflect the beautiful blue color of the Mediterranean Sea off the white walls of Casablanca. The movie was not in color, however, so the audiences couldn't see Bergman's blue gowns and Casablanca is on the Atlantic Ocean, not the Mediterranean.

It was said of Henreid that he had adopted the two orphaned children of his late gardener. The children were in Switzerland and he was trying to get them into the United States. Furthermore, it was claimed that Henreid was helping relieve the food shortage by raising chickens.

Praise From Censors

On October 26, 1942, four members of the local BMP/OWI office were shown *Casablanca* at a private screening. They were impressed and issued a public report saying that *Casablanca* was a positive contribution to America's war effort. The report said that, because the movie commented on Rick's activities in Ethiopia and Spain, it aided "in the understanding that our war did not commence with Pearl Harbor, but that the roots of aggression reach far back." The report also commented that the movie emphasized that "personal desires must be subordinated to the task of defeating fascism...(and) graphically illustrated the chaos and misery which fascism and the war has brought." The report went on to state that the movie shows America to be "the haven of the oppressed and homeless."

Casablanca In The News

By late October, General Patton's desert-trained troops were in staging camps in the Chesapeake Bay area and practicing amphibious landings at Solomons Island, Maryland; Little Creek and Virginia Beach,Virginia; and in Chesapeake Bay, all on the Atlantic coast. Such large-scale activities, despite government censorship, were hard to conceal from the media. The mere presence of this large force and its activities gave rise to a host of rumors that they would soon depart and go into battle at some location on the other side of the Atlantic. Several locations were suggested but, because of their desert training, it seemed pretty certain to the armchair strategists in the media that the destination was North Africa and very likely the Atlantic coast of French Morocco. In this respect, the city of Casablanca became prominent in the news because it was no secret that the capture of Casablanca's fine harbor and rail connections would be a military necessity for a continued advance inland. When the troops began loading aboard troop ships in late October and sailing off over the horizon, the rumors escalated. With the mention of Casablanca in the news almost daily, eyebrows began to rise at Warner Bros.

On Friday November 6, 1942, Hal Wallis and Jack Warner met to discuss the unfolding situation concerning the rumors about French Morocco and Casablanca. Their discussion centered around what, if anything, should be done about *Casablanca*. At that time, the release date for the movie had been set for June 1943. Nothing was decided that Friday and before Warner and Wallis could discuss it again on Monday, fate intervened.

In the early morning of Sunday, November 8, 1942, American troops began landing on the Atlantic coast of French Morocco at three locations. The primary object during the first days of the invasion was, as the rumors back home had predicted, the port city of Casablanca. A direct assault on the city from the sea was militarily unwise because of the French warships in the harbor. Instead, the Army forces assigned to capturing the city landed 24 miles to the north at the resort community of Fedala where, in the movie, Strasser and the German Armistice Commission had their offices. There were a few coastal gun emplacements at Fedala but the American planners believed that their guns could be neutralized by fire from the American ships and/or by air strikes if necessary. At Fedala the beach was flat and sandy and the surf light, both factors aiding an invader.

A second American force landed at Mehdia, 75 miles north of Casablanca, and moved inland to capture a much-needed air field.

The third force landed 140 miles south of Casablanca at the port of Safie which was lightly defended and had adequate dock facilities that could be captured intact and used to off-load tanks and other large vehicles from freighters. This operation was necessary because the soon-to-become-famous LSTs (Landing Ship Tanks), that could land tanks directly onto a beach, were not yet available.

The great question in the minds of the Americans was whether or not the French would offer resistance. They did. As Vichy had announced time-and-again the French armed forces under their command were ordered to defend French territory against *any* invader.

German soldiers, members of the German Armistice Commission, are captured by American troops at Fedala on the first day of the invasion.

Fortunately, the French resistance was brief. Unfortunately, though, both Americans and Frenchmen were killed in the process.

At the Miramar Hotel in Fedala, American troops captured a group of German soldiers, the real members of the German Armistice Commission.

While American soldiers were landing in French Morocco, other American and British soldiers, having sailed from Britain, were landing at Oran and Algiers in Algeria. There, too, the French offered some brief resistance.

When the Vichy French surrendered in French Morocco to the Americans, negotiations were held in the Miramar Hotel at Fedala.

On November 10, as one of their efforts to impede American reinforcements flowing to French North Africa, a German submarine had laid ten mines in New York Harbor about five miles east of Ambrose Light. They were discovered three days later and swept up by Navy mine sweepers. New York Harbor was closed, though, for 48 hours. The mines did no damage to shipping.

Within a few days, all of the objectives of the invasion had been met, including the capture of Casablanca, which was occupied on the 11th. Many of the French officers and men in both French Morocco and Algeria began showing a willingness to join the Allied cause. Within weeks, the rest of French Morocco was occupied by American troops and the vital rail line from Casablanca westward into Algeria was secured. Strategically, this rail line was important to the Allies in that it provided an alternative route from the Atlantic Ocean to Algeria for reinforcements and military supplies in the event the Axis Powers, or Spain, attempted to close the Strait of Gibraltar. That did

The American Army Air Forces' Air Transport Command acquired facilities at Casablanca Airport as part of their worldwide air transport system and named them Cazes Air Base. Here, American personnel are seen waiting for their planes. Refugees did not normally have access to these facilities.

not occur and the main Allied supply routes continued to funnel, unimpeded, through the Strait of Gibraltar throughout the remaining months of the North African campaign.

Instead of the colorful natives and beautiful belly-dancers that American movies had led them to expect, the American GIs discovered the city was full of vultures, con artist, thieves, prostitutes, beggars, bootleggers and, yes, pickpockets.

It's a sad commentary that when the Americans came to Casablanca and French Morocco, the European refugees became worse off than before. Because French Morocco had become a war zone, concerns for refugees plummeted to the bottom of everyone's priority lists. First of all, transportation by sea, land or air out of French Morocco, and in many areas within the country, was taken over by the American military and the rejuvenated French Military, and their needs superseded all others.

The anti-Semitic decrees issued by the Vichy Government were repealed but economic conditions for refugees changed little. Furthermore, by November 1942, most nations that had accepted refugees earlier in the war were beginning to, or already had, shut their doors to additional immigrants.

A Million Dollars Worth Of Publicity

Jack Warner and Hal Wallis woke up Sunday morning, November 8, the day of the invasion, to learn that a million dollars worth of free publicity had suddenly been dumped in their laps.

The next day, the big question at Warner Bros. was, should the film now be changed to reflect the invasion? And if so, how? The executives in the New York Office were thinking the same thing. They wired their suggestions to Burbank that Rick and Renault be shown on an Allied ship before the landing in Morocco. That idea was kicked around at Burbank. It would mean a new ending to the movie, one that might not be as dynamic as the one they already had. Furthermore, it would be difficult to justify historically since Rick and Renault joined the Free French who had not been invited to participate in the invasion. By stretching the imagination, though, Rick and Renault might have been depicted as Free French liaison officers acting as observers to the invasion. The former Prefect of Police of Casablanca and a former Casablanca businessman would certainly have been good candidates for such a job.

Jack Warner was against it, though, and wired the New York Office later in the day saying,

"HAVE JUST RUN 'CASABLANCA' AND IT'S IMPOSSIBLE TO CHANGE THIS PICTURE AND MAKE SENSE WITH THE STORY WE TOLD ORIGINALLY. STORY WE WANT TO TELL OF (ALLIES) LANDING AND EVERYTHING WOULD HAVE TO BE A COMPLETE NEW PICTURE AND WOULD NOT FIT IN THE PRESENT FILM. IT'S SUCH A GREAT PICTURE AS IT IS, WOULD BE A MISREPRESENTATION IF WE WERE TO COME IN NOW WITH A SMALL TAG SCENE ABOUT AMERICAN TROOPS LANDING ETCETERA, WHICH AS I HAVE ALREADY SAID IS A COMPLETE NEW STORY IN ITSELF...ENTIRE INDUSTRY ENVIES US WITH PICTURE HAVING TITLE 'CASABLANCA' READY TO RELEASE, AND FEEL WE SHOULD TAKE ADVANTAGE OF THIS GREAT

Germans Occupy Vichy And All Of Southern France

When the Allies landed in French North Africa, German troops occupied the remainder of metropolitan France, including the city of Vichy. The Petain Government remained in the city and continued to function, but now its freedom of action was greatly curtailed. That invasion caused a new wave of French refugees to swarm into northern Spain. As a result, the Madrid Government became hard-pressed to accommodate these people as well as the refugees already in their country. Many refugees were sent to Spanish Morocco and from there, with Spanish cooperation, were nudged across the border into French Morocco. Once across the border, many of the young Frenchmen joined the French Army in North Africa with the hopes of fighting for the Allies.

As for the many other refugees in French Morocco, it would not be until well after the war that their problems were finally resolved.

Road To Morocco

Paramount had a situation similar to that at Warner Bros., a movie "in the can" entitled *Road To Morocco* with Bob Hope, Bing Crosby and Dorothy Lamour. It was a zany comedy about two Americans (Hope and Crosby) shipwrecked on the coast of Morocco who encounter a beautiful native princess (Lamour), who is betrothed to a local sheik, but falls for both of the hapless Americans one after the other.

Paramount did the prudent thing as did Warner Bros. and released their film as soon as they could.

SCOOP. NATURALLY THE LONGER WE WAIT TO RELEASE IT THE LESS IMPORTANT TITLE WILL BE..."

Even though Jack Warner had made the decision not to alter the movie, Hal Wallis still wasn't sure. He had seen things change before. On Tuesday, the 10th, he began making arrangements to shoot a scene showing Rick and Renault in Free French uniforms on the deck of an Allied freighter. An existing set of a freighter was available on Stage 7, but Claude Rains (Renault) wasn't. He was in Pennsylvania on his farm so the scene could not be filmed until he returned and would, in turn, delay the release of the film.

On Wednesday, the 11th, David O. Selznick, who held Ingrid Bergman's movie contract, saw the movie for the first time in a special preview. He too was curious about the movie and its connections to the recent events in Morocco. After viewing the movie, Selznick wired Warner Bros. and advised them not to change the film. Selznick's opinion was respected at Warner Bros. and it helped confirm the decision, already made, not to alter the film. With this, Wallis called off the scene showing Rick and Renault on the freighter.

Plans, though, went ahead full-speed to release the film as soon as possible in New York City and with as much fanfare as the studio could muster. To this end, the Fighting French representatives in American (the phrase "Fighting French" had replaced "Free French") were contacted and asked to stage a military parade in front of the theater on opening night. They readily accepted.

Another concern for speed was the possibility that the Vichy Government, so prominently mentioned in the movie, might suddenly disappear. This didn't happen.

Warner Bros.' publicity went to work and cranked out news releases, theater posters and other bits of information announcing the coming release of the movie. One of their favorite slogans became "Casablanca captured by the Allies...but Hollywood got there first."

Casablanca Premieres In NYC On Thanksgiving Day

Casablanca premiered nationally at the Hollywood Theater in New York City on Thursday, November 26, 1942—Thanksgiving Day—just 18 days after the landings. Ads for the movie announced, "The Army's got Casablanca—and so have Warner Bros."

Left front: General Auguste Nogues, French Resident-General in French Morocco and still loyal to the Vichy French Government, is seen here with General Hobart Gay, Chief of Staff to General Patton. Negotiations were underway to bring the Vichy French over to the Allied cause.

Outside, in the street, before the initial showing, Fighting French soldiers marched in formation down Fifth Avenue with flags and banners waving and a band playing patriotic songs, including "La Marseillaise." The event was sponsored, with Warner Bros.' cooperation, by two Fighting French organizations, the "France Forever" Organization and the "Fighting French Relief Committee." Inside the lobby, booths had been set up to sell Fighting French souvenirs and enlist those who wanted to join the Fighting French cause.

The pre-show fanfare was so impressive that the Office of War Information copied the Fighting French activities and had them repeated when the movie premiered in other countries.

Reviews of the movie were mixed but they were more positive than negative. Critics agreed that the timing for the movie was excellent and that the scene showing the singing of "La Marseillaise" was outstanding. It was predicted that the movie would be a box office success.

Soon after the New York premier, General Charles De Gaulle contacted Warner Bros. from his headquarters in London asking for copies of the film to show to his headquarters' personnel and in liberated French areas around the world. Warner Bros., of course, obliged and made De Gaulle's interest in the movie known to the world.

After the New York premiere, *Casablanca* was screened at a number of selected theaters around the country. This was the normal pattern for a major film at the time before its general release. Some critics quickly put it on their "10 Best" movie lists for 1942. This was a strong indicator of what was to come.

Casablanca Not Shown In Casablanca

Casablanca was not shown immediately in Casablanca nor anywhere else in liberated North Africa. Since these areas had been liberated by the American and British, De Gaulle's influence did not yet exist here; but the OWI's did, and that organization nixed the showing of the movie.

The political situation in French North Africa was very complex and tense for several weeks after the invasion because many French leaders and individuals who had taken oaths of loyalty to the Vichy Government were reluctant to break their oaths and side with the Allies. The British and American military leaders were trying to work with them in an effort to bring them over to the Allied cause and, of course, to prevent any further bloodshed.

Because of the tense political situation in French North Africa, the OWI felt that the scene where Renault threw the bottle of Vichy water into the waste basket and kicked it over would be too offensive to those still loyal to Vichy. For this reason, *Casablanca* was not released in French North Africa until later in the war.

Good News From The War Fronts

On November 22, four days before Thanksgiving, came great news from the eastern front. A massive Soviet counter-offensive had succeeded in encircling and trapping the entire German 6th Army, along with some large Romanian and Italian units, at Stalingrad. The bloody battle for Stalingrad was not over, but with this action the Soviets had definitely gained the upper hand.

At his headquarters in Germany the Führer was visibly worried. Dr. Theodor Morrell, one of Hitler's several attending physicians, wrote in his notes for November 23, "(Hitler) getting scarcely any sleep because of huge responsibility and overwork."

On the other side of the globe, the Americans were still slugging it out with the Japanese on Guadalcanal and were slowly winning the day there, too. And, on nearby New Guinea, the Japanese advance had been stopped and the Allies had taken the offensive.

In North Africa, just before the Americans and British landed in French North Africa, the British 8th Army in Egypt had gone on the offensive at El Alamein and dealt Rommel's Afrika Corps a resounding defeat. Rommel and his Italian Allies were in head-long retreat back into Libya when the Americans and British landed in French Morocco and Algeria. With American, British and some French units advancing from Algeria into Tunisia, Rommel's German forces and his Italian allies were now caught between the jaws of a giant pincers and forced to fight on two fronts. Their only hope was to consolidate their forces in Tunisia and hope to strike out again from there.

On December 2, 1942, a group of scientists, headed by Enrico Fermi and working in a make-shift laboratory on the campus of the University of Chicago, attained the first controlled nuclear chain reaction in history. This fundamental experiment in nuclear physics indicated that an atom bomb was feasible. This event was top secret and not known to the public at the time.

Throughout the rest of December, hard fighting continued in Libya, Tunisia, Guadalcanal and New Guinea, and the Allies were slowly but surely, making gains.

In the Libyan Desert, General Rommel was becoming apprehensive about his future and that of his Afrika Corps. On December 11, he wrote to his wife in German,

"I would be grateful if you would send me by secret courier a small English-German dictionary. I think I'm going to need it."

On the eastern front in the Soviet Union, six Soviet armies were battering away repeatedly at the trapped German 6th Army at Stalingrad. That army, cut off from all supplies except for a desperate, but weather-plagued air lift, was getting weaker by the day. It was only a matter of time before the Soviets would have their first major victory of the war against the mighty German juggernaut that had successfully rolled across Europe over the last three years.

On Guadalcanal, that bloody battle had been in progress now for five months with the Americans making slow but steady gains against the Japanese. In some quarters, this lengthy struggle was likened to that in the Soviet Union and Guadalcanal was referred to as "The Stalingrad of the Pacific."

On December 30, the city of Casablanca blipped into the news again because a flight of four-engine German "Condor" bombers carried out a bombing raid on the city. This was the first time Casablanca was bombed during the war. The raid did very little damage.

New Year's Day 1943, was considerably different than New Year's Day 1942. On January 1, 1942, the war news was of one Allied defeat after another. Now, by January 1, 1943, the situation had been reversed and the Allies were taking the initiative on all fronts. The mood of the American public was decidedly upbeat now. It was a good time to release a war movie in which the good guys win.

Casablanca Released—Warner Bros. Receives Another Million Dollars Of Publicity

Warner Bros. chose a January release date, in part, because *Casablanca* could then compete in the Academy Awards for 1943 and not 1942. The movie, *Mrs. Miniver* (1942), was, by December 1942, considered the front-runner for the 1942 awards and the Warner Bros. executives chose not to compete with it.

So, on Saturday January 23, 1943, *Casablanca* was released for general distribution.

And, as luck would have it, the next day the American and British Governments handed Warner Bros. *another* million dollars worth of free publicity.

The Casablanca Conference

On Sunday January 24, 1943, it was announced simultaneously in Washington and London that President Roosevelt and Prime Minister Winston Churchill were holding a summit meeting in Casablanca, French Morocco, and had been there since January 14. This news made the headlines in every newspaper in the country and was accompanied by photographs of Roosevelt, Churchill and the other participants.

In the theater sections of many of those newspapers were the advertisements for the movie *Casablanca*. And, at theaters around the country, *Casablanca* was announced in the "Coming Attractions."

Actually, Roosevelt and Churchill were not in Casablanca. They were meeting at the Anfa Hotel in Fedala where the American invasion force had come ashore in November 1942. But, the conference was known then, as later, as the "Casablanca Conference." The conference, as well as the Casablanca location, had been suggested by Roosevelt for the purpose of discussing future operations in the Mediterranean area after the Germans and Italians had been defeated in North Africa—a prospect that was becoming more likely each day.

The Germans, who still had spies in Casablanca, knew of the meeting from the beginning, January 14, and announced that fact to the world. But, American censors prevented that report from reaching the American people. For the American Secret Service agents who were assigned to protect Roosevelt and Churchill, it was a time of great tension. They knew that the Germans were aware that the conference was in progress and that Casablanca had been bombed by German planes only two weeks earlier. Fortunately, though, the Germans made no attempt to harm the participants.

At one of his news conferences in Casablanca, Roosevelt mentioned what many people believed was an off-hand remark: that the Allies would now demand "Unconditional Surrender" of all the Axis Powers. This phrase was seized upon by the reporters and spread to every corner of the globe because it indicated, for the first time, that the Allies would not consider a negotiated settlement to end World War II. By making this demand on the Axis nations, some believed the war would be prolonged by forcing the enemy to fight to the bitter end.

Despite the murmur of opposition to this demand, "Unconditional Surrender" became the confirmed war policy of the Allied Powers and was repeated frequently in official proclamations, political speeches, propaganda announcements, slogans.

Now, Should We Change The Movie?

With the news of the Casablanca Conference still hot on the wires, Warner Bros.' New York Office suggested once again that the movie *Casablanca* might be altered in some manner to reflect the Conference. The insertion, somewhere in the movie of the phrase "Unconditional Surrender," would certainly have been appropriate. But, by the time this suggestion was mulled over in Burbank, reports were coming in that ticket sales were up about 50 percent more than anticipated. So, Jack Warner made the decision again to let the movie stand as it was.

Pay Attention, People

The "Coming Attractions" previews were, during 1943, somewhat shorter than in previous years. This was because of yet another government-imposed wartime restriction on the movie industry, limiting previews to 200 feet of film. This was an effort to save film and resulted in previews being a little over two minutes screen time.

The main participants at the Casablanca Conference in January 1943. Left to right: General Henri Giraud, President Roosevelt (seated), Gen. Charles De Gaulle and Winston Churchill. President Roosevelt flew to and from the meeting on the Pan American "Clipper."

Box Office Magic

In the weeks following its release, the movie *Casablanca* more than lived up to Warner Bros.' expectations at the box office. It ran for ten weeks in the Los Angeles area alone and grossed the then-healthy sum of $225,827. In New York City, the movie broke attendance records. Across the country, many movie houses held it over for a second or third week or pulled other movies in order to show it. Some theaters went to extra expense by displaying the flag of the Fighting French, the French *tricolore* with the Cross of Lorraine on the center white panel.

Above and beyond the money aspect of the film, *Casablanca* was praised as a movie of great quality and became a serious contender for Academy Award nominations. Critics praised it and it made some of the "10 Best" lists for 1943 as it had for 1942. Viewers admitted going to see it more than once, and, in some theaters, members of the audience would stand, sing or hum along during the singing of "La Marseillaise." Audiences roared with laughter at Rick's quip to Strasser that there were sections of New York City he wouldn't advise the Germans to try to capture. And, when Strasser was killed during the final scenes, audiences cheered their approval. At its height, some 5,000 fan letters a week poured into Warner Bros. concerning the movie or its cast members.

The careers of nearly everyone in the film were enhanced. Bogart's stock rose to new heights and he remained at the top of his profession for the rest of his life. With *Casablanca*'s release, Bogart replaced Errol Flynn as Warner Bros.' top box office star.

Bergman's career received a strong boost and offers from movie producers poured in, much to the delight of David O. Selznick. The Epsteins were praised for their work and Warner Bros. up-graded them from screenwriters to producers.

Michael Curtiz, with *Casablanca* to his credit, soon rose to be Hollywood's top money-making director and became the fifth-highest paid employee at Warner Bros.

The song, "As Time Goes By," enjoyed a healthy revival and was recorded by several artists including Dooley Wilson. Sales of records and sheet music exceeded those of a decade earlier when the song was first introduced. It was so popular that it remained on the popular radio program, *Your Hit Parade*, for 21 uninterrupted weeks.

War News Improves

As *Casablanca* was being seen across the nation, news from the war fronts continued to improve. And, correspondingly, the morale of the American people continued to improve. Now, high-ranking military personnel and other influential people began speaking more confidently and more often of the final victory.

On January 23, 1943, the day *Casablanca* went into general distribution, newspaper headlines and radio news casts throughout the United States proclaimed the good news that Tripoli, the capital of the Italian colony of Libya had fallen to the British 8th Army and that Rommel's Afrika Corps and his Italian allies were fast retreating towards Tunisia.

From the eastern front, reports came, on January 25, 1943, that the encircled German 6th Army at Stalingrad had now been cut into two pockets—a sign that their end was near. And elsewhere along the eastern front, the Soviets were making major advances. For the second year in a row, the Soviets were showing that they could outfight the Germans in the cold Russian winters.

From Europe, reports were being received almost daily of Allied air raids on German and other Axis cities. Berlin, Wilhelmshaven, Hamburg, Messina, Turin, Milan, Nuremberg, Essen and Palermo were some of the targets. Clearly, the Allies were gaining mastery of the skies over Europe and in the process devastating the Axis' industrial might and transportation systems.

On January 31, the end came for the German 6th Army at Stalingrad. Out of ammunition, fuel and food, the Axis forces surrendered. Over 160,000 Axis troops had been killed and some 90,000 captured. Isolated pockets of die-hards held out until February 2.

The Axis defeat at Stalingrad was a very serious blow to Germany's military situation on the eastern front and would prove to be the turning point of the war. The powerful Soviet forces used at Stalingrad were now free to strike elsewhere and they began maneuvering quickly to take advantage of their now-superior strength.

The Nazi Government in Berlin admitted the disaster at Stalingrad and Hitler called for a national period of mourning between February 4 and 6. During this time, all theaters, opera houses, night clubs and other places of amusement were closed.

In the Solomon Islands in the South Pacific, the United States Navy and the Army Air Forces had succeeded in stopping virtually all supplies and reinforcements from reaching the Japanese forces on Guadalcanal. The American forces on the island had made a steady string of advances, often against suicidal Japanese resistance, forcing the Japanese towards the north end of the island with their backs to the sea.

The end came for the Japanese on Guadalcanal during the night of February 7-8 when Japanese destroyers pulled off a daring rescue mission under the cover of darkness and evacuated most of the Japanese troops from the island. American forces quickly jumped into the void and by the 9th all resistance had ended on Guadalcanal. In their attempt to defend the island, the Japanese had lost over 9,000 men killed and less than 100 captured. Despite the lop-sided casualty figures compared to those at Stalingrad, both Allied victories were of great significance. In both instances, the enemy had been resoundingly stopped and beaten. The victories in Libya, at Stalingrad and on Guadalcanal were clear indicators that the tide of the war had changed and that the Allies were on the offensive. It was a time for rejoicing in America—a time to celebrate and have fun—like, maybe, taking in a picture show. Business reports for the summer of 1943 indicated that movie theaters, night clubs, resorts and other places of entertainment were having a banner year. With nearly full employment and good wages being paid by war plants, people had money to spend. There was a general feeling, too, that, because of the austere conditions of the Great Depression and the current war restrictions there was a lot of "catching up" to do.

On February 4, Rommel's forces retreated into Tunisia. All of Libya was under Allied control. The Axis defenses in Tunisia, though, were still strong and there was to be three more months of hard fighting there before the Allies could claim victory in North Africa.

On February 14, the Soviets captured the important sea port of Rostov, forcing other Axis forces to withdraw from the oil-rich Caucasus area. From this point on, Germany's oil reserve began to diminish towards a point of no return.

Two days later, the Soviets re-captured the major industrial city of Kharkov and continue their westerly advance.

On February 21, American soldiers occupied two islands in the Russell Group just north of Guadalcanal—a small step closer to Tokyo. There were no Japanese on the islands. This began the long march back for the Americans in the Pacific, a process which became known as "island hopping."

In Europe, the British and Americans stepped up their air war against the Axis Powers and began "Round-the-Clock" bombing of industrial and military targets. The Americans bombed during the day and the British at night.

On March 14, the Soviets suffered a serious setback when the Germans re-captured the city of Kharkov. This prompted Joseph Stalin, the Soviet dictator, to send an angry letter to Roosevelt on the 16th demanding a real second front be opened soon in Europe by the Western Allies. Stalin rejected the so-called second front in North Africa, calling it a side-show.

During the first week in April 1943, fighting on the eastern front once again came to a stand-still due to the muddy conditions caused by the spring thaw.

Conrad Veidt (Strasser) Dies

Like the others in *Casablanca*, Conrad Veidt's career received a significant boost and he followed *Casablanca* with a co-starring role in MGM's *Above Suspicion* (1943). But, fate intervened and Veidt, at the height of his career, died suddenly April 3, 1943, in Los Angeles while playing golf. *Above Suspicion* was released 25 days later on April 28. And, of course, *Casablanca* was still playing nationwide. He was 50 years old and the first *Casablanca* member to pass away.

Casablanca: A Sequel?

In Burbank Jack Warner was watching the money roll in from *Casablanca* and basking in the critics' praise for the movie. The movie magazines and movie columnists were commenting frequently on the film and rumors of various kinds began to circulate. Warner Bros. made no effort to stop them. One such rumor was that the movie was a parody on the relationship between President Franklin Roosevelt and Prime Minister Winston Churchill. Rick was Roosevelt, who lived in a white house (*casa blanca*), and Laszlo was Churchill, a clever and sophisticated European who was trying to draw Roosevelt into the fray—and succeeded as confirmed by the fact that Rick joins the Free French at the end of the movie.

There was also talk in the media, as well as at the studio, about the possibility of a sequel for *Casablanca*. Warner Bros. encouraged this activity too. *Brazzaville* was a name tossed about for such a film both at Warner Bros.' and in the media. The studio stimulated this discussion by suggesting that Bogart and Greenstreet would be in the film along with Geraldine Fitzgerald who would play a Red Cross nurse.

Gossip columnists had it that David O. Selznick wouldn't loan Bergman to Warner Bros. again for a sequel. That too made good publicity and brought about speculation on who might play opposite Bogart.

Screenwriter Frederick Stephani, who had written the *Flash Gordon* series for Universal, came forward and proposed a sequel which is worthy of note. It began with Rick and Renault walking off into the mist, only instead of it being December 4, 1941, it was November 8, 1942, the day the Americans landed in French Morocco. The script goes on to reveal that both Rick and Renault had been working for the Allies in Casablanca as secret agents.

After Casablanca is secured by American troops, Rick gets another spy mission. He is sent to Tangier to infiltrate a Nazi spy ring which is feeding vital information about Allied shipping to German submarines stalking the waters on both sides of the Strait of Gibraltar. Tangier is in Spanish Morocco on the south shore of the Strait of Gibraltar, and in 1943 was an international city and a hotbed of wartime intrigue. Rick opens a gambling house in Tangier as cover and successfully infiltrates the spy ring. One of the Nazi spies is the beautiful Maria, who soon falls head-over-heels in love with Rick.

Then, Ilsa shows up. She's a widow. Laszlo has been killed. She has just come from Casablanca where she was informed by Renault that Rick is in Tangier. Unbeknownst to her, Renault follows.

Rick now has a dilemma. He loves Ilsa just as always, but he hasn't yet been able to get the information he needs on the spy ring. He plays along with Maria and Ilsa understands. Meanwhile, the Nazi spy-master becomes suspicious of Rick and sets a trap. Rick walks into it and is about to be shot when Maria darts in front of the spy-master's gun and takes the bullet meant for Rick. Renault surges into the room at that moment and shoots the spy-master dead. Ilsa is close behind. Maria is now dying in Rick's arms and begs him to tell her he loves her. Rick looks at Ilsa, who is crying but nods her approval. Rick tells Maria he loves her as she dies in his arms.

Warner Bros. didn't like this story and rejected it. But the public wasn't told that. The studio wanted talk of a sequel to continue.

In May, Warner Bros. announced that their forthcoming movie *The Conspirators* was being re-written to be a sequel to *Casablanca*. It was, of sorts, but without Bogart and Bergman. Paul Henreid and Hedy Lamarr played the lead roles with Sydney Greenstreet and Peter Lorre in supporting roles. Max Steiner composed the musical score. *The Conspirators* was a story about a Dutch resistance leader (Henreid) operating in Lisbon who outwits a Nazis ring there involved in an international conspiracy against the Allies. The movie, released in 1944, got so-so reviews.

Even though *The Conspirators* went into production during 1943 the studio kept alive the rumors of other *Casablanca* sequels for their publicity value. Hal Wallis, it was said, was seriously looking for a story. Eventually, talk of a sequel faded as the film completed its run. But, as time went on and the film began to be recognized as a classic, rumors of a sequel returned.

While *Casablanca* was still running in the movie houses, Warner Bros. authorized a radio adaptation of the movie to be presented on CBS. This was a fairly common practice at the time and the studio welcomed it. The radio adaptation was performed on the evening of April 26, 1943, with Bogart, Bergman and Henreid reciting abbreviated versions of their movie roles.

War News Still Good

On May 7, 1943, British troops captured Tunis, the capital of Tunisia and one of the last Axis strongholds in that country. The same day, American troops took Bizerte, another enemy stronghold. On the 9th, most of the German and Italian forces in Tunisia surrendered unconditionally to the Allies. Mopping up operations continued until May 12. Thousands of Germans were taken prisoner by the Allies, but the Afrika Corps' famous leader, General Rommel, wasn't one of them. He was too valuable a war hero for the Germans to lose so Hitler had ordered him back to Europe several weeks earlier. General Jurgen von Arnim had replaced Rommel and he took the fall. Von Arnim spent the rest of the war in an American prisoner-of-war camp in Mississippi.

On May 11, American troops landed on Attu Island, one of the two Japanese-occupied islands in the Aleutian Island Chain of Alaska. The Japanese had been expecting the invasion and were well dug in. Thus began the bloodiest battle of the war fought on the North American continent. Hard fighting on Attu's rugged terrain lasted until

May 30. The Japanese garrison, completely cut off from supplies and without hope of rescue, fought to the bitter end. The Japanese lost 2,352 men killed, the last 500 committing suicide rather than being captured by the Allies. There were 28 prisoners of war, mostly men who had been wounded. This pattern of suicidal resistance on the part of the Japanese would be repeated over and over again as American troops began advancing across the Central Pacific from island to island. On Attu, American losses were 550 killed and 1,140 wounded.

In the Soviet Union, it was the third summer of the war but this summer was different. The Axis forces which had, during the last two summers, gone on the offensive and made significant territorial gains, were now noticeably weaker and could not muster their former strength. As a result, the battles there see-sawed back and forth with neither side gaining an advantage, that is, until the Battle of Kursk.

Chapter Eleven

Here's Looking At You, Kid

Leslie Howard Killed

On June 1, 1943, a commercial aircraft of the Dutch airline, KLM, left Lisbon, Portugal, for a routine scheduled flight to London. As the plane flew over the Bay of Biscay, eight German fighter planes appeared and shot down the unarmed aircraft. All aboard perished.

The belligerents of World War II did not normally attack each other's civilian aircraft unless they suspected that they were being used surreptitiously for military purposes or that there was some important individual aboard whom the enemy sought to eliminate. Another deterrent to attacking commercial air liners was that one's own secret agents and sympathizers frequently flew aboard commercial flights.

Aboard the plane was actor Leslie Howard, who had given Humphrey Bogart his big break in Hollywood when he insisted that Bogart get the role of Duke Mantee in the movie version of Howard's hit Broadway play *The Petrified Forest*.

Needless to say, Bogart was deeply saddened when he heard the news. Years later when his daughter was born he named her Leslie after his friend.

One of those not saddened by Howard's death was Joseph Goebbels, Germany's Propaganda Minister and movie czar. In Goebbels' eyes, Howard was an enemy propagandist. Howard had made two movies that Goebbels believed were directed against the German Nazi regime. The first was *The Scarlet Pimpernel* (1934) in which Howard played a British aristocrat who rescues fellow French aristocrats from the terrors of the French Revolution. The second was *Pimpernel Smith* (1941), a sequel to *The Scarlet Pimpernel*, in which Howard not only starred, but directed. In this film, Howard portrayed a British professor of archaeology who goes to Europe to rescue refugees from the Nazis. Furthermore, Howard had just starred in and directed a patriotic wartime movie titled *The First of The Few* (1942) about the development of the famous British "Spitfire" fighter plane.

Commenting on Howard's death, Goebbels' newspaper, *Der Angriff*, headlined "Pimpernel Smith Has Made His Last Trip."

Howard's trip to Portugal had been non-political. He had spent several weeks in Portugal and Spain lecturing on various aspects of the theater.

Postwar examination of the records of the German air squadron that shot down the airliner do not reveal why the civilian plane was attacked. Speculation has it, of course, that the Germans were after Howard. But, there were others on the plane who might have been targets, or perhaps the sum-total of those individuals might have made the attack justifiable in the eyes of the Nazis.

One theory is that Howard's manager, Alfred Chenhalls, was aboard the plane. Chenhalls greatly resembled Winston Churchill and, at the time, Churchill was known by the Germans to be in Algiers, Algeria, conferring with the Allied commanders. Possibly, some overzealous spy might have spotted Chenhalls in Lisbon, mistook him for Churchill on his way home, and reported it to his superiors. For a head of state to fly on a commercial air liner in wartime was a most unusual event and it is difficult to understand how such a report could have been taken seriously.

Other individuals aboard the plane included Ivan Sharp, a member of the British Government who had been in Lisbon negotiating wolfram (tungsten ore) exports to the United Kingdom. Another person of note on the plane was T.M. Shervington, Manager of Shell Oil Company operations in Lisbon, and believed by the Germans to be a British secret agent.

There were no Axis agents or sympathizers aboard the air liner, indicating that the attack was likely premeditated.

The War Continues

During the latter half of 1943, the Allies began to enjoy one victory after another on the war fronts.

On July 5, 1943, the biggest tank battle in history erupted in the Soviet Union near the city of Kursk. Against his generals' advice, Hitler committed Germany's best units to the battle. The Soviets knew of the German plans, and, due to German delays, had adequate time to prepare defenses. The Battle of Kursk lasted seven days and proved a disaster for the Germans and a decisive factor in the future course of the war. With their best units badly mauled at Kursk, the Germans were unable to recover the initiative on the eastern front. Soviet forces began a slow but steady series of advances that eventually forced the Germans out of the Soviet Union, back through Poland and into Germany itself.

On July 10, British and American forces from North Africa invaded the Italian home island of Sicily.

Fifteen days later, Mussolini was voted out of power by his own Fascist Grand Council and arrested by King Victor Emmanuel. The king then appointed Marshal

Pietro Badoglio to take his place as head of the government. Badoglio had been one of Mussolini's most outspoken opponents and it was believed that Badoglio would take Italy out of the war at the first opportunity.

Next Stop: Marseilles?

At Warner Bros., Bogart's new film, *Passage to Marseilles*, was awaiting release, but Jack Warner was holding it up, awaiting events in the Mediterranean area. It didn't take much of a military strategist to see that after the Allied victory in North Africa, the next step would be an invasion somewhere in southern Europe. There was much speculation in the press and elsewhere that the location might be southern France with Marseilles a primary objective. Warner had hopes of pulling off another publicity coup with the *Marseilles* film, similar to *Casablanca* and the invasion of French Morocco. But alas, President Roosevelt and General Eisenhower didn't keep Col. Warner adequately informed and invaded Sicily instead. Soon afterwards, the film was released. Warner didn't know it at the time, but if he had waited until August 1944, he could have had his publicity coup because at that time Allied forces did invade southern France and Marseilles was a primary target.

Back To The War

On August 12, 1943, the Badoglio Government sent a special envoy to Madrid, Spain, in utmost secrecy to meet with the British ambassador and begin negotiations for Italy's withdrawal from the war.

In the Aleutian Island chain of Alaska, a large American force landed on the island of Kiska on August 15 only to discover that the Japanese had secretly abandoned the island several days before. No more Japanese forces remained on the North American continent.

On the 17th, the last Axis forces withdrew from Sicily, leaving the island completely in Allied hands. Secret talks with the Italians regarding their surrender had moved to Lisbon where Italian General Giuseppe Castellano was negotiating with the Allies.

On September 3, British troops landed on the tip of the Italian "boot" near Reggio and began a rapid advance northward. Later that day, Italian representatives signed an armistice agreement with the Allies at Syracuse, Sicily.

Before dawn on September 8, Allied forces began landing at Salerno on the Mediterranean coast of Italy 25 miles south of Naples. Later that day, the Badoglio Government surrendered to the Allies unconditionally and fighting between Allied and Italian force ceased at once. Italy was out of the war but the war was far from over in Italy. German troops retreating from Sicily quickly converged on Salerno to contain the Allied beachhead as other German troops moved in from the north. On September 10, they occupied Rome, and the Badoglio Government and Royal family fled to Brindisi in the Allied-controlled south. Two days later, Mussolini was rescued by the Germans in a daring raid on his place of imprisonment, a ski lodge atop the Gran Sasso. His

Fascist Government was reinstated and he established new headquarters at Gargagno on Lake Garda in northern Italy.

In late September, American forces broke out of their beachhead at Salerno and on October 1, 1943, Naples was occupied. On the 13th, the Badoglio Government declared war on Germany.

German resistance stiffened at what they called the "Gustav Line" north of Naples and the battle for Italy see-sawed back and forth, plagued by cold and rainy weather, for the next three months.

On November 6, Soviet forces re-captured Kiev, the capital of the Ukraine and the Soviet Union's third largest city.

U.S. Marines invaded the islands of Tarawa and Makin in the Gilbert Island Group on November 20, 1943. This was the beginning of the American Navy's island hopping campaign across the Central Pacific that would eventually bring American forces directly into the Japanese home islands. The battle for Tarawa was extremely bloody and lasted four days with the Japanese garrison fighting virtually to the last man.

Entertaining The Troops—Bogart Goes To Casablanca And Bergman Goes To Alaska

Back in the States, virtually every entertainer of note not already in the armed services was doing his or her bit for the war effort by entertaining the troops. Most of these activities were handled through the United Service Organization (USO), a volunteer organization designed to provide personal services, comfort and entertainment for off-duty, traveling, returning and wounded servicemen.

To this end, the USO organized overseas tours of entertainers that traveled about the various war zones and behind the lines. These tours were not without their hazards. Each entertainer and tour member traveling in a war zone was given an official uniform so that, in the event they were captured, they would be accorded the status of a prisoner of war provided by the Geneva Conventions. No USO members were ever captured, but 37 USO personnel were killed during the war and others were injured.

In December 1943, both Humphrey Bogart and Ingrid Bergman gave up Christmases at home to participate in USO overseas tours. Bogart and his actress wife, Mayo Methot, toured North Africa and Italy with two other entertainers, Don Cumming and Ralph Hark. They called themselves the "Filthy Four." Bogart did some sloppy card tricks, recited lines from *The Petrified Forest* and made fun of his tough guy image. One of his lines went, "I'll tell you what I'm really over here for—to get a new mob. The draft took all my best rod men. Anybody want to get in on the rackets?" He also boasted that his movie six-shooter, able to shoot 30 shots without reloading, was a secret weapon that would win the war. Another of his lines to the GIs was, "I'm gonna let you in on the real inside dope. You want to know where you're going next? Well, I gotta be cagey about this, but you remember I made a picture called *Casablanca*? And where did you guys go after that? Uh-huh. Well, I just finished one called *Passage to Marseilles*. Get it? Don't tell anybody."

Ingrid Bergman, second from left, and her USO troupe in Alaska, December 1943.

When Bogart met up with war correspondent Ernie Pyle and director John Huston, he supposedly fired a machine gun inside a bar and knocked himself out after jumping off a bar shouting, "Geronimo!" And, he did daily combat with Mayo.

Mayo, a singer in her own right, sang requests for the boys, including her trademark, "Embraceable You."

Their travels in North Africa took them to Casablanca, French Morocco. By then, *Casablanca* had been released there.

Their tour lasted until February 1944, and they returned home from Italy. Bogart was scheduled to make another movie, *To Have And Have Not*, with an unknown actress named Lauren Bacall.

Meanwhile, Ingrid Bergman volunteered to entertain the troops in Alaska in the dead of winter.

Bergman had been offered a tour of the South Pacific but, thinking it would be full of insects and snakes, chose Alaska, an area where few entertainers wanted to go. Bergman developed a short song and dance routine, told stories, read poetry and just mingled, talked and danced with the servicemen. She was one of five performers in the troupe. During her tour, she handed out 5,000 signed photographs. Often, the "concert hall" was an aircraft hangar and the stage the bed of a truck. The strain was telling on Bergman. She caught pneumonia and spent New Year's Eve in an Army hospital.

During her tour, Bergman befriended Lt. Gen. Simon Bolivar Buckner, the top Army commander in Alaska and there were rumors of a love affair. After she returned to the States, they corresponded. "Buck," as she called him, was later transferred to the Pacific and he wrote to her asking her to come to there to entertain the boys. She wrote

General Simon Bolivar Buckner became Ingrid Bergman's pen pal after they met in Alaska during her USO tour there. Buckner was killed on Okinawa, June 18, 1945.

back, telling him of her dislike for insects and snakes, but that she'd think about it. Their last correspondence was his letter to her dated May 2, 1945. It was written from Okinawa where the bloody battle for that island was in progress and Buckner was in command. In his letter, Buckner wrote, "When I returned to my tent this evening, muddy and wet from watching the fighting on the front, I found your very welcome letter awaiting me...we have been fighting now for more than a month on this picturesque and beautiful island with a good climate and quaint and interesting villages...Up until today we have killed 28,000 Japs but we are up against the most powerful defense yet faced in the Pacific and have to proceed carefully and methodically...I hope that the next big fight will take me to Tokyo...and I hope that the war will end in time to see you on Broadway as Joan of Arc." By that time, Bergman was preparing for Maxwell Anderson's play *Joan of Lorraine* which was to begin on Broadway in New York City for the 1946 season.

Before Bergman wrote back, "Buck" was dead, killed by a Japanese artillery shell on Okinawa on June 18, 1945.

Paul Henreid (Laszlo) made a USO tour a couple of months before Bogart went to Morocco and Bergman went to Alaska. His tour stayed in the United States and was an extravagant affair called the "Hollywood Cavalcade." Other celebrities included Fred Astaire, Lucille Ball, James Cagney, Judy Garland, Betty Hutton, Mickey Rooney, Harpo Marx, and Kay Kyser and his band.

While Bogart and Bergman were overseas, *Casablanca* made the radio again. On the evening of January 24, 1944, Alan Ladd and Hedy Lamarr played Rick and Ilsa respectively in a radio adaptation of the movie on the *Lux Radio Theater* program. Cecil B. De Mille hosted the program.

About two months after Bogart and the "Filthy Four" did their thing in Casablanca, actor John Garfield and his troupe, the "Flying Showboat" arrived there. They entertained the GIs in much the same manner as Bogart's group. Garfield said of Casablanca, "It looks like Beverly Hills, but smells bad."

Moroccan troops, shown here at their camp near Cassino, Italy in January 1944, were a part of the Allied forces trying to fight their way through the "Gustav Line." The Moroccans were brave but ruthless fighters. It is doubtful that they were entertained by Bogart's "Filthy Four."

With so many stars running around the globe on USO tours, there was something of a star shortage in Hollywood. This was aggravated by the fact that movie personnel continued to leave for military service. In early 1944, it was announced that 22 percent of Hollywood's pre-war work force was now in service.

Hard Fighting Continues

On the world's war fronts, the Allies still had the initiative, but the enemy was still strong and determined. Although the sense of victory was growing in the Allied nations, it was by no means a certainty. And men were still dying in the war at the rate of thousands per day.

The bloodiest fighting was, as usual, on the eastern front in the Soviet Union and was turning out to be a very costly battle of attrition for both sides. The American news media was full of reports of battles in places the American people never heard of: Vinnitsa, Kirovograd, Rokitno, Zhlobin, Krasnogvardeisk and Krasnoye Selo.

While Bogart and the "Filthy Four" were entertaining the troops in Italy, the American Army carried out a second amphibious landing on the Mediterranean coast of Italy at Anzio on January 22, 1944. Anzio was only 30 miles south of German-occupied Rome, but Rome was not the objective. The troops were there to outflank the "Gustav Line" north of Naples where the Germans had all but stalled the Allied advance.

In the Central Pacific, U.S. Marines and soldiers invaded Kwajalein Island in the Marshall Islands Group on January 31, 1944. Kwajalein was 750 miles north west of Tarawa and that many more miles closer to the Japanese home islands. The Japanese on the island put up another fight-to-the-death defense and it took four days of hard fighting to secure it.

On February 17, 1944, U.S. Marines and soldiers invaded yet another island in the Central Pacific: Eniwetok, 400 miles northwest of Kwajalein. The Japanese garrison there was smaller, but, like the garrison on Kwajalein, they fought to the death. Again, it took four days of hard fighting to secure that island.

In the South Pacific, American forces under General MacArthur landed on the Admiralty Islands north of New Guinea on February 29. MacArthur's objective was to recover the Philippines and threaten the Japanese home islands from the south.

Casablanca Wins Best Picture

The Academy Awards for 1943 were held in Hollywood on the evening of March 2, 1944, at Grauman's Chinese Theater with Jack Benny as master of ceremonies. Up until now, the ceremonies had been held in hotels and were closed to the public. This ceremony, though, was held in a theater for the first time and was open to the public for $10 a seat. The proceeds went to the War Relief Fund.

It had been a big year for the movie makers. Over 200 feature films had been produced to satisfy the strong public demand for quality pictures. The overwhelming theme for movies in 1943 was, of course, World War II. The war was such a multi-faceted event that there was material galore for screenwriters. Besides, since the Americans and their Allies began winning victories on the war fronts, the movie-going public wanted to see those victories portrayed on the screen. The list of war movies made in 1943 reads like a history book on the war: *Action in the North Atlantic, This Is The Army, The Cross of Lorraine, Guadalcanal Diary, Passport to Suez, Reunion in France, So Proudly We Hail, Stage Door Canteen, Bomber's Moon, Bombardier, Bataan, Air Force, Hitler's Children, Mission to Moscow, Paris After Dark, Two Tickets to London, Sahara, Watch on the Rhine, Five Graves to Cairo, Commandos Strike at Dawn, Hostages, The Immortal Sergeant, Adventure in Iraq, Aerial Gunner, Appointment in Berlin* and *I Escaped From the Gestapo.*

Even comedies had a war theme. Laurel and Hardy did their patriotic bit in MGM's *Air Raid Wardens* and Donald Duck played an overworked Nazi stooge in Disney's *Der Fuhrer's Face.* Leonid Kinskey (Rick's bartender) narrated that movie and later dubbed in the Russian for the version shown in the Soviet Union.

Serial heroes did their part too. Sherlock Holmes returned from the 19th century with his friend, Dr. Watson, in Universal's *Sherlock Holmes and the Secret Weapon.* In this story of derring do, released in January 1943, the inimitable detective keeps the Nazis from stealing the plans of a secret bombsight. *Sherlock Holmes in Washington* followed in April 1943, in which Holmes and Watson foil a Nazi gang in Washington, DC, from stealing some of America's top military secrets.

In Columbia's *The Return of the Vampire*, Dracula survives the London Blitz and searches for some unsuspecting, but tasty, victims.

The Falcon in RKO's *The Falcon Strikes Back*, finds himself framed for stealing war bonds and shooting a bank messenger but is able to track down the real culprits and clear his name.

Then, there was Republic's *The Masked Marvel*. In this film, the popular movie hero of the 1940s is hired by an insurance company to prove that a gang of Japanese spies is trying to sabotage America's war effort.

MGM's *Lassie Come Home* (1943) had been such a success that a sequel was inevitable. In *Son of Lassie,* the first of several films about this incredible collie, the dog-hero follows his master to war and helps him do in a few Nazis. Peter Lawford and June Lockhart played opposite Lassie's offspring. It would have been a sure bet that if Warner Bros.' dog star of the 1930s, Rin Tin Tin, had still been alive he, too, would have been in the fray chasing Nazis.

Not all of the movies mentioned above were contenders for Academy Awards in 1943, but there were several high quality films that were. *Casablanca* was one of them and won the day.

Tarzan, Batman and Charlie Chan

The Allies were most fortunate in having some very important secret operatives on their side, all eager to fight against America's enemies.

In 1942, America's favorite Ape Man, Tarzan, did battle with the enemy in RKO's *Tarzan Triumphs*. In it, a band of Nazis parachute into his jungle domain to look for oil and tin. With the help of Boy, a jungle princess and a band of white natives, Tarzan forms a jungle-style volunteer militia that chases some of the Nazis into the most dangerous part of the jungle where they are eaten by wild animals. The head Nazi escapes, though, but Tarzan, assisted by Cheetah the chimpanzee, catches up with him and gets him in the end.

Beginning in 1943, Columbia gave the Saturday matinee crowd 15 episodes of a serial in which Batman and Robin tangle with Japan's arch spy, Dr. Daka, played by J. Carrol Naish. In the serial, Daka has acquired a team of Caucasian criminals, traitors and other criminal-types as well as a number of not-so-willing accomplices who have been subjected to Daka's brain machine and turned into zombies. As a sideline,

the good doctor keeps alligators as pets.

As the serial unfolds, Dr. Daka and his evil band try to wreck a train carrying war supplies, steal a secret new airplane and generally thwart the Allied war effort. In the process, Batman gets thrown off a tall building, dropped through a trap door and hit by a truck. He miraculously survives these perils, and, in the last chapter, Batman and Robin are seen chasing Daka back to his secret hideout. Just as they are about to catch him, Daka falls into his alligator pit and disappears beneath the thrashing and churning water.

After the war, Columbia put the serial on video cassette but the word "Japanese" was erased and the word "Hoodlums" inserted so that they would not be offensive to Japanese viewers. By that time, Columbia was owned by the Sony Corporation, a Japanese firm.

In 1944, America's favorite Chinese detective, Charlie Chan (the Chinese were on our side), took a war job with the Government in Monogram's *Charlie Chan in the Secret Service*. In that film, Chan helps the Feds round up a gang of Axis bad guys.

The movie was voted Best Picture, the Epsteins and Howard Koch won awards for Best Screenplay and Mike Curtiz won Best Director. Humphrey Bogart, Claude Rains, Max Steiner (composer), Arthur Edeson (head cameraman) and Owen Marks (editor) all received Academy Award nominations. The movie was also a great financial success. It had cost $1,039,000 to produce, and, by the time it had concluded its first run, it had brought in $3,015,000. It was not the industry's biggest money-maker for 1943, though, ranking seventh in total revenues.

There was an unfortunate incident that evening that ended the already faltering relationship between Jack Warner and Hal Wallis. When *Casablanca* was announced as the winner of the Best Picture award, both Warner and Wallis rose from their seats to go to the stage and receive the Oscar. Warner got there first. Wallis claimed that Warner family members had blocked his way as he tried to get out of his seat and into the aisle. Wallis was enraged that he was not given the honor of receiving the Oscar. Later, Wallis asked for the Oscar and Warner wouldn't give it to him or even let him be photographed with it. The breach between Warner and Wallis was widely publicized in the press and on April 4, Warner canceled Wallis' contract on a technicality. But, the feud went on. Warner Bros. sent Wallis a bill for $7,000 for photographic equipment installed in Wallis' home over the years. And, years later, when Jack Warner wrote his autobiography, he mentioned Wallis only once and indicated that he was stupid. *Casablanca* was mentioned only once also.

After leaving Warner Bros., Wallis started his own production company, Hal Wallis Productions. Wallis became associated with Paramount and spent the next 25 years working under this arrangement, winning three more Oscars.

On the night of the Awards, though, Wallis didn't go home empty-handed. He won the Thalburg Award for consistent high quality productions during 1943.

Warner Bros. won other awards that night and walked away with a total of eight.

After winning the Academy Award for Best Picture, *Casablanca* had a short revival, but then began to fade away.

On the Monday after the Academy Awards, March 5, Bogart started his new movie at Warner Bros., *To Have And Have Not* (1945), which was based on an Ernest Hemingway novel. His leading lady was a newcomer, 19-year-old Lauren Bacall, whom he would later marry. Also in the film were *Casablanca's* Marcel Dalio (croupier) and Dan Seymour (Abdul). This was another war story set in an exotic French colonial locale, the French-owned and Vichy-controlled island of Martinique in the Caribbean. Once again, Bogart played an American expatriate fighting Nazis and the scoundrels loyal to Vichy. The film's similarity to *Casablanca* was not accidental.

More War News

Soon after the 1943 Academy Awards came the welcome news from the eastern front that Soviet forces had entered Poland. On that sector of the front, known as the Central Front, Axis forces had been pushed out of the Soviet Union. Three days later, Soviet troops on the Southern Front entered Romania.

On May 9, Soviet forces reached the easternmost frontier of Czechoslovakia and all along the eastern front Axis forces continue to retreat.

During the last days of May 1944, Allied troops in Italy penetrated the Gustav Line and broke out of the Anzio beachhead. The Germans retreated to a new defense line north of Rome and, on June 4, American forces captured that city.

Two days later, the invasion that everyone had been predicting would come, occurred. It was known then, and now, as "D-Day." The largest naval armada in history appeared off the coast of Normandy in northern France and Allied forces began streaming ashore. The heavy German defensive fire was met by equally heavy fire from Allied warships and aircraft. Allied troops were brought ashore all through the day, and, by nightfall, some 155,000 men had secured the landing beaches and, in some places, penetrated several miles inland. This was the real "second front." In the days that followed, the Allies consolidated their gains, advanced further inland, and, on June 27, captured the important sea port of Cherbourg.

Meanwhile, on June 15, U.S. Marines landed on Saipan Island in the Marianas Group in the Central Pacific. The Japanese garrison was much larger than the Americans had anticipated and the fighting was bloody and prolonged. The island was secured on July 9.

With the capture of Saipan, the Americans began building airfields from which the new super-long-range B-29 bombers could reach Japan. American strategy was to devastate Japan from the air and then to invade the Japanese homeland.

On July 20, 1944, German Army officers who hoped to take Germany out of the war attempted, but failed, to kill Hitler. Hitler's revenge was awesome. In the next few months, thousands of high-ranking German officers thought to be disloyal to Hitler were executed or arrested. Field Marshal Rommel was one of those to die.

On the 21st, American forces landed on Guam, an American possession before the Japanese occupied it in December 1941. From Guam, B-29 bombers could reach both Japan and the Philippines.

On the 27th, a very powerful American armored force broke out of the Normandy beachhead west of St. Lo, deeply penetrating the German defenses. The race for Paris was on. In the east, the Soviets were approaching Warsaw.

A very large American and French force landed on the southern coast of France on August 15. On the 16th, Marseilles was captured by the Allied forces although pockets of German troops still resisted in the city and held out for several days. That same day, Allied forces began advancing rapidly up the Rhone River Valley. They, too, were heading for Paris.

On the 23rd, Romania dropped out of the war as an Axis partner and surrendered unconditionally to the Allies. Two days later, Romania declared war on Germany.

On August 25, 1944, Paris was liberated by Allied forces.

On September 3, Brussels, the capital of Belgium, was liberated by the British and the next day Finland dropped out of the war as an Axis partner and signed an armistice with the Soviets. On the 7th, Bulgaria, under strong Soviet pressure, declared war on Germany.

American troops march down the Champs Elysées in Paris after its liberation on August 25, 1944.

On the 15th, American forces entered Germany near Aachen, and Luxembourg was liberated. The Germans, desperate for soldiers, began drafting 16-year-olds.

Every day and night, now, American and/or British bombers attacked German cities, railroads, industrial complexes and military targets. The same was being planned for Japan.

In the Pacific, American forces invaded the Philippines on October 20. American soldiers landed on the island of Leyte, south of the main island of Luzon. Three days later, the Japanese resorted to a desperate new weapon, the *kamikazes* (divine wind). These were suicide pilots who flew their bomb-laden aircraft into Allied targets, mainly warships. There were also suicide boats and mini-submarines.

About this time, B-29 bombers had begun regularly attacking targets in the Japanese home island from newly-constructed air fields on Saipan and Tinian Islands in the Marianas and from Guam. Other B-29s, flying out of fields in China and the Aleutian Islands of Alaska, were attacking targets on the Japanese home islands.

On December 16, 1944, the German Army launched a major attack against British and American forces in the Ardennes area of Luxembourg, Belgium and France. The attack succeeded in penetrating the Allied lines more than 50 miles and became known as the "Battle of the Bulge." The Allies, after a maximum effort, were able to stop the offensive, and, by early 1945, had succeeded in eliminating the bulge.

Casablanca Clones

For Hollywood, the year 1944 was pretty much like 1943. The public still wanted to see war movies and the movie studios obliged. The desert locale and Vichy French themes were still very much in evidence. Near the end of the year, though, there was a noticeable change in the public's desire to see less of the heavy war themes and more of what they had watched before the war.

Curiously enough, only one of Bogart's films, *Passage to Marseilles*, and one of Bergman's films, *Gaslight*, were released that year. Bogart did appear in a documentary produced by the National Screen Service on behalf of the Red Cross titled *Report from the Front*.

Many *Casablanca* cast members found employment in *Passage to Marseilles*, a story about several convicts who escape from France's notorious prison camp, Devil's Island, and join the Free French. Claude Rains, Peter Lorre, Sydney Greenstreet, Helmut Dantine and Corinna Mura were in the movie.

Also in 1944, Paul Henreid and Sydney Greenstreet got fourth and fifth billing respectively in Warner Bros.' World War II-related drama, *Between Two Worlds* about a number of air raid victims and two lovers who have committed suicide, all sailing on a luxury ship bound for the next world.

Then, Paul Henreid, playing opposite Ida Lupino, fought the Nazis one more time in Warner Bros.' *In Our Time (1944)*, the story of an English girl who marries a Polish count targeted for elimination by the Nazis. Howard Koch co-authored the script.

Warner Bros. put Peter Lorre and Sydney Greenstreet back in the desert again, and gave them starring roles in *The Mask of Dimitrios*, a drama about a timid Dutch novelist who finds himself caught up in a nasty intrigue in the Middle East.

The desert theme was popular with other studios, too. RKO came forth with *Action in Arabia*, starring George Sanders and Virginia Bruce who get involved in a three-way armed clash in the Damascus desert between Nazis, Vichy French and Free French. Marcel Dalio (Rick's croupier) had a part in this film.

A British-made film, *The Man From Morocco*, circulated in American movie houses with Anton Walbrook and Margaretta Scott starring as members of an international brigade who are captured by the Vichy French and sent into the Moroccan desert as forced laborers to help build a railroad for the Nazis. This film had a historical basis because the Vichy French were building a road, not a railroad, through the Moroccan desert from Algeria to Dakar on the coast of French West Africa. The Allies feared that the Vichy French would allow the Germans to use that road to supply a submarine base at Dakar and thereby more effectively threaten Allied shipping routes in the Central and Southern Atlantic. At the time of the story line in *Casablanca*, some refugees and others who ran afoul of the Vichy Government were sent to labor camps in the desert to work on the road. It was to such a camp that Victor Laszlo might have been sent if he hadn't escaped the clutches of Major Strasser and Captain Renault.

MGM offered the American movie-goers the desert theme twice in 1944, first in the musical, *Kismet*, a re-make of Warner Bros.' 1930 film of the same name in which an oriental magician becomes a wicked vizier. *Kismet* starred Ronald Coleman and Marlene Dietrich, and Joy Page (Annina) had a supporting role. MGM's second desert theme offering was a comedy, *Lost in a Harem*, with Bud Abbott and Lou Costello.

Columbia came forth with *The Desert Hawk* starring Gilbert Roland and Mona Maris as twin brothers in a desert kingdom. The bad brother tries to overthrow the good one who has inherited the throne.

The Last Year Of The War

The year 1945 began on a positive note because there was light at the end of the tunnel, indicating that this terrible war could possibly end with an Allied victory before the year was out. It did just that, but in January 1945, the Allied planners in Washington and London could see that only Germany could be defeated by the end of the year. Japan's defeat would not be completed until mid-1946—unless, of course, there were some unforeseen developments. These facts were withheld from the American public in order to keep up public morale. Meanwhile, the carnage continued.

On January 9, 1945, American troops landed on the northwest coast of Luzon, the main island in the Philippines. The ultimate objective was Manila, the capital.

On the 17th, Soviet forces captured Warsaw after a two-month-long battle both inside and outside the city that left the Polish capital and its citizenry decimated.

On the 20th, Hungary surrendered to the Allies, and, on February 13, Soviet forces captured Budapest, the capital of Hungary, after a bloody month-and-a-half long struggle that also decimated that city and its inhabitants.

In the Western Pacific, American Marines landed February 19 on Iwo Jima in the Volcano Island Group. Iwo Jima was 850 miles due south of Tokyo and the closest approach yet to the Japanese home islands. Once again, the Japanese defended the island to the last man in a bloody battle that lasted until March 26.

In the Philippines, American troops captured Manila on February 24 after several weeks of hard fighting. The Japanese defenders, in an ugly act of revenge, slaughtered thousand of innocent Filipino civilians before withdrawing.

On March 5, the German Government began drafting 15-year-olds. Two days later, American forces surged across the Rhine River on a partially destroyed but still standing railroad bridge at Remagen. The Rhine had been the last natural defense line for the Germans in western Germany. That same day, American troops captured Cologne, Germany's third largest city and the first major German city to be captured by the Allies. On the 9th, American forces captured Bonn. Three days later, Soviet spearheads reached a point on the Oder River only 50 miles east of Berlin. On the 19th, American troops took Koblenz, another major city in western Germany. On the 27th, British and American troops reached a point 200 miles west of Berlin. On the 29th, Frankfurt was occupied by the Americans. The next day, Soviet troops captured the port city of Danzig on the Baltic Sea.

On April 1, 1945, American and British troops surrounded the Ruhr Basin, the heart of Germany's industrial area. On that same day, American soldiers and Marines began the invasion of Okinawa, one of the Japanese home islands, 1,000 miles southwest of Tokyo. The Allied amphibious assault on the island was the largest yet carried out in the Pacific. The Japanese put up one of their strongest defenses ever, an indication of what the Americans might encounter when invading other home islands. The battle for Okinawa would last until June 21 and cost the Americans over 50,000 casualties. The Japanese would lose twice that number.

Also on April 1, the Japanese Government closed all schools for a year. The teachers, administrators and older students were absorbed into Japan's military and industrial labor forces.

In Germany, they began drafting 14-year-olds.

On April 4, American troops liberated the Nazi concentration camp outside Ohrdruf, the first of several they would encounter. The conditions of the camp and the cruelties imposed on the inmates were so outrageous that Gen. George Patton vomited when he saw them. Patton forced all of the residents of Ohrdruf to go through the camp and see what the Nazis had done to their victims. Ohrdruf's burgermeister and his wife returned home after seeing the camp and hanged themselves out of shame.

President Roosevelt Dies

With victory so near, President Franklin Roosevelt wasn't able to see it attained. He died suddenly of a brain hemorrhage at his cottage near Warm Springs, GA, on April 12, 1945. Vice-President Harry S Truman was sworn in later that day in Washington, DC, as America's new President.

Nazi Germany Dies

On the day after President Roosevelt died, Soviet troops occupied Vienna, Austria, after several days of hard fighting. On the 19th, U.S. troops captured Leipzig and the next day they took Nuremberg. On April 20, Hitler turned 56. The next day, Soviet troops entered the outskirts of Berlin while other Soviet forces began encircling the city. Also that day, Fighting French troops took Stuttgart, and American and Polish troops took Bologna in Italy's Po Valley.

April 1945: A Time For Dying

During April 1945, three of World War II's most important leaders died: Franklin Roosevelt (April 12), Benito Mussolini (April 29) and Adolph Hitler (April 30). Each had their mistress with them when they died.

On April 25, American and Soviet troops met for the first time at Torgau on the Elbe River. Nazi Germany was split in two. Later that day, Soviet troops completed the encirclement of Berlin. Hitler was in Berlin, deep in his bomb-proof bunker, and had vowed to remain there and fight to the end. His end came on the afternoon of April 30. With Soviet troops only yards from his bunker, he and his bride of 37 hours, Eva Braun, committed suicide.

Before he died, Hitler passed political control of Germany to Admiral Karl Doenitz who surrendered to the Allies unconditionally on May 7. The war in Europe was over. It was called V-E Day.

The Horror Of The Holocaust Reaches Into Hollywood

With the liberation of the Nazi concentration camps came the terrible realization that the reports about them received throughout the latter part of the war had not been false or exaggerated. They were all ghastly places of suffering and death.

As the Allied armies took over the camps, various military and government agencies, the Red Cross and other charitable organizations delved into camp records, interviewed inmates and camp personnel to put together a picture of what had really happened in these awful places. Then word was sent out to relatives around the world about the fates that had befallen their loved ones. Some of those reports came to Hollywood and to the people who had been a part of *Casablanca*.

Marcel Dalio (Rick's croupier) suffered, perhaps, the greatest loss. His mother and father died in the camps. Lotte Palfi (woman selling her jewelry) lost her mother and S. Z. Sakall's (Carl) wife lost a sister, a brother-in-law and a niece.

Michael Curtiz' sister and her family were sent to Auschwitz concentration camp from Hungary. She survived but her husband and their two sons did not.

Paul Henreid had no one in the camps, but he was concerned about his mother who had lived through the war in Vienna. He had been able to correspond with her occasionally through the Red Cross. Now, with Vienna in the Soviet zone of occupation, there were new concerns. Fortunately for Henreid, though, he had befriended General Mark Clark during the war and now asked him to have someone check on his mother. Clark obliged and sent a lieutenant to see her when the Americans were allowed to enter Vienna under agreement with the Soviets. The lieutenant found Frau von Henreid (the family's true name) in humble circumstances but in good health. Clark arranged for her to get to Paris aboard a military aircraft and from there, Henreid brought her to Los Angeles. She eventually went to live in South Africa with her other son, Robert.

Madeleine Lebeau (Yvonne) lost touch with her brother who had been living in Paris during the war. She eventually learned that he had been drafted by the Vichy Government and sent to Germany to do forced labor. He survived the war, however, and returned to France.

American forces discovered this train carriage filled with dead and dying concentration camp inmates. An Army doctor is seen looking for "live ones."

Another War Ends—The Bogarts' War

Humphrey and Mayo's USO trip to French Morocco and Italy in 1944 had been hard on their marriage and it was visibly in trouble. When Bogart returned to Hollywood, he began work on *To Have And Have Not* with Lauren Bacall. As Mayo had feared all along, and had falsely accused him of having done in *Casablanca*, Bogart fell in love with his leading lady. The movie was released in January 1945, and soon afterwards Humphrey and Mayo split. In April, Mayo went to Nevada for a quickie divorce. It was final on May 10, 1945, and on the 21st Humphrey and Lauren Bacall were married. The tabloids had a field day, calling them "B & B."

Warner Bros., anxious to cash in on the publicity generated by the Bogart-Bacall marriage, cast them together again in *The Big Sleep* (1946).

Bergman Goes On Another Tour

In June 1945, Ingrid Bergman returned to Europe for the first time in six years, on another USO tour. The tour group included Jack Benny, Larry Adler, Martha Tilton and others. As she did in Alaska in 1943, she performed short skits and read lines from her Broadway play *Joan of Lorraine*. The tour went to Berlin and she recorded in her notes, "The city had been blown to bits." Then, the group went on to Czechoslovakia, then Heidelberg, Germany, and eventually to Paris. While in Germany she met General Eisenhower. On one occasion, the members of her group went to see a concentration camp, but Bergman couldn't stomach it and didn't go. On another occasion, a trigger-happy American GI took at shot at their group and almost hit Larry Adler.

World War II Ends

World War II ran its bitter course in the Pacific after Germany surrendered, and, to everyone's surprise and relief, ended suddenly, and much sooner than expected, in August 1945. The Americans had secretly developed a new and terrible weapon of destruction that could obliterate a city in an instant: the atomic bomb. After the dropping of two of these terrible bombs on the Japanese cities of Hiroshima and Nagasaki, and the declaration of war on Japan by the Soviet Union, the leaders in Tokyo, realizing that they had no defense against such a weapon and such overwhelming odds, accepted America's demand for unconditional surrender. That was August, 15, 1945, V-J Day.

Celebration—Celebration—Celebration

In every city in the nation and in most of the cities of the world, the same phenomena occurred. Upon hearing the news of Japan's surrender, people stopped what they were doing and poured into the streets in an atmosphere of wild celebration. Strangers hugged, danced and kissed each other; they drank, cheered, marched, hung from light posts, splashed in the pools of public fountains, careened wildly about in taxis, buses and private cars, carried servicemen on their shoulders, blew horns and did a thousand other things of joy. This worldwide celebration was, like the war itself, a spectacle the world had never seen before.

Ingrid Bergman was in Paris that day and she and her friends were caught up in the celebration like everyone else. She rode down the Champs Elysées on the hood of a Jeep driven by photographer Robert Capa waving and shouting. When the Jeep was forced to stop because of the crowds, she jumped off and kissed the first GI she encountered.

Paris Spurns *Casablanca*

Casablanca began showing in Paris during the latter part of 1945 and it was not popular. So many of the French people still had respect for Marshal Petain and his now-defunct Vichy Government that they didn't appreciate the way he and his regime were depicted in the movie.

More War Movies

Despite the changing whims of the public, there was still a strong market for war movies in 1945. And, like everyone else, the movie makers couldn't foresee that the war would suddenly end a little over half way through the year.

Warner Bros. did one more desert-oriented film. *Escape in the Desert* co-starred Philip Dorn and *Casablanca*'s Helmut Dantine (Jan) and told the tale of an American flyer stranded in the desert of North Africa who outwits a renegade Nazi. Some compared the film to *The Petrified Forest* (1936), but with the Nazis as the bad guys.

With Bogart's leading lady from *Casablanca*, Ingrid Bergman, having dashed off to do a movie on the Spanish Civil War (1936-39), the powers at Warner Bros. though it wise to send Bogart's new leading lady, Lauren Bacall, off to the same war. Thus evolved *Confidential Agent*, starring Charles Boyer and Lauren Bacall, about one of Generalissimo Franco's closest aides, a bad guy played by Boyer, going to England in an effort to buy weapons for the Spanish Government. But, instead of weapons, he finds love in the arms of a tycoon's daughter. Peter Lorre gave another of his fine supporting roles in this film.

Bogart appeared in another Government film, *Hollywood Victory Caravan*, sponsored by the U.S. Treasury Department to sell war bonds.

With the defeat of Germany, the emphasis on war movies shifted more to the Pacific and the war with Japan.

Warner Bros.' box office attraction, Errol Flynn, was put in a film titled *Objective Burma* about the Allied effort to liberate that country from the Japanese.

The studio pulled off a major box office coup in 1945 by producing the movie version of Col. Robert Lee Scott, Jr.'s best-selling book *God is My Co-Pilot*. This was a war story about the adventures of an American air crew in the Pacific. Dennis Morgan, Dane Clark and Raymond Massey starred.

European films began to reappear on American screens again in 1945 and they too had war themes. From not-so-neutral Switzerland (that country had been accused of dealing with the Nazis) came an image-improving film titled *The Last Chance*. In this film, an Englishman and an American escape from an Italian prisoner-of-war camp in northern Italy, and, with the help of some peace-loving, pro-Allied Swiss citizens, escape safely to Switzerland.

The Italian film, *Open City*, directed by Ingrid Bergman's future lover and husband, Roberto Rosselini, made the rounds in America. It told of a band of pro-Allied Italian resistance fighters who defy the Nazis in German-occupied Rome just before that city is liberated by the Americans.

From the Soviet Union, which was still America's fighting Ally (the Cold War had not yet begun), came a documentary in English titled *Berlin* relating the bloody battle for that city between Soviet and Nazi forces during the last days of the war.

With the end of the war, there appeared a new movie theme in Hollywood, highlighting individuals who were now returning from the war and those who wouldn't return. In this latter category, United Artists came forth with *The Story of GI Joe*, the touching tale of the life and death of the much-loved war correspondent, Ernie Pyle. Pyle was killed by a Japanese sniper in the last months of the Pacific war on an island off Okinawa. Burgess Meredith played Pyle.

RKO produced *Tomorrow is Forever*, written by Lenore Coffee (a *Casablanca* writer) and starring Orson Welles and Claudette Colbert. In this film, an ex-GI thought to be dead, returns from the war with a disfigured face to learn that his wife has remarried.

Warner Bros.' *Hotel Berlin*, starring Raymond Massey, Peter Lorre and Helmut Dantine, was about a group of people in a hotel in Berlin and how their lives intertwine as the war in Europe comes to an end.

The year 1945 gave us the first atomic bomb movie. Following the dropping of the atomic bomb on Hiroshima on August 6, Twentieth Century-Fox rushed into production on *The House on 92nd Street* starring William Eythe, Lloyd Noland and Signe Hasso. It was released before the year ended and was a fictional account of how the FBI foil a gang of Nazi spies in New York City who are trying to steal the atomic bomb formula.

Hollywood's Contribution

With the end of the war, Hollywood could look back with pride on the things it did to help the war effort. In 1942, the Federal Government asked Hollywood to support the war effort with movies that met a six-theme guideline laid down by the Office of War Information. This was done willingly and on a generous scale by the movie industry. Between 1942 and 1945, some 1,700 films were produced by Hollywood and over 500 of them had war themes that met the Government's criteria.

Furthermore, hundreds of movie people, including many famous stars, served in the armed forces. Some of them gave their lives. Those who would not be returning were: Carole Lombard, Leslie Howard, Glenn Miller (band leader) and Lee Powell (the original Lone Ranger).

Chapter Twelve

Vultures, Vultures Everywhere!

The Cold War Begins

With the shooting war over, the alliance between the Western Allies and the Soviet Union quickly began to crumble. By the end of 1945, the Soviets controlled all of Eastern Europe, one-fourth of Germany, all of Mongolia and Manchuria, much of Northern China and half of Korea and they were showing signs that they meant to impose Communist regimes in all those lands. The Soviets were very slow to disarm their huge military forces, many of which remained in Eastern Europe, capable of launching attacks into Western Europe on short notice.

The situation was of grave concern to virtually every Western leader and to most of the people of the Western world. The words of Communism's founders were still remembered: that since Communism was so obviously the panacea for all mankind, it was perfectly acceptable to spread Communism by force of arms if necessary. Premier Joseph Stalin, the Soviet Union's dictator, had renounced this claim and called for peaceful co-existence, but his actions indicated otherwise.

In the West, the reaction was to stay well armed as long as the Soviets remained armed and to root out all elements of Communism within one's own borders.

Bergman's FBI File

It was in the atmosphere of the emerging Cold War that Ingrid Bergman, in December 1945, accepted an invitation to participate in a program put on by an organization known as "The American Youth for Democracy." FBI Chief, J. Edgar Hoover, had identified this group as a Communist-run organization and the successor to the prewar "Young Communists League." As a result of her participation, Bergman acquired a dossier in the FBI's files and was one of an increasing number of Hollywood celebrities believed by the FBI and others to be sympathetic to Communism. Other Hollywood personalities were acquiring FBI dossiers, too.

Popularity Of War Movies Wanes

Quite understandably, by 1946, the American public was tired of war. At the local movie houses this translated into an interest in movies without war themes. Older war films were affected, too, and re-runs of films like *Casablanca* were of little interest to the public.

This new trend was evident in the Academy Awards of March 1945, in which Ingrid Bergman won the Best Actress award for her performance in *Gaslight*. *Going My Way*, the story of a parish priest in the slums, swept most of the other awards.

The trend continued in the Academy Awards of 1946 when all but one award went to non-World War II films. The one exception was for Best Original Story to Charles D. Booth for *The House on 92nd Street*.

War movies were not dead, though. Movies with World War II themes in 1946 included Universal-International's *Paris Underground* with Constance Bennett, Gracie Fields and George Rigaud. This was a story of two women in occupied Paris involved in the resistance movement. In England, the film was named *Madame Pimpernel*, an obvious reference to the late Leslie Howard and his *Pimpernel* films.

MGM's melodrama *The Best Years of Our Lives* addressed the problems of three servicemen who returned to their home town and faced a variety of postwar problems. This film swept the 1947 Academy Awards winning Best Film, Best Actor (Frederic March), Best Director (William Wyler), Best Supporting Actor (Harold Russell) and Best Screenplay (Robert E. Sherwood).

A Night in Casablanca

Despite the decline in interest in war movies, *Casablanca* was not altogether forgotten in 1946. The Marx Brothers made a zany comedy entitled *A Night in Casablanca*. Groucho, Chico and Harpo played hotel employees in a Casablanca hotel who get into some very weird entanglements with refugees and a gang of Nazis operating out of a night club. Dan Seymour (Adbul) had a role in the film.

Jack Warner, so the story goes, took offense with the Marx Brothers' use of the word "Casablanca" and had his legal department send a letter threatening legal action. Groucho wrote back, threatening a countersuit, claiming that they had used the word "Brothers" professionally long before the Warner brothers did. The case never went to court.

During 1946, *Casablanca* was shown in Germany but, in compliance with new anti-Nazi laws, the word "Nazi" was not used.

The Postwar Years

With the end of hostilities, many of the European refugees who had sought sanctuary in Hollywood returned home. Most of them had not done well in Hollywood and hoped to revive their careers in Europe. The future did not look bright for them in Hollywood. With the decline in war movies, roles for movie Nazis and people with foreign accents diminished significantly. Curt Bois (pickpocket) was one of the first to return to Europe and was able to successfully rebuild his career. Marcel Dalio (croupier) soon followed and re-established his career in Europe.

For those who returned to Germany, a new problem arose. Many of those who had gone along with Goebbels' takeover of the German movie industry were still there and many of those who returned were Jews. Expecting these people to work together harmoniously was difficult at best.

One *Casablanca* member who did not return home was S. Z. Sakall (Carl). He loved America, had a long-term contract with Warner Bros. and was doing quite well in Hollywood. In December 1946, he and his wife became American citizens. They were so proud of their citizenship papers that they had them framed and placed over their fireplace mantel.

By now, Bogart was at the top of his profession. For 1946, he reported earnings of $432,000 to the IRS. In 1947, he signed a new 15-year contract with Warner Bros., guaranteeing him $200,000 per year with casting, script and director approval. He was allowed to form his own production company on the side. Soon afterwards, Bogart formed the Santana Corporation. That year, 1947, was a very good one for Bogart. He reported earnings of $467,361 to the IRS and was the highest paid actor in America.

Warner Bros. didn't do too badly either that year. They reported corporate earnings of $21.1 million.

Cold War films became popular and Bergman and Claude Rains appeared together in RKO's *Notorious* (1946). Directed by Alfred Hitchcock and set in Rio de Janeiro, the plot centered around a woman who marries a runaway Nazi. In the film, Rains has a stash of uranium stored in wine bottles in his cellar.

The team of Peter Lorre and Sydney Greenstreet was on a roll so Warner Bros. took advantage of it and co-starred them in two films. In the first, *Three Strangers* (1946), Lorre and Greenstreet, along with Geraldine Fitzgerald, portray three sweepstakes winners who find both fortune and tragedy in their winnings. Howard Koch co-authored the screenplay and Arthur Edeson was the chief cameraman.

The second Lorre-Greenstreet film, *The Verdict* (1946), was about a Scotland Yard inspector who, after his retirement, works on a case he was previously unable to solve. This was Lorre and Greenstreet's last film together.

Warner Bros. starred Paul Henreid in *Of Human Bondage* (1946), a remake of the 1934 film in which a rich Englishman is brought down by his infatuation with a sluttish waitress. The movie did not do well at the box office and, as a result, Warner Bros. and Henreid became mutually disenchanted with each other and Henreid's contract was terminated later that year by mutual consent. Henreid's career was in trouble. Roles for continental lovers, as he played in *Of Human Bondage*, were slowly disappearing in the fickle field of filmdom. In 1947, Henreid received more bad news when he was criticized for having joined an organization called "Committee for the First Amendment" which was accused of being a Communist front organization. Humphrey

Bogart was also a member of the organization but, for some reason, was not singled out.

On March 14, 1947, Jack Warner received the "Medal of Merit" from the War Department for his and his company's services to the war effort. Warner, no longer an Army Colonel, received the award from General Harold "Hap" Arnold, his military mentor, in a ceremony at March Field, east of Los Angeles. Warner was the first in the movie industry to receive this award.

In 1947, Ingrid Bergman's contract with David O. Selznick expired and she became a free-lance actress. She was one of the first actresses to do this and it was a gamble. During the last year of their contract, Selznick was paying her $2,000 a week for a guaranteed 40 weeks per year. Bergman's action was one of many indications that the studio system of the 1930s and 1940s was breaking down. Bergman made a prudent move because the studio system continued to deteriorate.

Murray Burnett (co-author of the play *Everybody Comes To Rick's*) found employment writing for radio programs. He was not able to use any of the material from his play or the movie because he had sold the rights to Warner Bros., but he did write along the same theme for a radio series called *Cafe Istanbul*. Marlene Dietrich was the star of the show.

The Hollywood Ten

In Washington, DC, the U.S. House of Representatives established the House Committee on Un-American Activities to investigate the extent of Communist infiltration in American society. One of the segments of society investigated was the movie industry because of the unusual influence it could exert on public opinion. Evidence that Hollywood had tried to influence American political opinion was cited in the fact that the movie industry had made several pro-Communist movies during and immediately after the war. It followed, then, that the people who wrote and produced those movies must be Communist sympathizers and that they should therefore be exposed to the public and their activities suppressed. To this end, and backed by the extensive files of the FBI, the Committee subpoenaed ten prominent Hollywood personalities whom they suspected of having Communist ties. They were: Herbert Biberman, producer-director; Edward Dmytryk, director; Adrian Scott, producer-writer; Alvah Bessie, and screenwriters Lester Cole, Ring Lardner, Jr., John Howard Lawson, Albert Maltz, Samuel Ornitz, and Dalton Trumbo.

These gentlemen were brought before the Committee in October 1947, and asked probing questions, under oath, about their political beliefs and activities. To some or all of the questions each man claimed protection under the Fifth Amendment, the right to protect oneself against incrimination, and/or their individual rights to free speech. This was highly publicized in the news media and those individuals were dubbed "The Hollywood Ten."

Back in Hollywood, many were outraged at what they perceived to be the high-handed methods used by the Committee to discredit fellow members of the industry.

Twenty-five friends and associates decided to do something about it. They chartered an airplane and flew to Washington to testify on behalf of the Hollywood Ten. Humphrey Bogart, Lauren Bacall and Paul Henreid were among them. Their arrival in Washington caused a sensation and their testimony before the Committee was covered in great detail. That testimony turned out to be a disaster. More than once, the Hollywood stars and the congressmen got into shouting matches. It was an ugly scene and it changed nothing.

Humphrey Bogart, quite understandably, got considerable attention from both critics and supporters of the Committee. Among the most ardent critics of the Committee was the Communist newspaper, *The Daily Worker*. That publication ran Bogart's picture on the front page and made glowing references to his support of the beleaguered Ten.

Information was leaked to the press that early in the war an FBI informant had identified Bogart and several other well-known Hollywood personalities as having pro-Communist leanings. The accuser was later exposed as a pathological liar, but the damage was done. This accusation had gone into the FBI's file on Bogart which, by the time he testified before the Committee, was several hundred pages thick. In this file were other derogatory comments such as those on his film *Passage to Marseilles*. This movie, according to the file, followed the Communist Party line. Another Bogart film, *Action in the North Atlantic*, had been written by John Howard Lawson, one of the Hollywood Ten. Bogart, like other prominent people, had been mentioned occasionally over the years in *The Daily Worker* and this, too, was noted in his file. The recent issue with his picture on the front page was undoubtedly added to his dossier.

The linking of Bogart's name to any form of Communist activity, true or not, was obviously detrimental to his career.

Bogart realized that he was being used as a political pawn. Once back in Hollywood, he began making public comments that his trip to Washington had been a mistake. He made additional statements of regret and eventually apologized publicly for his actions.

Paul Henreid made no apologies and came to resent Bogart's doing so. As a result, their friendship deteriorated. This was most unfortunate for Henreid because his faltering career was dealt a serious blow by his refusal to apologize for his actions in Washington.

The Committee pressed forward with its investigation and other testimony strongly indicated that all of the Hollywood Ten were, or had been, members of the Communist Party or one or more of its front organizations. This was not illegal under the laws of the day, but it was damning to the careers of the ten individuals in question. Back in Hollywood, the consensus was that it was best not to try to buck the Committee but to let the investigation run its course. After all, Hollywood's business was entertainment, not politics.

By November, it was made known publicly that Hollywood would have no more need for the services of the Hollywood Ten. The era of blacklisting in Hollywood had begun. It would continue for a decade.

Paul Henreid continued to defend his actions and he too was eventually "gray-listed" by the major studios. To make a living, he turned to producing and directing and took some supporting roles that came his way. Never again did he play a lead role in a movie.

Back in Washington, the Hollywood Ten were cited for contempt of Congress for refusing to divulge their past and present political affiliations. They were eventually tried before the Federal Court in Washington. In April 1948, all ten were found guilty and given the maximum sentence of one year in jail and fined $1,000 apiece. The Committee had won the day and Hollywood took note. After the Hollywood Ten were released from jail, they found themselves unwelcome in the movie industry. Some went abroad to work and others worked under pseudonyms.

The Committee, flush with victory, continued its investigation of Hollywood. Individual movies were scrutinized for their pro-Communist content and individuals connected with those movies were, by association, suspected of having Communist leanings. One movie raked over the coals was Warner Bros.' *Mission to Moscow* (1943). The fact that President Roosevelt had personally asked Jack Warner to make the movie was overlooked and the ax fell upon Howard Koch, author of the screenplay. Before this happened, though, Jack Warner, who was greatly embarrassed that the film would even come before the Committee, offered to send 12 employees to Washington to explain the studio's position. The Committee, nevertheless, had its way and accused Koch of having Communist leanings, in part because his FBI file showed that he had supported several left-wing causes in the past.

None of the other Warner Bros. personnel associated with the movie were condemned, but Koch's career was ruined. He eventually moved to Europe and wrote under the pseudonym of Peter Howard. Some insiders have since hinted that Jack Warner had, in some manner, influenced the Committee and allowed Koch to be thrown to the wolves in order to save himself and his stars.

Declining Fortunes

In the late 1940s, director Michael Curtiz seemed to lose his touch. He had formed a production company of his own to make films that would be distributed by Warner Bros. The overall project lost money and he and Warner Bros. became entangled in legal problems. Curtiz' association with Warner Bros. was permanently damaged. Curtiz' last really successful movie was *Mildred Pierce* (1947). After that, his films did poorly at the box office.

Peter Lorre was still getting good roles, but rumors were circulating that he, too, had extreme leftist political views. These disturbed Lorre considerably and he became disillusioned with Hollywood. In 1949, he returned to Europe where he co-wrote, directed and starred in a German movie *Der Verlorene* (The Lost One) (1951) about a good German doctor who is forced to kill for the Nazis. The movie flopped. Lorre did a film in England and then returned to Hollywood. His first employer was his old friend, Humphrey Bogart, who gave him a role in the Santana production *Beat the Devil* (1954).

Sydney Greenstreet had no particular political problems but he left the industry in 1948 after making his last film, *Malaya* (1949), a World War II story about smuggling rubber out of Malaya for the Allies, starring Spencer Tracy and James Stewart. Greenstreet was 69 and he simply wanted to retire. His health was failing. He had diabetes and Bright's Disease (a kidney disorder).

Leonid Kinskey (Sacha) became disenchanted with Hollywood in the late 1940s and left to try other endeavors. He returned, though, in the mid 1950s.

Madeleine Lebeau's career was at a standstill in Hollywood, so she went to England in 1949 and appeared in *Cage of Gold* (1950).

Ingrid Bergman, too, left Hollywood in 1949 to do work in Italy. She had a contract to do a film for the famous producer Roberto Rossellini.

The Times, They Are A Changin'

This could be the lament of the entire movie industry in the late 1940s. Television was coming on strong, the House Un-American Activities Committee was continuing its political cleansing of Hollywood and movie stars were rebelling against the studio system. Furthermore, there was new competition now for the public's entertainment dollar, such as cheap vacations, theme parks, Nevada gambling meccas and an explosion in professional sports.

To make matters worse for the movie makers, the U.S. Supreme Court, in 1948, decided that "block booking," the grouping of good films and bad films together in a take-it-or-leave-it leasing arrangement, was unconstitutional. This opened the door to smaller production companies that could get their films booked on a per film basis. The next year, the Supreme Court decided that movie studios owning movie theaters was a restraint of trade and ordered the studios to divest themselves of their theater chains.

In order to re-coup some of these losses, Warner Bros. tried their luck on television with a program titled *Warner Bros. Presents*. The format was to show old Warner Bros. movies. One of the first movies shown on the series was *Casablanca*. *Warner Bros. Presents* lasted for a while, but was then discontinued.

Casablanca Lives On

While other movies faded into obscurity, *Casablanca* continued to pop up now and then in the late 1940s and early 1950s. When Warner Bros.' *Key Largo* was released in 1948 with Bogart and Bacall it was not compared to previous Bogart and Bacall films, but to *Casablanca*.

And, *Casablanca* became one of the most popular "old movies" shown on TV.

Warner Bros. noted this happy situation and released the movie for another theater run. It made good profits this second time around and Jack Warner smiled all the way to the bank.

In 1951, Julius Epstein tried to interest investors in producing *Casablanca* on Broadway as a musical. Warner Bros. wasn't impressed with the idea and refused to grant Epstein the rights to the story. On February 7, 1952, at the age of 42, Philip Epstein died of cancer. He was the second of the *Casablanca* members to die. Conrad Veidt (Strasser) had died in 1943. From then on, Julius Epstein wrote alone.

Bergman and Rossellini

Ingrid Bergman's trip to Italy to do a film for Roberto Rossellini turned into more than a business deal. Although she was still married to Peter Lindstrom, she fell in love with her director and became pregnant with his child. When the news of the Bergman-Rossellini affair broke, it was the scandal of the decade. Newspapers across the Western world headlined "Bergman Pregnant With Another Man's Baby." This marked the end of Bergman's Hollywood career and box office receipts for her film, RKO's *Joan of Arc* (1948), plummeted.

Bergman divorced Lindstrom and married Rossellini in 1950, but professionally she was tarnished goods as far as the American public was concerned. She was denounced in America by the press, by religious groups, women's clubs and from the floor of the U.S. Senate where she was called "Hollywood's apostle of degradation" and "a free-love cultist." The film she had gone to Italy to make, *Stromboli*, was not commercially or critically successful.

She and Rossellini continued to make movies together in Europe, but they were unwelcomed in the American film market.

Bogart's Star Rises—*Casablanca* Follows

As Bergman's star crashed to earth, Bogart's continued to climb. He did film after film. Some of them were masterpieces, such as *The Treasure of Sierra Madre* (1948), *Key Largo* (1948), *The African Queen* (1951) and *The Caine Mutiny* (1954).

And, Bogart was still doing his bit for the war effort—the Cold War. In 1952, he made a movie short under MGM's guidance, encouraging citizens to buy U.S. Savings Bonds. Also that year, at the age of 53, his second child was born, a daughter he named Leslie, after Leslie Howard.

Bogart was still a favorite of the fan magazines, but now he was touted as a happy family man, expectant father (on two occasions) and a hard-working no-nonsense Hollywood star. And, occasionally, his role in *Casablanca* was referred to. No one in the early 1950s was referring to Ingrid Bergman in *Casablanca*.

His independent company was doing well, too. In 1951, Santana Corporation produced its fourth film, *Sirocco*, in which Bogart played a gun runner supplying arms to the rebels in Damascus in 1925. The comparisons in the media to *Casablanca* were abundant. Bogart and his associates had often considered the possibility of doing a remake of *Casablanca*, but it never came to pass. This did not keep Bogart from borrowing parts of *Casablanca* and pieces from his other old movies and cranking them out again in his new ones. In *The African Queen*, he was a cynical American once again in a remote part of Africa doing the righteous thing for the woman in question. This won him an Academy Award for Best Actor that year. The formula still worked. Bogart and Africa were a dynamic combination.

In Santana's second production, *Tokyo Joe* (1949), Bogart was a night club owner again and in Santana's fifth and last film, *Beat the Devil* (1955), he was one of three escaped convicts from Devils Island—a la *Passage to Marseilles* (1944). Michael Curtiz, who had directed him in *Passage to Marseilles* directed him again in *Beat the Devil*. Bogart's old friend, Peter Lorre, had a role in *Beat the Devil*. He played a villainous blond-haired German named O'Hara.

That same year, 1955, Bogart did *The Desperate Hours* for Paramount and was again one of three escaped convicts.

In 1953, Bogart dabbled again in politics and, once again, got his fingers burned. He worked for Democratic candidate Adlai Stevenson's presidential campaign. He got bad press for this effort; critics again telling him that he should stay out of politics and stick to acting. He apparently took their advice because this was his last venture into the political arena.

Also that year, Dooley Wilson died, the third cast member of the movie to die. He was 59 years old. Wilson had worked up to the end, mostly in stage plays. His last film was a western, *Passage West* (1951).

Sydney Greenstreet was the next to die, on January 19, 1954. He was 74 and had been retired for several years.

The Search For More "Pinkos"

Beginning in 1951, the House Committee on Un-American Activities launched another political cleansing campaign against Hollywood. By now, the Korean Conflict had begun and the Cold War had become more serious. There were those in high places who saw Communists and other "Pinkos" under every rock. Not only were Hollywood types targeted, the Committee investigated stage actors, novelists, newspaper columnists and even those who fought for the Loyalists in Spain. This campaign was much more intensive than the campaign of the late 1940s and lasted it for several years. Some 300 people of the arts were brought before the Committee and exposed as having some connection to Communism or at least extreme left-wing views. None of the principals in *Casablanca* were involved this time. A self-appointed vigilante group calling itself "Aware" actually drew up a blacklist condemning individuals based on the testimony brought out before the Committee. That list was circulated widely with the help of the American Legion.

In Hollywood, the movers and shakers were still kow-towing to the Committee and most of those "exposed" by the Committee found themselves out of work in tinsel town.

Casablanca On TV

The country's TV stations came to recognize the value of old movies and *Casablanca* became one of the highest rated old films on television. It was shown sometimes in prime time and, on occasion, would have a larger audience than the network programming.

In 1955, ABC Television brought back the former radio format *Warner Bros. Presents* and had old Warner Bros. films dramatized on TV. When it came to *Casablanca*, Charles McGraw played Rick Jason (Rick Blaine), Marcel Dalio (Rick's croupier) became Captain Renault, Dan Seymour (Adbul) became Ferrari, and Clarence Muse, who had screentested for the role back in 1942, played Sam. Ludwig Stossel (the German going to America) became Carl. Ilsa's role was omitted and different actresses appeared for the various episodes. The time frame for this version of *Casablanca* was post-war and the enemy was the Communist Party. *Warner Bros. Presents* lasted one season.

Warner Bros. was reaping profits from *Casablanca* once again from theater re-runs and television. The movie fit very nicely into a two-hour time slot on TV and was edited down to fit a 90-minute slot. By 1955, the studio's total profits on the movie had risen from $3,015.000, after its initial run in 1943, to $6,819,000. Because the film was shown so often, the popularity of the stars remained high—even that of Ingrid Bergman.

Bogart And Bergman Meet In Italy

In the 1950s, Italy was a popular, and inexpensive, place to make films. Bogart and his Santana Productions crew went to Italy in 1954 to do some filming for *Beat The Devil* (1954). There, he met Ingrid Bergman and her husband, Roberto Rossellini, for dinner along with other friends.

Bergman said of that evening, "He felt sorry for me because he had thought I had ruined my career by stepping away from the Hollywood scene and into Italian movies." Bergman, indeed, was into the Italian movie scene. She was busy making a film in Italy in which she was playing Joan of Arc, for the third time in her career, this time in her husband's *Joan of Arc at the Stake* (1953). *Casablanca* was the only film she and Bogart made together and was the basis for their friendship.

S. Z. Sakall Dies

In 1955, S. Z. Sakall died at age 71. Sakall was still accepting movie roles until his death. His last film was MGM's *The Student Prince* (1954). Sakall was the fifth *Casablanca* member to die.

Come Back Ingrid, All Is Forgiven

Even though Ingrid Bergman was living in self-imposed exile in Europe, she was still the subject of movie magazines and gossip columns. With time, her image improved. She and her husband, Roberto Rossellini, had established what appeared to be a stable family and she gave birth to twins, a boy and a girl. She and Rossellini were demonstrating their professionalism by consistently making quality films together for the European market. In the eyes of the Puritanical Americans, they were proving to be a responsible couple after all. But still, her only exposure to American audiences was through her old films such as *Casablanca*.

In 1955, she starred in the movie *Anastasia*, the story of the supposed survival of the youngest child of Czar Nicholas of Russia who was executed, along with his family, during the Bolshevik Revolution in Russia. The film had universal appeal and was made in England for worldwide distribution by Twentieth Century-Fox. That was a gamble for the studio. Upon release in the U.S., it proved to be very successful, but a cloud of suspicion still hovered over Bergman and she was the subject of much discussion in the media. In 1956, popular TV host Ed Sullivan conducted a poll of his viewers on their feelings about Bergman. The results were overwhelmingly in her favor and she soon returned in triumph to accept her second Academy Award for Best Actress for her role in *Anastasia*.

"Goodbye, Rick. God Bless You." (Ilsa To Rick At The Airport)

Around Christmas 1955, Humphrey Bogart experienced some coughing spells and pain in swallowing. His doctors gave him the horrible news that he had throat cancer. This was devastating because he and his wife, Lauren Bacall, had long-range plans for the future including making a movie together titled *Melville Goodman, USA*. The doctors recommended an immediate operation and advised Bogart to quit smoking and drinking. He submitted to the former, but ignored their advice on the latter. The operation revealed that the cancer had spread and the surgeons removed as much of the cancer as they could find, hoping that they had removed it all. They didn't. The coughing and painful swallowing returned. Bogart was then treated with radiation and seemed to rebound throughout most of 1956. He continued to sail on his yacht, the "Santana" and won the Ensenada Race that year. By the end of the year, though, his conditioned worsened and he didn't have the strength to sail his beloved yacht anymore, so he sold it. He soon became homebound and spent much of his time in a wheel chair. Humphrey Bogart died in his sleep at his Hollywood home on January 14, 1957. He died nine days prior to his 58th birthday and was the sixth of the *Casablanca* crew to die. His family scattered his ashes at sea.

Later that same year, Harry Warner, the oldest of the Warner brothers, died. He was 74.

The Cult Begins

Bogart didn't live to see the rise of the "Casablanca Cult." In the penetrating book, *Round Up the Usual Suspects*, Aljean Harmetz pegs its inception as April 21, 1957, the first time *Casablanca* was shown at the Brattle Theater in Cambridge, MA.

For about a year or more before that date, a new craze had been sweeping the country—the revival of old movies. In almost every major city, there sprang up one or more movie houses, known as art theaters, that began showing old movies, foreign films, avant-garde and "artsy" films. All facets of the film world were offered: western, musicals, comedies and even some of the old silent movies.

In the forefront of this artistic movement were the nation's college students, and many art theaters came into being near college campuses. The Brattle was one of them. It was located near the campus of Harvard University. When the Brattle management began showing *Casablanca*, they were very pleasantly surprised. Harvard students flocked to see it and the Brattle held it over for a second week.

The Brattle brought back *Casablanca* time and time again and attendance was always good. Soon, the Brattle management began having "Bogart Festivals." Bogart's death was, undoubtedly, a factor here. He was becoming an icon.

Then, down the street from the Brattle Theater, the Blue Parrot Cafe opened. Seeing another opportunity, the Brattle opened "Club Casablanca" in the basement of the theater.

Harvard students came time and again to see *Casablanca* and memorized some of the lines. When the lines were spoken on the screen the students would recite them aloud.

In the "Marseillaise" scene, more often than not, the entire audience would stand and sing along, substituting "da-da" for the French lyrics. This phenomenon had also occurred in 1943.

It was like this in other towns too. In New York City, some of the art theaters consistently broke attendance records when they showed the movie *Casablanca*.

At some Bogart Festivals around the country, people would come dressed in *Casablanca*-era costumes and there would be pre- and post-show *Casablanca* parties.

Movie buffs began compiling "Best Film" lists for old movies and *Casablanca* made the best ten for the years 1942 and 1943.

At the same time the art theaters were spreading across the country, the movie industry, in general, was experiencing a rejuvenation at the box office. By now, television was being referred to as "The Great Wasteland," and viewers were rediscovering the pleasures of going to an air-conditioned movie house, sitting in the dark, seeing a well-made first-run movie, eating a bag of popcorn and sharing the moment with a significan other. It was just as much fun as it used to be.

Casablanca Becomes A Classic

Webster's *New Lexicon Dictionary* defines a "classic" as something that has been "received into the accepted canons of excellence." By the late 1950s, *Casablanca* had met this standard. Virtually every educated person knew that the word "Casablanca" referred to both a city and a movie. Around the country, restaurants and night clubs with names like "Rick's Cafe Americain," "Rick's Place," Rick's Cafe" and "The Casablanca Cafe" opened. Some restaurants modeled their interiors from the Warner Bros. set.

Products and services also made use of the *Casablanca* name. The Casablanca Fan Co. offers ceiling fans, advertising agencies occasionally use clips or bits of dialogue from the film, comedians imitate Bogart (years after his death) and every now and then a Bogart Festival appears.

*Rick's Cafe Americain in
Indianapolis, Indiana.*

Sociologists, psychologists, Freudians, feminists and other lofty thinkers analyzed the movie over the years and came to fascinating conclusions about its value. Howard Koch referred to the movie as "political church" and devotees acquired the label, "Casablanquistas."

In 1957, Julius Epstein tried once again to convert *Casablanca* into a Broadway musical. But, again it didn't happen.

By the 1960s, collecting *Casablanca* memorabilia had become a hobby for many people. Posters of Bogart and the others in the movie hung on many college dormitory walls. The price for original posters and lobby cards began to take off so that only the serious collectors could afford to purchase them. All sorts of souvenir items appeared: t-shirts, cups, note books, beer mugs, etc.

Books on *Casablanca* were published, and Bogart and some of the other *Casablanca* members wrote their autobiographies. When they did, they usually devoted considerable space to the movie. Films and documentaries on *Casablanca* were narrated at times by individuals associated with the film.

Eight, Nine, Ten And Eleven

On April 10, 1962, Michael Curtiz died in Los Angeles of cancer. His age was thought to be 72 as he had quoted different ages at different times. He was the eighth *Casablanca* member to die. In his lifetime, he had directed more than 150 movies. After leaving Warner Bros. in 1954, he worked as an independent director for other studios. During those years, he directed some of the biggest names in Hollywood and made a respectable number of outstanding films. Curtiz slowed down in his later years but never really retired. His last film was a John Wayne western, *The Comancheros* (1961). Curtiz had been nominated for Academy Awards four times but won only once—for the movie *Casablanca*.

The next *Casablanca* member to die was Peter Lorre on March 23, 1964, in Los Angeles. Lorre died of a stroke. He had become considerably overweight in his latter years, suffered from high blood pressure and was said to have problems with alcohol and drugs. He had steady work, though, until his death at age 59. His last film was a Jerry Lewis comedy for Paramount, *The Patsy* (1964).

On May 30, 1967, Claude Rains died in Sandwich, NH. Like Peter Lorre, Rains had good roles offered to him until his death. His last film was Universal's *The Greatest Story Ever Told* (1965). Rains had third billing among a host of big-name stars. He played Herod the Great. Rains was nominated for Academy Awards twice (1939 and 1946), but never won. He never made a western, was rumored to be a secretive drinker, especially in his later life, and was married six times. Rains didn't like to see himself on the screen and went to very few movies. It has been said that he never saw himself in *Casablanca*.

Rains designed his own headstone and the engraving on it reads "Claude Rains 1889-1967. All Things Once, are things forever. Soul, once living, lives forever."

That same year, 1967, Abe Warner died. He was 81. Of the original four Warner brothers, only Jack remined alive in 1967.

Casablanca In The Sixties

In the 1960s, the Brattle Theater in Cambridge, Massachusetts continued to be the Mecca of the Casablanca Cult. The theater was still showing old films and their "Bogart Festival" had become an annual affair. *Casablanca* was, of course, shown at every festival. In 1964, some 15,000 people attended the event.

There were similar Bogart and *Casablanca* events elsewhere in the country. In 1965 alone, four Manhattan art theaters held Bogart revivals at which the showing of *Casablanca* became a constant. That same year, six books were published about Bogart and a scene from *Casablanca* was on the cover of each of the books.

Casablanca crept onto the American scene in dozens of little ways. In Ft. Lauderdale, Florida, a well-known Mafia boss built a mansion and named it "Casablanca South" and everybody knew what "Play it Again, Sam" referred to.

The mid-1960s was a period of internal turmoil for many Americans. The very unpopular Viet Nam War was in progress, the Cold War threatened to evolve into World War III, or perhaps a nuclear holocaust and there were racial problems in the the United States. Under this atmosphere, a movie such as *Casablanca* offered a release from the cares of the day.

In March 1965, the old Jack Warner/Hal Wallis feud surfaced again at the Academy Awards. Warner's *My Fair Lady* and Hal Wallis' *Becket* were both up for Best Picture of 1964. Both men had personally produced their respective films. History repeated itself that night and Jack Warner got the award.

In 1967, Warner Bros. was sold to Seven Arts Corporation and Jack Warner walked away with $32 million. In the years that followed, the company changed hands several more times.

With the change of ownership at Warner Bros., Julius Epstein tried for the third time to get *Casablanca* on the stage. He collaborated with composer Arthur Schwartz and lyricist Leo Robin and wrote a musical based on the movie. One scene had Rick and Sam singing a song together, and, in another, a group of refugees about to board the plane for Lisbon sing a choral arrangement about going to America, asking whether or not it is really a worthwhile place to go. Seven Arts wasn't impressed and Epstein's idea died again.

In 1967, writer-producer-actor Woody Allen brought a successful play to Broadway based on *Casablanca* titled *Play it Again Sam*. This is a phrase that had come to be associated with the film, but was not actually one of its lines. In the play, Allen plays Allen Felix, a film critic and bumbling lover whose wife has left him. He calls upon Humphrey Bogart's spirit for advice and gets it. There is much to-do about refugees and a final tongue-in-cheek scene based on *Casablanca*'s airport scene. Bogart was played by Jerry Lacy. In 1972, Allen starred in the movie version of the play for Paramount.

Casablanca In The Seventies

In 1971, Max Steiner died at the age of 83. He had retired in 1965. In his career, he had written over 300 musical scores for movies. His last film was for Warner Bros.' *Two on a Guillotine* (1965).

In 1973, *Casablanca* was on the radio again in the *Lux Radio Hour*. A lot of new dialogue was written for this program which got excellent reviews.

And, the laurels for *Casablanca* continued to pour in. In 1972, a University of Southern California poll of the most significant films in cinema history placed *Casablanca* 18th out of 53. In 1975, a poll of 1,500 film and television executives placed the movie second out of 30. By 1977, *Casablanca* was sold into syndication and soon became the most frequently seen movie on TV. That same year, the American Film Institute took a poll of the best movies ever made. *Casablanca* came in third behind *Gone With the Wind* and *Citizen Kane*. Also that year, *Casablanca* made it to Broadway in the musical review *The Bogart Years in Song*. Julius Epstein was not involved in this venture.

In 1978, screenwriter Casey Robinson died. He was 76 and had been retired for some years. His last film was *The Son of Captain Blood* (1962).

Casablanca In The Eighties

In 1980, the TV movie *The Man With Bogart's Face* appeared across the nation. Robert Sacci played Bogart. A few years later, a similar TV movie was made titled *Bogie*. Kevin O'Connor starred in that film as Bogart. In 1981, a popular song came out titled "Playing Bogart." It was a minor success.

In that same year, Jack Warner died at the age of 89. He was the last of the four original Warner brothers and the youngest of the 12 Warner children. Jack Warner outlived all of the other film moguls of his day.

On August 29 (her birthday), 1982, Ingrid Bergman died in London of cancer. She was 67. Soon after her return from Europe in 1957 her marriage to Roberto Rossellini was annulled and in 1958 she married theatrical producer Lars Schmidt but divorced him in 1975. Her career remained strong during the 1960s and 1970s. She appeared in movies, on the stage and in TV dramas both in the United States and in Europe. She won a third Academy Award, this time for Best Supporting Actress, in *Murder on the Orient Express* (1974). Four years later, she received an Academy Award nomination for Best Actress in *Autumn Sonata* (1978), a story that paralleled her own life. Soon afterward, though, she discovered that she had cancer. In 1980, she wrote her autobiography titled *My Story*. Her last movie was *A Woman Called Golda* (1982). She completed work on this movie in June 1982. Two months later she was dead.

Helmut Dantine (Jan) also died in 1982. He had returned to his native Austria and died in Vienna. His last film was Universal's *The Killer Elite* (1975) for which he was executive producer. He was 65.

As a gag, joke writer Chuck Ross, in 1982, copied the script of *Casablanca*, renamed it *Everybody Come to Rick's*, changed Sam's name to Dooley and sent it out to 217 movie agents asking if they would be interested in representing the script. Of those agents that replied, 33 recognized it as the *Casablanca* script, eight said it resembled *Casablanca*, three replied saying that they would represent the script and one of those said that they had already submitted it to a movie studio. One agent replied that it wouldn't make a good movie, but might make a good novel.

In 1983, Marcel Dalio (croupier) died on November 20 in Paris. He was 83. Dalio had returned to Europe in the 1960s, lived mostly in Paris, and continued his career there although he returned to the United States on occasions to do films in Hollywood. In 1976, he wrote his memoirs, and, in 1978, he made his last film.

In 1983, NBC Television produced a summer series titled *Casablanca*. It began in April, ran three shows, got unfavorable reviews, ran two more shows in August, got more unfavorable reviews and was then canceled. Part of the original set of Rick's cafe had miraculously survived and a lot of people, some of whom had worked on the original movie, went to the NBC studio just to take a look at it.

In the NBC series, David Soul played Rick, Hector Elisondo was Renault, Scatman Crothers was Sam and Ray Liotta was Sacha. The time frame for the TV series was changed from December 1941, to June 1940, (the fall of France and the arrival of Rick in Casablanca) through November 1941, (just prior to Ilsa's arrival in Casablanca). David Soul's marriage, like that of Bogart and Mayo's in 1942, was in serious trouble during the filming of the series, and Soul was drinking heavily. The Souls eventually divorced.

That same year, 1983, *Casablanca* received another laurel when the British film Institute voted it the best film ever made.

Bogey's Buick. This 1940 Buick Limited four-door convertible phaeton was used in the airport scene in the movie **Casablanca.** *It has had several owners and is a highly valued collector's car today.*

Hal Wallis was the next *Casablanca* member to pass away. He died in 1986 at the age of 86. Wallis retired in 1975 and was awarded an honorary Doctor of Philosophy from his home-town university, Northwestern University, in Evanston (Chicago), IL, and the Order of Commander of the British Empire from the British Government.

The 1940 Buick Limited phaeton model 81C that Bogart and the others took to the Casablanca Airport in the closing scenes of the movie had become a cherished collector's item by the 1980s. The automobile was used by Warner Bros. until 1970 and was in over 50 movies. In the studio's fleet of cars it was simply known as #325. The car was sold that year to musician Lyle Ritz for $3,457, a respectable collector's car price for that time. Sixteen years later, though, it was put on the auction block for $33,000. Its original price in 1940 was approximately $2,000. There were only 230 of these cars made and this was the only one with a cloth upholstery. In the upholstery are cigarette burns said to have been made by Bogart. Its original color was Aztec Brown with a beige top.

Twenty of these cars were exported in 1940 thus making the scene in *Casablanca* historically accurate. One of the exported cars could have gone to Casablanca, French Morocco—at least in the realm of movie fiction.

Maintenance records showed that in 1955 the 15-year-old car had only 4,310 miles on it. When it was sold at auction it had over 40,000.

The Lockheed 12A Electra airplane used in the movie's airport scene as the "plane to Lisbon" wasn't so lucky. After its life as a small transport plane it was converted into a lowly crop duster. In 1987, it was discovered and purchased by Disney World at Orlando, FL, restored and made a part of their Great Movie Rides attraction.

In the late 1980s, Turner Entertainment Corporation bought the rights to *Casablanca* and other old Warner Bros. movies. *Casablanca* was colorized and made its color debut November 9, 1988, on Turner's TBS Superstation, angering many film purists. In 1989, the video of *Casablanca* was put on the market and is, today, available in color or in black and white. Through the years, it has consistently been one of the most popular movie videos sold.

In 1988, Congress expanded the national treasures program and created the National Film Registry for the preservation of "culturally, historically and aesthetically significant" films. In September 1989, the first 25 films were selected. *Casablanca* was one of them. Another Bogart film, *The Maltese Falcon*, was also one of the 25.

That year, another poll was taken among 22 of the world's top movie critics on the all-time popularity of famous movies. They ranked *Casablanca* ninth out of the 100 listed.

At the Oakland Airport in Oakland, CA, "The Casablanca Aviation Company" went into business offering airplane rides in World War II vintage aircraft. One of the main events was a *Casablanca* dinner flight around the Bay area in a converted World War II DC-3 transport plane.

In 1988, another relic from the movie went across the auction block. It was Sam's piano. It was sold by Sotheby's Auction House for $154,000 to C. Itoh & Co., a Japanese firm.

And still they speak of a sequel.

In 1988, Howard Koch, one of the movie's original screenwriters, proposed a sequel in which Rick's illegitimate son by Ilsa returns to Casablanca to find out what happened to his father. This idea was still-born.

In the absence of an authorized sequel, there are those who persist in comparing other movies to *Casablanca*. That was the case for Warner Bros.' *Tequila Sunrise* (1988), about an ex-drug dealer who is offered one more major drug deal and has to compete with his friend for the affection of the film's leading lady. Mel Gibson and Michelle Pfeiffer starred.

Then, in 1990, Universal's *Havana* was, likewise, compared to *Casablanca*. *Havana* was the story of an American gambler who becomes involved in Cuban politics during the last days of the Batista (pre-Castro) Regime. Robert Redford and Lena Olin starred.

Casablanca In The Nineties

In 1990, another big business deal went down in Hollywood and it had a *Casablanca* connection: the purchase of Warner Bros. by the Sony Corporation, owners of Columbia Studios. To celebrate their acquisition, the new owners painted "Warner Bros." again on the water tower of the old Burbank Studio and then held a large party on Stage 8 where the scenes in Rick's Cafe were filmed. For the party, the set of Rick's Cafe was reconstructed. Both the Henry Mancini Orchestra and Quincy Jones were hired to play music and, of course, they both played their versions of "As Time Goes

By." Waiters in fezes served drinks to the thousand-plus guests who attended, many of them Hollywood's top stars. The party cost $4.5 million—$1.5 million more than the movie *Casablanca* cost to produce in 1942.

In 1991, *Casablanca*'s real-life lovers, Paul Andor (the man shot in the opening scenes) and Lotte Palfi (the woman selling her jewelry) both died. It will be remembered that they were courting during the making of *Casablanca* and later married.

After *Casablanca*, Andor and Palfi pursued theatrical careers with modest success. They lived in New York City, working in plays and television. After retirement, Andor developed Parkinson's Disease and longed to go back to Germany to die. Palfi, who wasn't in the best of health herself, didn't want to go, so they had an amicable divorce. Andor later married his nurse and Palfi attended the wedding. In 1991, Andor died in Berlin at the age of 90. Two weeks later, Palfi died in New York city at the age of 88.

Curt Bois (pickpocket) died in 1991 on Christmas Day. Bois returned to Germany in the early 1950s and eventually moved to Communist-controlled East Germany. By doing so, he lost his U.S. citizenship. He died in East Berlin at the age of 90.

In 1991, 80-year-old Murray Burnett (co-author of the play *Everybody Comes to Rick's*) had a dream come true. He saw his play finally produced on the stage in London. After acquiring Warner Bros.' permission, he re-wrote the original three-act play into two acts and re-named it *Rick's Bar Casablanca*. British actor Leslie Grantham was Rick and American actress Shelley Thompson was Lois Meredith. Unfortunately, the reviews were not good and the play ran for only a month. Burnett died in Sepetember 1997 at the age of 87.

The year 1992 marked the 50th anniversary of the making of *Casablanca*. To celebrate that event, the film's current owner, Turner Entertainment Corp., threw a lavish party at the Museum of Modern Art in New York City. In attendance were the King of Morocco and Bogart's son, novelist Stephen Bogart.

And, the prices of *Casablanca* memorabilia kept going up. A postcard with one of Bogart's chess moves mailed to a pal in the 1940s sold for $1,750. Original *Casablanca* theater posters were going for between $3,000 and $12,000 each. Reprints cost about $10.

The year 1992 also saw the demise of Paul Henreid. Henreid died in Santa Monica, California, on March 29, 1992, of pneumonia following a stroke. He was 84.

Howard Koch died on August 17, 1995, of pneumonia in Kingston, NY. After returning from his self-imposed exile in Europe in the 1980s, he returned to the area he called home in upstate New York, dabbled in liberal politics, wrote letters to magazines and various individuals, helped save a cornfield from developers in the Woodstock area and wrote a play titled *The Trial of Richard Nixon*. Koch was 93.

Casablanca has become a part of the Moroccan culture over the years. Stories persist that part of the film was actually filmed there and tour guides in Casablanca are apt to point out any old bar and tell unsuspecting tourists that this was Rick's original cafe. They also point out old hotels as being the place where the movie stars stayed during filming.

In Casablanca, the "vultures" are still at workand the myth and magic of *Casablanca* continues.

Recommended Reading

Allen, J.C.; *Conrad Veidt: From Caligari to Casablanca.* Pacific Grove, CA, Boxwood Press, 1981.

Barber, Joel; *The Week France Fell.* New York City, Stein and Day, 1976.

Behlmer, Rudy; *Inside Warner Bros. (1935-1951).* New York City, Viking Press, 1985.

Berton, Pierre; *The Great Depression 1919-1939.* Toronto, MacMillan Pub., 1980.

Delzell, Charles F.; *Mediterranean Fascism: 1919-1945.* New York City, Doubleday & Co., 1990.

Duignan, Peter, and Gann, L. H.; *World War II In Europe: Causes, Course and Consequences.* Palo Alto, CA, Stanford Press, 1995.

Garland, Brock; *War Movies,* New York City, Facts on File Publications, 1987.

Greenfield, Richard; *Ethiopia: A New Political History.* New York City, Fred A. Praeger Co., 1984.

Harmetz, Aljean; *Round Up the Usual Suspects: The Making of Casablanca—Bogart, Bergman and World War II.* New York City, Hyperion, 1992.

Howe, George F.; *U.S. Army in World War II: The Mediterranean Theater of Operations: Northwest Africa.* Washington, DC; Center of Military History, U.S. Army, 1991.

Hyams, Joe; *Bogie: The Biography of Humphrey Bogart.* New York City, The New American Library, 1966.

Korbel, Josef; *Twentieth Century Czechoslovakia.* New York City, Columbia University Press, 1977.

Lebo, Harlan; *Casablanca: Behind the Scenes.* New York City, Simon & Schuster, 1992.

Murphy, Robert; *Diplomat Among Warriors.* New York City, Doubleday & Co. 1964.

Ready, J. Lee; *World War II Nation by Nation.* London, Arms & Armour Press, 1995.

Rosenstone, Robert A.; *Crusade of the Left: The Lincoln Battalion in the Spanish Civil War.* New York City: Pegusus, 1969.

Sennett, Ted; *Masters of Menace: Greenstreet and Lorre.* New York City, E. F. Dutton, 1979.

Thomas, Bob; *Clown Prince of Hollywood: The Antic Life and Times of Jack Warner.* New York City, McGraw Pub. 1990.

Wallis, Hal, and Highm, Chas; *Starmaker: The Autobiography of Hal Wallis.* New York City, Macmillan & Co., 1980.

Index